Buddhism

Buddhism

A Philosophical Approach

Cyrus Panjvani

broadview press

Library and Archives Canada Cataloguing in Publication

Panjvani, Cyrus, author
    Buddhism : a philosophical approach / Cyrus Panjvani.

Includes bibliographical references and index.
ISBN 978-1-55111-853-6 (pbk.)

    1. Buddhist philosophy.   I. Title.

B162.P35 2013   181'.043   C2013-907132-6

Broadview Press is an independent, international publishing house, incorporated in 1985.

We welcome comments and suggestions regarding any aspect of our publications—please feel free to contact us at the addresses below or at broadview@broadviewpress.com.

North America:
PO Box 1243, Peterborough, Ontario, Canada K9J 7H5
2215 Kenmore Ave., Buffalo, NY, USA 14207
Tel: (705) 743-8990; Fax: (705) 743-8353
E-mail: customerservice@broadviewpress.com

UK, Europe, Central Asia, Middle East, Africa, India, and Southeast Asia:
Eurospan Group, 3 Henrietta St., London, UK WC2E 8LU
Tel: 44 (0) 1767 604972; Fax: 44 (0) 1767 601640
Email: eurospan@turpin-distribution.com

Australia and New Zealand:
NewSouth Books, c/o TL Distribution
15-23 Helles Ave., Moorebank NSW, Australia 2170
Tel: (02) 8778 9999; Fax: (02) 8778 9944
Email: orders@tldistribution.com.au

www.broadviewpress.com

Broadview Press acknowledges the financial support of the Government of Canada through the Book Publishing Industry Development Program (BPIDP) for our publishing activities.

Edited by Robert M. Martin

The inside pages of this book is printed on paper containing 100% post-consumer fibre.

Book design and composition by George Kirkpatrick
PRINTED IN CANADA

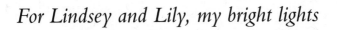

For Lindsey and Lily, my bright lights

Contents

Preface

THIS BOOK PHILOSOPHICALLY INTRODUCES basic truths, doctrines, and principles of Buddhism. It presents reasoning, provides arguments, raises critical considerations, and considers responses. Its goal is to explain the teachings of the Buddha and the concepts and doctrines of Buddhism clearly and consistently. It is meant to be an accessible guide for those who have no background in Buddhism, and to be beneficial to the understanding of those who do.

The explanations in this book aim to be clear and true, and it is worth giving some thought upfront to these objectives. Providing clarity is like casting light. Clarity allows us to see better and eases the path to understanding. And just as one light source need not deny the illumination of another but can add to it, the understanding gained through one explanation can stand to gain from another even if they are different in approach. Truth is more exclusive: if an explanation is accurate or true, then a differing one is liable to not be. But while the explanations provided in this book strive for truth, they do not presume to possess truth. This is not simply about modesty, and nor is it hesitancy. It is about what is important for gaining clarity and furthering understanding: an

openness of mind and a non-attachment to views. An attitude of possession towards truth is not helpful for gaining philosophical understanding,
and particularly so concerning Buddhism.

Ashoka was a renowned Indian warrior king of the Maurya dynasty
from the third century BCE who later gave up his conquering ways to
devote himself fully to Buddhism. He is reputed to have cut the following message into a rock: "Do not quarrel about religions, concord is
meritorious. Do not imagine that you have complete hold on Truth. You
may not have it; no religion has a monopoly of Truth."[1] This is quite
a message to write with the point of a sword, and especially from one
committing wholeheartedly to a religion as Ashoka is said to have done.
But it is an attitude appropriate to the Indian philosophical religious
milieu, including Buddhism, as we will come to see. It is also an attitude
appropriate to philosophical writing: while it aims for truth, it does not
benefit from an attitude of possession of truth and in fact suffers for it.
Whether Ashoka intends so or not, he describes not only an approach
towards religion but a good approach towards explanations of religion.

This same attitude of non-possession of truth is evident in a famous
Buddhist simile. The Buddha, in the *Alagaddupama* sutra, describes a
man who comes to an expanse of water with no way to cross. He builds
a raft and then asks himself, after he has crossed, whether he should
carry the raft which he has just built along with him on his journey.
The Buddha describes this to be an encumbrance and not useful. He
states, "'This raft has been very helpful to me, since supported by it and
making an effort with my hands and feet, I got safely across to the far
shore. Suppose I were to haul it onto the dry land or set it adrift in the
water, and then go wherever I want.' Now, bhikkhus [monks], it is by so
doing that that man would be doing what should be done with that raft.
So I have shown you how the Dhamma is similar to a raft, being for the
purpose of crossing over, not for the purpose of grasping."[2] The Buddha

---

1 As quoted in Radhakrishnan (1984), p. 10.
2 *Alagaddupama Sutta, Majjhima Nikaya* I 22, p. 229.

likens his teachings—the *Dhamma* in Pali, or *Dharma* in Sanskrit—to rafts. Teachings, as with rafts, are to be used and then put aside when no longer of use. They are not to be objects of attachment and possession; they are not to be carried around as rafts on one's back when it is not beneficial to do so. This attitude of non-attachment to teachings is part of a wider attitude of non-attachment. Attachment to self, it will be discussed, is the key source of suffering in the Buddhist sense and overcoming this is the focus of Buddhist practice and discipline. A book about Buddhism's teachings such as this can be described as a teaching itself, and in this respect, a kind of raft. A raft for accessing other rafts, perhaps. Its value lies in the clarity of understanding it helps deliver about Buddhist teachings. It does not befit the writing of such a book to presume possession of truth, or present an attitude of attachment to its views. This would not communicate well the manner in which Buddhist teachings and doctrines are supposed to be appreciated.

Chapter One presents the Indian philosophical tradition within which Buddhism arose and some general themes of this tradition. The legend and life story of the Buddha are meant to impart important lessons about Buddhism, and these are discussed in Chapters Two and Three. Chapters Four through Seven successively discuss each of the Four Noble Truths concerning the nature of suffering; its cause in cravings; the release from suffering that is Nirvana or Enlightenment; and the means to its realization through the Noble Eightfold Path. And Chapters Eight, Nine and Ten respectively discuss the doctrines of No Self, Impermanence, and Dependent Origination. These truths and doctrines, and the connections between them and the concepts they raise, are critically important for philosophically appreciating Buddhism, and accordingly they are closely attended and analysed over seven successive chapters. Collectively this discussion is the greater part of this book. The notions of karma and rebirth raise important questions about the continuity of self over time and these are assessed in Chapter Eleven. Chapter Twelve addresses the concept of dharmas in the Abhidharma tradition and Chapters Thirteen and Fourteen address key concepts of Mahayana Buddhism. These three chapters focus on discussing and assessing central concepts and aspects, and therewith provide thematic presentations rather than broad overviews of these traditions and their several schools. The former chapter on Mahayana Buddhism focusses on the concept of emptiness and the response this provides to the metaphysics expressed in the Abhidharma. The latter chapter focuses on the role of compassion, the figure of the Bodhisattva, and the idea that the Buddha taught with what is called "Skillful Means." The Abhidharma and Mahayana Buddhism each claim to uphold the original understanding of the Buddha. And so in this respect, even though the book treads beyond the Buddha's life, in particular with these chapters, it remains throughout a philosophical discussion and elaboration of the Buddha's thought. This concern with philosophically understanding the Buddha's thought circumscribes this book. The book concludes with a discussion of the Buddha as he is presented in the Parable of the Burning House from the *Lotus* sutra. This is a coda that returns the book to the question of the connection between truth and teachings in Buddhism.

A philosophical explanation aims to determine and assess underlying reasoning, reconstitute arguments, consolidate views, and find internal consistency. This is not different from the aims of non-philosophers such as Indologists, Buddhologists and other specialists in religious studies and the history of Buddhism, but there is a difference in how these aims are addressed and fulfilled. While there is history in this book, the objective is not a specifically historical presentation but a philosophical one. It is focussed on ideas and reasons that, while historically contextualized, are conceived and assessed in their own right, as if they are meant to apply independently of historical circumstances of time and place. Philosophers writing on Buddhism build and draw heavily upon the cautious and meticulous work of other scholars, and this book presents no exception. Gaining understanding depends on others; we do not achieve understanding alone. The aim of this book is to provide its reader with a philosophical understanding of Buddhism. If it succeeds, this owes much to the work of others. If it fails then it may be a leaky raft, in which case it is best to find another.

Lastly, I would like to say 'Thank-you' to the following: First, to my late parents, for their love, nurturing, and for placing me on the long path and walking the beginning with me. I continue to be influenced by them, even when I don't know it, or forget it. Second, to Grant MacEwan University. I have been given opportunity, means, and encouragement in pursuing this project. Included in this was funding from a MacEwan Research, Scholarly Activity and Creative Achievement Grant and a MacEwan Faculty of Arts and Science Research Grant for two research trips: one to the College of Buddhist Studies at Dongguk University in Seoul, South Korea, and the other to the Central Institute for Higher Tibetan Studies in Sarnath, India. The discussions I had, and the study I was able to complete during both these trips, are much valued. Third, to the many students I have had over the years who have taken Buddhist and Asian Philosophy classes with me. I have improved in my ability to talk about Buddhism, and to think about Buddhism, as a result of our involved discussions. I have received more from them than I have given to them. Fourth, to an undisclosed referee and the copyeditor at Broadview Press, Bob Martin: both provided pointed and valuable feedback in the late stages of this manuscript. Last, and most of all, to my wife Lindsey. We joked for a long time that the dedication of this book should state that without her this book would have been completed years earlier. This idea for a dedication was in jest, but not entirely so. There is truth to it, although "years" is almost certainly an exaggeration. I did not end up saying this in the dedication but I will say it to her here, in the Preface: My dear, this book would have been written much earlier if not for your interruptions. But it would have been a poor book and I a poor author. Each interruption enriched me, even if at the time it did not seem so. I learned about Buddhism with you and from you, in ways that neither of us may fully fathom.

I

Indian Contexts

General Themes of the Indian Philosophical Tradition

BUDDHISM IS CONSIDERED AN unorthodox school within the Indian philosophical tradition. It is unorthodox because of its rejection of key principles or doctrines, but it does share the Indian tradition's concerns and themes. Generally speaking, its concerns are comparable, but its responses are often not. This section will present a general description of these shared themes.

The primary theme in the Indian philosophical tradition is a concern with suffering, particularly with overcoming suffering. While we may all be experiencers of suffering, it does not follow from this that we properly understand suffering. Overcoming suffering, it is thought, requires first understanding the nature and causes of suffering. And this involves understanding desire, for this is thought to be at the root of suffering.

When we desire what we do not have, or to be rid of what we do have, there is suffering. This is to say that suffering arises when there is a gap between what we have and what we desire. Or more simply put, suffering results from unsatisfied desires. Accordingly, there are two general approaches to close the gap between our actual condition and our desired condition, and thereby lessen and overcome suffering.[1] The first is to try to satisfy our desires. If we achieve all we desire, then there will be no suffering caused by unsatisfied desire. However, in the Indian tradition, this approach to alleviating suffering is held to be unsatisfactory. It is held to be impossible to fully satisfy our desires, and so impossible to fully close the gap between our desires and our actual state in this way. One reason for this is that we are creatures who do not easily stay satisfied with what we have and are prone to want more. Our minds often jump in quick succession from the satisfaction of one desire to the pressing demands of another. Also, many desires – such as hunger, thirst, and sexual desire – often do not stay satisfied for long before they rise again. If many of our desires, once satisfied, arise with regularity, then the gap between desires and our actual state cannot be permanently closed. Another key reason that suffering cannot be effectively eradicated by satisfying desires is that there are many desires that we, being mortal human beings, simply cannot satisfy. These include the desires never to die, to remain ever youthful and healthy, and never to feel pain or displeasure. Clearly, if suffering is caused by a gap between our desires and our actual state, then this gap cannot be closed by trying to fully and permanently satisfy all of our desires.

And so a second approach is offered for dealing with suffering and closing the gap between our actual and desired state. This involves trying to overcome our desires. If we manage to desire less, then our desires will outstrip our actual state by that much less. If we desire very little, then the disparity between our actual state and desired state will be reduced to very little. This might seem odd, for it might seem that if one doesn't give into desires, then one suffers more for it. But the point is not simply to resist pressing desires; it is rather not to feel the pressure and temptation of desires, and in this way the suffering of desire is to be overcome. It was thought that this was the proper way to understand and

---

1 J.M. Koller makes this observation in speaking of the Indian tradition in his (2007), p. 9.

deal with the problem of suffering for it deals with suffering at its root, which is desire, and tries to dig out this root. One might think that the most promising route should be a mixed one: try to satisfy those desires that can be satisfied, and try to undo or uproot others. But a mixed solution, which would be divided in focus, would not focus squarely on undoing the root cause of suffering which is desire. It would also not offer a full solution for there will still be desires, such as for food, that cannot be permanently satisfied, or eradicated, and insofar as unsatisfied desires remain then suffering remains. The objective is to eliminate and not just lessen desire-caused suffering and so an approach that tries to overcome some desires while retaining other desires will not ultimately suffice. Although Buddhism differs in its view of the root cause of suffering, it shares the view that the root is to be fully uprooted, that is, that suffering is to be eliminated at its source rather than just lessened.

Removing desires, as opposed to satisfying them, requires much fortitude and strength of character. It involves not only being unmoved by temptation, but ultimately not even feeling temptation (for to feel temptation is to feel desire, and hence suffer). And so a highly disciplined life is called for. In the Indian tradition, the emphasis on suffering, by way of its connection to desire, leads to an emphasis on discipline – bodily, moral, and mental – as a means towards overcoming suffering. And with this emphasis on self-discipline comes an emphasis on self-knowledge, for one must know well what one seeks to control.[1] Knowledge of self in turn involves self-observation and reflection. And thus, as a result of this connection between suffering and desire, a meditative and introspective approach gains importance in the Indian tradition as a means towards the goal of overcoming suffering.

Another important characteristic of the Indian philosophical tradition, again speaking quite generally, is a preoccupation with subject-object dualism. This is a dualism between, on the one hand, our selves or our subjective awareness and, on the other hand, the objects of our awareness.

---

1 These points are observed by J.M. Koller in his (2007), p. 9.

The objects of our awareness can be objects in the external world around us or our own states of mind (internal states, such as desires and fears, are objects of introspective awareness and in this respect fall under the object side of this dualism). This dualism is thought to involve attachment to self, and release from this dualism to be a release from self and also from suffering.

In the history of the Western philosophical tradition, the dualism that is the main preoccupation, and this is to still speak quite generally, is the dualism between the physical and non-physical or the material and immaterial. We see this, predominantly, in the concern with whether there exists an immaterial god or immaterial soul (which, by virtue of its immateriality, need not perish with the death of the material body). We see this concern in Socrates, who was so confident in his reasons for the existence of the immaterial and, he thought, immortal, soul that he did not fear his impending execution.[1] We see this concern among Western medieval and theologically-minded philosophers, such as St. Augustine. And we see it, most famously, with Descartes and his argument for the indubitable and immaterial self. Descartes thought that it was possible to entertain doubts about the existence of the body and of anything else material (for instance, it is conceivable that we may be under the deceptive sway of a powerful, evil demon who makes us believe we have a body by giving us false sensory information). But he thought that it was not possible to doubt the existence of one's self (for if one is doubting, one must exist to doubt; if one is thinking anything at all, one must exist to do the thinking). He concluded that the existence of the self is indubitable and that it must be immaterial and different from the body. The philosopher George Berkeley and his metaphysical idealism opt for the immaterial side of this dualism as capturing the nature of reality. In the scientifically minded philosophical tradition of the twentieth century, there is an opting for materialism as capturing the nature of reality. Materialist views of the mind and world show a preoccupation with the dualism between the material and the immaterial by virtue of arguing for one side of this dualism.

---

1 C.f. Plato's *Phaedo*.

In contrast, in the Indian philosophical tradition, a preoccupation with the dualism between the material and the immaterial is comparatively much less pronounced. The concern with whether the world and human beings are to be thought of in purely material terms, or as a composite of material and immaterial elements, or even as purely immaterial, is not widespread. There are, certainly, thinkers or movements that ventured into this debate (e.g., the materialist school Carvaka), but subject-object dualism was much more the object of concern. This is different from the dualism between the immaterial and the material and it implies no position on the material and/or immaterial constitution of the world. In the Indian tradition, overcoming this divide between subject and object, or self and world, was taken to be a principal objective, integral to eradicating suffering. An awareness was sought wherein the division between one's subjective experience of the world and the world being experienced is overcome, resulting in an experience of unity or oneness with reality. In the Upanishads, realizing the identity between true subjective reality – which is termed 'Atman' or True Self (as opposed to one's individual, ego-self), and true objective reality – termed 'Brahman', was thought to be a complete and monistic experience of reality (these notions will be elaborated in the sections below). With subject-object dualism in place there is thought to be a limited and divided existence; a disparity between self and world that results in an excessive focus on self, and an experience of isolation, forlornness, incompleteness, and suffering.

Implicit in the concern with overcoming subject-object dualism is a concern with overcoming, in some sense, the subject or self. In the tradition of the Upanishads this involves overcoming the individual ego-self or psychophysical self – the self we are most familiar with – in favour of the egoless and non-individuated True Self or Atman. While Buddhism rejects Atman or True Self – and this rejection is a key reason it is considered an unorthodox school in the Indian tradition – it retains the idea that attachment to an ego-self is the root of suffering and to be overcome. The connection between attachment to self and suffering will be discussed specifically in Chapters Four and Five, and is also a theme running through the book. In Chapter Six, non-dualism will be discussed in connection with the indescribability of Nirvana. And in

Chapter Thirteen on Mahayana Buddhism, the topic of non-dualism will be revisited and discussed in terms of a notion called 'emptiness'.

In sum, while in important respects Buddhism presents a repudiation of the Indian Tradition in which it originates, in other important respects Buddhism and its concerns fit squarely within this Indian Tradition. It rejects the notion of True Self or Atman, but agrees with the point that the attachment to the ego-self is suffered and to be overcome. Buddhism also agrees that the division between actual state and desired state causes suffering, and further, that this suffered gap is to be bridged through overcoming rather than satisfying desires. But, as will be seen, Buddhism does not advocate trying to overcome all desires, but rather a carefully conceived subset of problematic desires called 'cravings' (*trishna*). In short, despite its differences with the Indian tradition in which it develops (and for which it is deemed an "unorthodox" school in the Indian tradition), Buddhism is still very much a part of this tradition in its preoccupation with suffering; its connection of suffering with desire (in the form of cravings); the call for discipline in overcoming desire; and in its concern with subject-object dualism and with overcoming attachment to self.

A Short Account of the Vedas and Upanishads

The Vedas are the ancient religious texts of India, dating as far back as 1500 BCE, and perhaps even further.[1] The concluding portions of the Vedas are called 'Upanishads'. They represent the height of philosophical or spiritual thought of the Vedas. They are also called 'Vedanta', which literally means "the end of the Vedas," both because they are the concluding portions of the Vedas and also, again, because they are viewed as the unsurpassed thoughts of the Vedas.

Within the Upanishads there is an affirmation of a metaphysical monism, but in other portions of the Vedas there is an espousal of both

---

1 Radhakrishnan and Moore (1957), p. 3.

polytheism and monotheism. This section will elaborate these distinctions. In early portions of the Vedas the worship of natural forces is advocated, and they are identified with deities or gods. For example, Varuna is the god of the sky, Agni is the god of fire, and Indra of thunder and lightning. Varuna is an overseer, ever observant of good and bad; Agni represents powers of creation and destruction; and Indra is a very popular god in the Vedas for, being a god of thunder, Indra symbolizes the power and strength that is needed in life to vanquish enemies and defend one's family and livelihood. In these ways, the powers associated with these deities extend beyond the natural forces themselves. This is a naturalistic polytheism as there are many gods and they are associated with forces of nature. While these various gods are responsible for these forces, and serve to maintain them, they are not the creators of these natural forces.

Behind these natural forces, and the functioning of the universe in general, lies an ordering principle to the universe. This ordering principle is called 'Rita'. 'Rita' literally means "order" or "that which is fitted together."[1] The universe was seen to be a well-ordered whole and the word 'Rita' refers to this universal order and serves to make the universe intelligible. And so, the various gods, by upholding and maintaining the forces of nature, uphold and maintain the universal order, Rita. They do not create Rita, just as they are not the creators of natural forces, but they are charged with maintaining the natural forces and, by extension, maintaining the universal order of Rita. While the gods serve to maintain Rita, Rita is still asserted to be prior to and more fundamental than all the gods. And so, behind the movement and diversity of the forces of nature, and behind all the various deities, lies a single, underlying principle. Rita came to refer not only to the physical ordering of the universe but also to an ideal moral ordering. And so the various deities, by upholding Rita, were also serving to maintain justice and an ideal ordering to the universe.[2]

---

1 Collins (1982), p. 41.
2 But not just the gods for, as Collins notes, this "divine ordering activity is to be supplemented by human effort ..." Collins (1982), p. 41. (*continued*)

While polytheism is espoused in portions of the Vedas, in other portions there is an espoused belief in one supreme god. This is monotheism, or at least something approximating monotheism. Note that, even without an explicit espousal of monotheism, the principle of Rita provides a basis for this way of thinking: Rita, as a single principle of order in the universe, conveys that there is something that ties the universe together, and that is responsible for its functioning and makes it a well-ordered whole. Rita is thus consistent with the idea of a single supreme god responsible for maintaining this order. A prominent (but not the only) conception of this supreme god is Prajapati. The name 'Prajapati' translates as "father god," and this name is meant to convey that all created beings are his children. The Rig Veda describes Prajapati as the "lord of all creatures." Some early portions of the Vedas convey that Prajapati is the creator of the universe and that the universe came into existence out of Prajapati himself. However, it is also suggested that Rita is prior to Prajapati, and the significance of this is that there may still be something more fundamental than even this supreme god. Prajapati is also identified with Shiva and Vishnu who are likewise viewed as supreme gods among different Hindu traditions. This view of god is henotheistic in that it involves the worship of one god but is also accepting of other deities or other conceptions of god.

Further in the Vedas, in the Upanishads, concerns are raised that apply to both monotheism and polytheism. It was held that the true nature of reality is one, that is, a whole without fundamental divisions or distinctions. Monotheism and polytheism presume fundamental divisions and distinctions: distinctions between gods, or distinctions between god and the world, or creator and creation. Distinctions were thought to be limitations, and to not be representative of the true nature of reality which was thought to be singular and undivided. And so, in the Upanishads,

---

Kalupahana adds: "The search was on for one single, ordaining, sustaining, coordinating principle of which all known forces, laws, and movements are manifestations. The earliest conception that satisfied all these conditions was rta [rita], and for a while it proved sufficient because it embodied not only physical but also spiritual (= sacrificial or ritualistic) and moral laws. It was not created, but found a guardian in Varuna." Kalupahana (1992), p. 7.

polytheism and monotheism give way to monism. In monism we find the idea of a single underlying reality, a reality that does not admit of a split between god and world, or between creator and creation. The universe, gods, humans, and all reality are fundamentally one or the same in essence. This monism was thought to escape description. This is because any linguistic description involves making distinctions between objects. And so, this monistic principle is simply referred to as That One (*tat ekam*). With monism, god(s) and the universe are no longer seen as separate; there is no division between creator and creation; nature and the power behind nature are not distinct. Everything is fundamentally one. The idea of monism is regarded as the philosophical height of the Vedas. The entire universe, in all its complexity and its infinite extent, is held to be essentially one. Everyday appearances are, of course, to the contrary, and thus monism implies that these appearances are mislead-ing. The idea of monism conveys that there is something underlying and unifying behind the multifariousness of appearances.

The Philosophy of the Upanishads

The word 'Upanishad' translates as "sitting down near," as in sitting down near a teacher or guru to receive a transmission of knowledge. The Upanishads deal with the question of what is the true nature of reality, or what is ultimate reality. The ancient authors – *rishis* or sages – were seeking a reality more fundamental, more substantial, than the transi-tory world of everyday appearances. The sages were searching for what underlies and makes possible the world we see around us. This reality was taken to be without changes and distinctions but, at the same time, underlie the appearances of change and distinction we see. It was a search for an underlying monistic principle. The name given to this principle was 'Brahman' (as noted earlier, it was also referred to as "That One"). 'Brahman' translates as "greatness" or "that which makes great" (and is derived from the root 'Brh' which means to grow or enlarge). In the Upanishads, Brahman comes to stand for the ultimate reality, the highest truth, and the essence of the universe. Brahman is that which gives life and existence to the universe.

There cannot be an origin to Brahman, the monistic principle, and neither can there be change in Brahman. Monism does not allow for this. Having an origin implies development, and the unfolding of distinctions over time, whereas monism holds that there are no ultimately real distinctions (for again, everything is fundamentally one). And so there cannot be real change or movement. This means that, fundamentally, the universe is not only one, or non-dual, but that this oneness implies that it is unchanging and without origin or end.

Monistic Brahman is also regarded as being beyond accurate description in language (for linguistic descriptions must employ concepts and terms that make distinctions between things). And if Brahman cannot be described, it follows that Brahman cannot be adequately conceived either insofar as we must make distinctions when we think with concepts (and note that this includes even elementary conceptual distinctions such as between is and is not, or existence and non-existence). And thus, Brahman is held to be beyond the possibility of conceptual understanding. Thus, the very words used here cannot convey a full and true understanding of Brahman. Paradoxically, to assert the indescribability of Brahman is itself to offer a description, but it is considered to be inadequate and, as with all descriptions, insufficient for appreciating the true nature of Brahman. Indescribability is a theme to which we will return in the discussion of Nirvana in Chapter Six.

If we cannot accurately describe Brahman in words, or conceptualize Brahman in thought, then this raises an obstacle to knowing Brahman, and thus to knowing the alleged Ultimate Reality. This is an epistemological problem: how can we *know* the true nature of things when our very means of knowing – be it conception or sensation or discursive thought – involve noticing distinctions or applying distinctions and thus raise obstacles to acquiring the knowledge we seek? Our ordinary means of knowing and cognizing are, by their nature, inadequate to this task. With this consideration in mind some of these ancient sages turned their attention inward, to the self, and asked an apparently different question:

"What is the true self?" or "What is the self in its most fundamental existence?" Just as it was thought that there was something more to the changing world around us – something unchanging and unifying – it was also thought that there was something more to the self than what we are familiar with. Something more to our selves than what we see in a mirror; something more than our egos, and our ever-changing bodies, and ever-changing minds with their unceasing desires. This something more was deemed to be our "True Self."

The word given for this "True Self" is 'Atman'.[1] The word 'Atman' originally meant breath, and then gradually acquired the meaning of self or soul. There is a distinction drawn between our individual selves – which vary, and undergo change in body, thought and mind, and the absolute, unvarying and unchanging True Self. The former will be called the ego-self, and sometimes also the empirical or psychophysical self, and the latter, as noted, is Atman. With this view of Atman or True Self, a key is found to the realization of Brahman or Ultimate Reality: while Brahman cannot be known through the ordinary means of knowing available to our individual selves, it was thought that Brahman can be known through a direct realization of our innermost and truest Self. That is, it was held that we can have direct access to the True Self, without the mediation of language, thought, or sensation, and through this direct inward experience we can encounter Brahman or Ultimate Reality.

The Identity of Brahman and Atman

Since Brahman was said to be beyond definition, beyond language, and beyond the categories of human thought, the search for knowledge of Ultimate Reality or Brahman appeared to be thwarted. Other than

---

1 Atman is also commonly transliterated as atman, beginning with a lowercase 'a'. A reason for this is that there are no capital letters in Sanskrit. The capitalized transliteration will be used herein in order to convey the appropriate connotation in English and to remain consistent with the transliterations of other Sanskrit words.

stipulating a name, nothing can effectively be said about this Ultimate Reality. However, it was realized that if Ultimate Reality is truly monistic, then Ultimate Reality – Brahman – must not be distinct from the ultimate and True Self – Atman. Thus, an experience of Atman would be an experience of Brahman. That is, if the True Self or Atman can be experienced – not through conceptual thought or description but through direct unmediated experience – then this is an experience of Brahman. Ultimate Reality, quixotically perhaps, is to be experienced through a turn inwards. The identity of Atman and Brahman, and the realization that Brahman could be experienced through an experience of Atman, are key conclusions of the Upanishads. The Upanishads proclaim "*Tat tvam asi*," meaning "Thou art that" (i.e., True Self is Ultimate Reality). Note, though, that in realizing our True Self we would not be realizing an individuated or personal self; this would not be Atman. The True Self is not different for different people, as this would violate the monism of Brahman. Presuming that reality is ultimately monistic, the experience of this reality by way of an experience of the truest and deepest self is not an experience that is essentially *mine*, or of *me* as an individual person. It is not an experience of what I ordinarily identify with my personal self or personality. It is an experience in which self in an individuated sense disappears; it is an experience in which the distinction between self and not self is overcome. In other words, the truest self on the Upanishadic view is not individuated or distinct or personal; the truest self is undifferentiated reality itself; it is Brahman. The key to the experience of reality as a monistic whole lies in the inward path of a direct and unmediated experience of the non-personal and yet truest self. An excerpt from the *Brhadaranyaka* Upanishad describes this:

> Whoever knows thus, 'I am Brahman,' becomes this all. Even the gods cannot prevent his becoming thus, for he becomes their self [Atman]. So whoever worships another divinity (than his self) thinking that he is one and (Brahman) another, he knows not. He is like an animal to the gods ... One should meditate only on the Self as his (true) world. The work of him who meditates on the

Self alone as his world is not exhausted for, out of that very Self he creates whatever he desires.[1]

Once again, the True Self is not to be conceived of as the self of change; the self that we describe in language; that we cognize through thoughts; or that is moved by desire and fear. Rather, it is held to be an immutable Self – Atman – and the experience of this is thought to involve an unmediated and undivided conscious experience. The Upanishads hold that knowledge of Atman is not an item of ordinary knowledge gained through ordinary means; it is not knowledge gained through sensation, or as the conclusion of an argument. It is an unconceptualized and unmediated experience gained through discipline and concentration. It is an inwardly gained experience and so is strictly a first-hand experience or knowledge. And thus, the identity of Atman and Brahman would remain a hypothesis until one realizes this alleged truth within oneself. Indian philosophy differs here from traditional Western philosophy, for this great conclusion of the Upanishads would remain a mere conjecture in the Western tradition, which, by and large, relies on discursive reason and the requirement that knowledge be describable and objectively verifiable. In the Indian tradition, while many truths can certainly be recognized and known by reason, argument and empirical observation, the most important truths of the universe and self can only be fully realized by way of direct experience.

The nature of monism, we may say, severely limits epistemic approaches. The means to knowledge must be direct, unmediated, without cognizance of differentiation or variation but an experience nonetheless. The ancient sages or *rishis* held that such an experience is possible, but, due to the nature of monism, ultimately incommunicable; it must be experienced by oneself to be known and realized. Those who do realize Brahman would be mystics in the proper sense of the term since the reality they experience is beyond clear communication (i.e., it is mysterious to those who have not experienced).

---

1 *The Principal Upanishads* 1.4.10/15, pp. 168 and 171.

The idea that Ultimate Reality or Brahman can only be experienced through an inward turn to one's deepest and truest self raises to importance specific practices for carrying out this inward turn. These practices involve an introspective and meditative approach as means for delving within. They also involve self-discipline and perhaps ascetic approaches, and this is because to realize one's True Self or Atman one has to overcome identifying oneself with one's thoughts, desires, fears, etc. To desire Atman, for instance, is to remain mired within the distinction of desired end and desiring agent. One's attachment to ego must not intrude in the effort to experience Atman (for this would be to be caught up with one's ego-self, and not to approach the True Self). Overcoming desire and attachment, and disentangling from one's individual ego-self, places much importance on techniques of self-discipline. These disciplining methods are termed 'yoga'. 'Yoga' is a general term referring to discipline or technique; the original meaning of the term involved the connotations of 'yoke' or 'join', as in yoking or joining with god, or Atman. Yoga involves bodily, mental and moral disciplining techniques, and is to lead to the realization of Atman (the yoga practice we are most familiar with – Hatha Yoga or bodily postures – is but one aspect or technique within the disciplines of yoga). Yoga, and the ideal of self-discipline in general, is of profound importance in the spiritual practices of the Indian tradition. And as will be seen, discipline techniques – mental, moral and physical – are important in Buddhism as well.

II

The Legend and Life of the Buddha

Introduction

THE WORD 'BUDDHA' MEANS awakened one, or enlightened one. Anyone who achieves enlightenment is thus a Buddha. It is held within Buddhism that there have been many enlightened figures, many buddhas. But generally speaking, Buddhism is still centred around one enlightened figure in particular – Gautama Buddha – whose life story and teachings are regarded as providing illumination and needed guidance on the path to enlightenment. While the figure of Gautama Buddha is indeed central within Buddhism, Buddhism does not depend on Gautama Buddha as, say, Christianity does on the figure of Jesus Christ, for Gautama is still one buddha among many.[1] Indeed, as the path towards enlightenment requires overcoming attachment to self and personality – something which will later be discussed in detail – placing exaggerated importance on the person of the Buddha, with a veneration

---

1 Peter Harvey states, "As 'Buddha' does not refer to a unique individual, Buddhism is less focused on the person of its founder than is, for example, Christianity." Harvey (1990), p. 1.

that manifests as attachment to the personality of the Buddha, would be an obstacle on the path towards enlightenment. Notwithstanding, the life of Gautama Buddha is regarded as vital for the example it conveys and the lessons it imparts for following the path to enlightenment.

What we know of the life of Gautama Buddha is largely a matter of legend. Scriptures providing details of his life were written after he died, and a canonical account of the Buddha's life was developed in the first two centuries after his death. Also, the information we have of the Buddha's life, including scriptural accounts, has been handed down through many a telling and retelling. This is the basis we have for an understanding of his life, but it is often difficult to separate what is fact from what is myth. It is clear that much has been embellished and mythologized in the accounts of the Buddha's life. As Thomas states, "The only firm ground from which we can start is not history, but the fact that a legend in a definite form existed in the first and second centuries after the Buddha's death."[1] There is good historical evidence that the Buddha was a real figure, but again some aspects of his life have been added upon or embellished, and this varies depending upon the source. Nevertheless, despite variation, a fairly canonical account of the life story of the Buddha does exist. While historical accuracy may not be available, the ability of the Buddha's life story to convey key principles of Buddhism – its pedagogic value – remains. This is a story of enlightenment, and an education in the method for reaching enlightenment.

The Early Life

'Siddhartha' is thought to have been a personal name of Gautama Buddha. Gautama Buddha is also known as Sakyamuni Buddha. 'Muni' means sage, and Sakya was an area at the foothills of the Himalayas where his father was said to have ruled. Sakyamuni thus means sage of the Sakyan clan. Hereon we will refer to him as Gautama when speaking

---

1 Thomas (1949), p. 2.

of him prior to his experience of enlightenment, and 'Gautama Buddha' or just 'Buddha' or 'the Buddha' after his alleged enlightenment.

The date of birth of the Buddha is thought to be around 486 BCE. This date is an educated stab, more likely to be wrong than right as a specific date, but does serve well in providing a rough approximation.[1] He is said to have left home when he was twenty-nine, achieved enlightenment at the age of thirty-five, and died at the age of eighty.

It is said that Gautama was born an aristocrat and a prince, the son of a great king. Some details in the Buddha's life, as commonly depicted, are clearly not accurate history, for example miraculous and superhuman feats (such as being able to speak at birth). This also applies to the widely held claim that Gautama Buddha was the son of a great king of the Sakyas. This could not have been since, as Williams says, "We know that his clan of the Sakyas had no king."[2] As Gethin notes, in portraying Gautama as what we would call a king, "the tradition is effectively recording little more than he was, in European cultural terms, a member of a locally important aristocratic family."[3] Portraying the Gautama as a prince, who lived in luxurious palaces with servants to cater to his every whim conveys to us that, in material terms, Gautama had all that he could ask for.

According to legend, Gautama's mother, Maya, had a dream that a white elephant entered into her from her right side. Brahmin priests predicted from this, and from thirty-two subtle but significant bodily signs found on Gautama's infant body, that he would become a "great man." More specifically, it was predicted that Maya's child would either become a great conquering king, or a spiritual leader of great consequence. Gautama's father, Suddhodana, did not want a priestly life for his son; he did not want his son to become a holy man. Instead, he wanted him to follow in his own footsteps, and become a commander and a warrior. And so, as legend has it, Gautama's father did his utmost to steer his son away from this spiritual fate by shielding him from certain

---

1 C.f. Williams (2000), p. 24.

2 Williams (2000), p. 26.

3 Gethin (1998), p. 15. See also Williams (2000), p. 26.

troubles of life that might, were he to encounter them, lead him to take up this spiritual path.

According to this legend, Gautama was intentionally kept away from all sights of suffering. He was intentionally deceived by his father about the inescapable troubles and maladies in the world. His father did this to ensure that his son would not fall into a concern for the suffering of humanity, and from this be inspired to take up the path of a spiritual leader. Everything was done to promote a view of life as undying, young and fresh. Gautama was attended to by good looking and youthful servants, male and female. He ate delicious food. Anyone who became ill was taken away. Dirt, dead flowers, and decay were swept away. The Buddha, later in life, is reported to have described his luxuriant palace life to his disciples:

> I was delicate, O monks, extremely delicate, excessively delicate. In my father's dwelling lotus-pools had been made, in one blue lotuses, in another red, in another white, all for my sake. I used no sandalwood that was not of Benares, my dress was of Benares cloth, my tunic, my under-robe, my cloak. Night and day a white parasol was held over me so that I should not be touched by cold or heat, by dust or weeds or dew. I had three palaces, one for the cold season, one for the hot, and one for the season of rains. Through the four rainy months, in the palace for the rainy season, entertained by female minstrels I did not come down from the palace …[1]

The legend continues that one day, at the age of twenty-nine, he wanted to leave the palace in order to see what was outside On some accounts, this was done with the acquiescence of his father, but only after his father had set a path (which was cleaned of decay), from which Gautama then veered. On more common accounts, he left of his own accord, with the compliance of his chariot driver, and without his father's knowledge. Either way, it is said that he ventured out of the

---

1 *Anguttara Nikaya* i 145, as quoted in Thomas (1949), p. 47.

palace four times, before ultimately leaving for good, and that each time he witnessed a "sign."

The Four Signs

The first time out he saw an old man. The encounter with this first sign – an old man, and the king's response to his son's encounter is described thus:

> [The man was] worn out with old age, with broken teeth, grey hair, bent, with broken down body, a stick in his hand, and trembling ... [Gautama] asked his charioteer ... "what man is this? Even his hair is not like that of others," and on hearing his reply said, "woe to birth, when the old age of one that is born shall be known." With agitated heart he thereupon returned and ascended his palace. The king asked why his son had returned so quickly. "O king, he has seen an old man, and on seeing an old man he will leave the world." "By this you are ruining me. Get together dancing girls for my son. If he enjoys luxury, he will have no thoughts of leaving the world." And so saying he increased the guards, and set them in all directions to the distance of a league.[1]

On the second trip outside the palace he encountered a sick man. Again a similar scenario ensued. Gautama asked why he appeared the way he did and his driver explained that he was sick and what it meant to be sick. Gautama asked whether he too may become sick and the driver said yes, that we are all liable to get sick. Gautama once again returned, troubled, to the palace.

On the third trip outside the palace Gautama saw a shrouded corpse attended by a crowd of mourners. He asked his driver what was going on and the driver said that the shrouded person had died. He asked his

---

1 *Mahapadana Sutta, Digha Nikaya* ii 22 & 23, as quoted in Thomas (1949), p. 52.

driver whether the same would happen to him and the driver said yes, eventually, we all will die. And again, Gautama returned to the palace troubled and unnerved.

On the fourth trip outside his palace he encountered a man with shaven head, saffron robes, and a calm demeanour. He asked his driver who this was and the driver said "One who has gone forth."[1] Gautama wanted to know more and so spoke to the man about what it means to "go forth." The monk responded that he has gone forth from normal societal life to lead a life in truth, goodness, compassion and contemplation. The serenity of this ascetic monk impressed Gautama very much.

While the first three signs are associated with suffering, the fourth is a sign of the potential for a release from suffering. With the peaceful demeanour of the "one who has gone forth," despite the obvious and inevitable sorrows and troubles of daily life, there is a sign of the possibility of a release from suffering through a spiritual life. It was this sign that ultimately led Gautama to leave behind his luxuriant life and lead a simpler, ascetic life. Gautama doesn't yet fully know what is involved in "going forth" – he receives no specific teachings – but he is nonetheless moved by the physical demeanour and comportment of the monk. He is moved by his expression of peace and serenity in the midst of a troubled world, seeming quite different from the expressions of anxiousness and licentiousness displayed in neglect of a troubled world.

The king tried to maintain a certain lifestyle for Gautama by shielding him from all sights of sickness, old age, and death, but it is very unlikely that Gautama would not have ever encountered any of this, to that point, of twenty-nine years. We would think that he must himself have been sick at some point. He must at some point have witnessed or felt pain, discomfort and distress. But the point of this life story, or at least of this aspect, is not its historical veracity but its symbolic and pedagogic value. It is a story of clear contrasts, between a luxuriant life in which the sight of suffering is kept at bay and, in its next step, a life of ascetic deprivation in which Gautama wilfully takes on hardship rather than unknowingly

---

1   *Mahapadana Sutta, Digha Nikaya* ii 28.

avoiding it. As we will see in the next chapter, the "Middle" path that Gautama is ultimately led to is rendered all the clearer for these contrasting lifestyles.

Sickness, old age, and death are signs that led Gautama to find an alternative path in life. They are thought of as paradigmatic examples of suffering and also, importantly, inevitable examples. Sickness is, for most if not all, an inevitable feature of life at some time. Old age, unless one dies young, is also inevitable (and aging is inevitable for all, young and old). And death is truly inevitable for all mortals. This inevitability is emphasized to Gautama in each of his first three trips outside the palace walls by his charioteer, and each time this inevitability upsets Gautama. The luxuriant life in the palace is meant to respond to these paradigms of suffering by keeping them in abeyance, outside the walls of the palace. It is a life that tries to attain bliss through enforced ignorance of the inevitable. This life signifies a certain approach to dealing with life's difficulties: indulgence in comfort while keeping the troubles of life out of sight and thereby, hopefully, out of mind. But once Gautama realizes the inevitability of sickness, old age and death, his ignorance is shed, and he realizes that his palace life does not provide a true remedy. The palace life offers a temporary reprieve at best. Once knowledge of the temporariness of this reprieve, and of the inevitability of sickness, old age, and death are gained, the palace life cannot keep the realities of life in abeyance anymore, no matter how high the walls. Gautama cannot return to his earlier ignorance.

These paradigmatic and inevitable examples of suffering lead Gautama to abandon his palace life. It is telling that Gautama recognizes their inevitability, and is very troubled by it, but still decides to leave. It is telling because Gautama already realizes that overcoming suffering cannot involve overcoming the experiences of old age, sickness and death (for again, these are inescapable). A luxuriant palace life may offer comfort, as long as one can keep these eventualities out of mind, but not a remedy. But neither does any life outside the palace walls offer a remedy. In leaving the palace, Gautama chooses against a life of comfort as the best way to deal with the inevitabilities of sickness, old age and death. He leaves to find a way to be at peace with these inevitabilities. Gautama's palace life was likely as good an attempt as possible to evade old age, sickness, and death. Since he leaves the palace to find a way to overcome suffering, he must believe that old age, sickness and death are not really suffering in themselves. Or at least, they are not the suffering he means to overcome. He realizes, or is beginning to realize, that it is his desires to never be old, get sick and die that need attending. In line with the Indian tradition as discussed in the previous chapter, Gautama is making an important connection between desire and suffering. It would be one thing to leave the palace to find a cure for old age, sickness and death, for this would be quite an exchange. But he left knowing he would find no cure for old age, sickness and death. Instead, he left to find a cure for his heart's agitation at the prospect of inevitable old age, sickness and death. The end of suffering that he seeks is the end of this agitation of his heart.

One approach to avoid suffering from old age, sickness and death is to seek to transcend human mortality – to become a deity of a sort. And there are stories of the Buddha that portray him as a deity (with supra-human abilities to suit). Another approach is to seek to not be troubled by, and *in this way* not suffer from, one's mortality. When Gautama encounters the "one who has gone forth," the fourth sign, he encounters someone who, by all appearances, is still subject to old age, sickness and death. But, despite these inevitabilities, he retains a calm and peaceful nature. He is untroubled by his mortality. It is this fourth sign that moves Gautama to follow suit, and this says something about the understanding of suffering to come. Namely, suffering is not equated with pain, old age, sickness or death. Rather, suffering results from one's attitude towards these inevitabilities; it is a result of one's attachment or cravings to never be sick, get old, and die. As a consequence, overcoming suffering requires overcoming deeply set cravings and attachments, and this in turn requires self-discipline and control. And so Gautama sets out on a journey to better understand suffering, and to lead a life of greater discipline and denial than he had previously led in his luxuriant palace life. The following passage conveys the Buddha's reflections, at this junc-ture before leaving the palace, on old age:

Then, O monks, did I, endowed with such majesty and such excessive delicacy, think thus, "an ignorant, ordinary person, who is himself subject to old age, not beyond the sphere of old age, on seeing an old man is troubled, ashamed, and disgusted, extending the thought to himself. I too am subject to old age, not beyond the sphere of old age, and should I, who am subject to old age, not beyond the sphere of old age, on seeing an old man be troubled, ashamed, and disgusted?" This seemed to me not fitting. As I thus reflected on it, all the elation in youth utterly disappeared.[1]

This passage is followed by similar passages concerning sickness and death. Note that the Buddha recounts here that it is not fitting for him to be "troubled, ashamed, and disgusted" at the sight of an old man, in particular when aging is also inevitable for him. Again, the implication is not that he should not be made to grow old, but that he should not be troubled by the prospect of becoming old, and he is upset with himself for this. Gautama is questioning the nature of his desire (in this case, his desire to not grow old), and is coming to realize that it is not by satisfying his desire that he will obtain success, but by quelling his desire.

And so, as legend has it, after having seen the fourth sign, and the possibility it seemed to convey of a peaceful life, Gautama at the age of twenty-nine made a decision to leave his palace life. In leaving, it is said he left behind his wife and child. At the age of sixteen he was married, as was the custom for an Indian nobleman of this age. His wife's name was Yasodhara (although this name is not used in all accounts; for instance, in the Pali canon, Bhadda Kaccana is also used). He had a son with her, named Rahula (which means 'chain'!). Being married and having a male child is important in the Indian custom of the time (as it remains today). It showed that Gautama had fulfilled his duties as a male and householder: he was a husband, fathered a son, and leaving them with material means, he was thus ready to take the step of "going forth." Today we may view leaving behind a wife and child as reprehensible, even for the

---

1 *Anguttara Nikaya* i 45, as quoted in Thomas (1949), p. 51.

purpose of pursuing a spiritual life. But in that time and context it was seen as appropriate that a man fulfill these functions in life before leaving to pursue a spiritual life. This makes discriminating legend from fact even more difficult, particularly as early texts do not mention his having a wife or child.[1]

In any event, unable to deal with his troubled thoughts he decided to confront what seemed to be the cause of his misery: his desires to never grow old, sick, or die. There is a gap here between his actual state and his desired state which, as explained in Chapter One, is a suffered gap. Given the inevitability of old age, sickness and death, the gap between actuality and desire can never be closed by trying to satisfy these desires. Luxury may help to keep one's mind away from thoughts of the inevitable through a steady stream of comforts, but it cannot close this gap. It may seem that the next course of action should be to try to close this gap by facing one's desires and untangling oneself from them. As noted above, this requires discipline, denial and self-mastery as one tries to overcome deep set desires. Accordingly, Gautama was led to renounce his former life, and the comforts and luxuries it offered. And so, in the middle of the night, after looking once more at his wife and son but without waking them, and without his father's knowing, he left the palace. Once in the forest, he sent back his horse, cut off his hair, cast off his fine robes for coarse and simple cloths, and began his quest for liberation from suffering.

---

1 Thomas states, "... the persons [the wife and son] are not mentioned in the older tradition at all. The name Bhaddā Kaccānā [in the Pali canon] is only one of the three or four persons identified by the later tradition with Buddha's wife, and the identification is not made by the older texts. The case stands exactly the same with Rāhula. He is never mentioned in the older texts as Buddha's son." Thomas (1949) p. 59. Thomas continues, "That Buddha should have had a wife is not only natural but according to Indian ideas inevitable. To marry is one of the duties of a person living in the world. The chroniclers did not need to start from the historic fact that the Buddha had a wife and son ... it is certain that the tradition has preserved no information about them." Thomas (1949), p. 60. And Kalupahana adds: "Doubts have been raised about whether the Buddha was married and had a family because there are no specific references to these matters in the early discourses." Kalupahana (1992), p. 23.

Renunciation

Having left the palace, Gautama was in need of some instruction and guidance, and sought out spiritual teachers – gurus or yogis – from whom he could learn. The first he encountered was a yogi named Alara Kalama. It was reported of Alara Kalama that he practiced a special kind of meditation, one that allowed him to enter a "sphere of nothingness." This was "a mystical trance attained by yogic concentration, in which the mind goes beyond any apparent object and dwells on the thought of nothingness."[1] He taught this technique to Gautama, who quickly mastered it, so much so that Alara Kalama offered him joint leadership of his group. But Gautama was not interested; he did not feel that the state of meditation that Alara Kalama taught would lead to the cessation of suffering. While it was of value, and brought him stillness for a time, he did not think this meditational trance carried enough insight into the nature of suffering, and so he went on and found himself another teacher.

This next yogi was Uddaka Ramaputra. Uddaka Ramaputra taught a meditational state described as a "sphere of neither cognition nor non-cognition." This is alleged to have been a deeper state of stillness than that taught by Alara Kalama, one where "consciousness is so attenuated as to hardly exist."[2] It was also one Gautama quickly mastered, so much so that Uddaka Ramaputra recognized Gautama as his own teacher, and Gautama was once again offered a position of leadership with Uddaka Ramaputra. But Gautama again refused. He was not satisfied. He did not think that he had found the answer to the cessation of suffering. Mishra nicely elaborates Gautama's dissatisfaction with these first teachers:

> The Buddha wasn't convinced, however, that meditation, as practiced by the ascetics of his time, alone could lead to spiritual transcendence. For one, the states achieved by meditation, no matter how deep, were temporary, 'comfortable abidings', as he put it,

1 Harvey (1990), p. 18.
2 Harvey (1990), p. 18.

'in the here and now'. One emerged from them, even after a long session, essentially unchanged. Concentration and endurance were important means, but without a corresponding moral and intellectual development, they by themselves did not end suffering. The Buddha saw this more clearly later. At the time, he knew only that the techniques of both Kalama and Ramaputra had taken him thus far and no further – an important awareness in that it already set him apart from those sramanas [ascetics] who were merely seeking to justify their escape from social obligations, and easily fell prey to pseudo-wisdom.[1]

If the meditational states that Gautama first learns are "temporary, 'comfortable abidings'" then in this respect they are on par with the comfortable abidings of his former palace life. Whether one finds psychological comfort via pleasant physical surroundings, or through trained mental states, both are escapist comforts that are a temporary reprieve from the suffering that Gautama was trying to overcome. They are a tempting deterrence from finding the path out of suffering.

Gautama certainly learned from both these gurus, but he needed to learn and experience more. He felt he understood what he could from the teachers available to him and needed a different approach. And so, at this juncture, Gautama turns away from teachers. He begins to pursue his own understanding, but not yet independently through his own path. He turns to a practice that was (and still is) a time-honoured approach to spiritual realization in India: asceticism.

Indeed, Gautama turned to an extreme asceticism, and soon attracted five ascetic disciples of his own who were impressed by his devotion to poverty and deprivation. Asceticism, especially in the extreme manner allegedly practiced by Gautama, presented a different challenge than he had experienced with Alara Kalama and Uddaka Ramaputra. With them the challenge was to reach certain meditative states, and this presented itself as a kind of cerebral challenge. As Mishra notes above, he could

---

1 Mishra (2004), p. 168.

emerge from these states "essentially unchanged." Asceticism presented a different challenge: a very physical one that challenged his body and its desires, and suggested the possibility that he may be able to defeat his desires. The meditative states he learned may have allowed him to better observe the desires at work in his mind, but asceticism presented the opportunity to truly challenge his desires, and temptations, on the battlefield of his own body.

Legend holds that Gautama took to asceticism as much as is humanly possible with dire consequences for his physical state. In the following passage, the Buddha reports on his physical condition:

> The bones of my spine when bent and straightened were like a row of spindles through the little food. As the beams of an old shed stick out, so did my ribs stick out through the little food. And as in a deep well was the deep low-lying sparkling of my eyes through the little food. And as a bitter gourd cut off raw is cracked and withered through wind and sun, so was the skin of my head withered through the little food. When I thought I would touch the skin of my stomach, I actually took hold of my spine, and when I thought I would touch my spine, I took hold of the skin of my stomach, so much did the skin of my stomach cling to my spine through the little food. When I thought I would ease myself, I thereupon fell prone through the little food. To relieve my body I stroked my limbs with my hand and as I did so the decayed hairs fell from my body through the little food.[1]

Eventually, after six long years of ascetic practice, Gautama was led to believe that this severe mortification was not sufficient for achieving a cessation of suffering. He learned to train and contain many of his desires, to the extent of leaving himself emaciated, but had still not reached his objective. In his ascetic life he tried, not to overcome the suffering that comes with desires by satisfying them, but by trying to confront and

---

1 *Mahasaccaka Sutta, Majjhima Nikaya* i 245-6, as quoted in Thomas (1949), p. 66.

uproot them. But Gautama found this course was also unsuccessful.

So he left his ascetic disciples, and ate some solid food. According to legend, he was offered a meal of sweet milk and rice, and then he bathed himself. He regained some strength and felt refreshed. He then sat down under a tree – a pipal tree (botanical name *ficus religiosa* – sacred fig), and this tree has come to be known as the 'Bodhi Tree' or 'Tree of Enlightenment'. He resolved then and there not to stir until he found peace and freedom from suffering. He affirms: "Let only skin, sinew and bone remain, let the flesh and blood dry in my body, but I will not give up this seat without attaining complete awakening."[1] After six days of being seated in meditation, he is said to have emerged "enlightened." Upon enlightenment, at the end of this six day meditation, the Buddha touched the earth. The gesture conveys that the earth is witness to the Buddha's enlightenment, and the symbolism also suggests that enlightenment is a grounded, and not a transcendent, experience; it is not other-worldly. The results of this meditation, which led to his alleged enlightenment or freedom from suffering, were the insights that form the basics of Buddhist teachings. And the first of these to be discussed is called the Middle Way.

---

1 *Jataka* i 71, as quoted in Gethin (1998), p. 22.

III

Reading the Middle Way

Steering the Middle Course

THE BUDDHA WENT FROM a life of luxury in his palaces, where he lived for twenty-nine years, to a life of extreme poverty and asceticism for six years. He found that both approaches were inadequate for overcoming suffering. Upon enlightenment, the Buddha began preaching what is called the "Middle Way" or "Middle Path."

At first, the Middle Way may seem to be a mid-point between the extremes of palatial luxury and ascetic poverty. This would suggest that the path to enlightenment involves a mean between extremes: a middle-class and middle-income lifestyle rather than upper or lower – analogous to the story of Goldilocks who found the first bowl of porridge too hot, the next too cold, before hitting upon the third which was in-between and just right: tepid. Such a mid-point is subject to change over time, and varies from region to region, as standards of living change and vary, and as available luxuries also vary and grow with material and techno-logical change. A middle way construed as an arbitrary and fluctuating mid-point involves a too literal reading of "middle." The Buddha did not turn to asceticism only to learn that he turned too far, and that he should have stopped mid-way between his princely and ascetic lives. A more apt reading is to interpret the Buddha as advocating modesty and moderation. There is merit to this reading, and it is an element of what the Buddha preached. However, it is also a simplification. Moderation does not by itself deal with the attachments and cravings that cause suffering (for one can still have cravings and attachments while living moderately or modestly). Indeed, one can even crave and be attached to living moderately or modestly, and thereby suffer from any shortfall in, or perceived threat to, this lifestyle.

In both the extremes of luxury and poverty, the Buddha noticed a concern with the body: one in trying to grant its every wish and the other in trying to deny its every wish. Asceticism places a great emphasis on the body, specifically on bodily denial and deprivation. This is problematic on two counts. First, overcoming attachment and craving is largely a mental achievement, requiring mental discipline. The Buddha did practice techniques of mental discipline prior to and during his ascetic period, but there was still a focus during this ascetic period on bodily denial, and this excessive focus undermines the capacity for having a clear and well-functioning mind. A clear head requires that the body be sufficiently fed. If the body is malnourished, the mind is debilitated. The mind is embodied, after all, and the extremes of asceticism undermine the clear mental functioning needed to deal with craving and attachment.

Second, if the objective of the ascetic life is to overcome desire fully, then this objective cannot be obtained. It is impossible to never feel hungry or thirsty, or to not desire to breathe air when gasping for breath or to sleep when long without sleep. This would be to try to overcome the demands of human embodiment. As long as we remain creatures of flesh and blood, overcoming desires such as these is impossible. Earlier it was noted that old age, sickness and death are inevitable. Hence, overcoming the suffering associated with these cannot involve eliminating old age, sickness and death; instead, it seems it must involve overcoming the desires to never be old, sick or die. This seems to be the reasonable next approach, and the ascetic path opts for this, finding the cause of suffering in desire. However, this view of desire, and the scope of desires needing to be overcome, is much too broad. As noted, one cannot eliminate certain desires and still be a functioning human being. And so while eliminating sickness, old age and death is impossible, so is eliminating all desire. And so both ends of the traditional approaches to dealing with suffering – through the satisfaction of desires and the elimination of desires – are insufficient for fully dealing with the problem of suffering. The Buddha's life story, in moving from one extreme to the other, shows the inadequacy of these traditional approaches. And even a lifestyle that adopts a measure of both approaches – trying to fully satisfy some desires while trying to fully eliminate the remaining – will bear the challenges of both these approaches. This is because the objective is to eliminate suffering entirely, and not just to reduce it. Simply put, unsatisfied desire, at least to some extent, seems ineradicable from the human condition.

There is an important connection between suffering and desire; but the ascetic path, according to Buddhism, does not get to the core of this connection. The luxuriant life tries to satisfy desires as much as possible while the ascetic path tries to undermine desires as much as possible. In the life story of the Buddha, neither approach is presented as effectively discriminating among the desires that are problematic and cause suffering from those that need not lead to suffering. The Middle Path tries to rectify this by being more cognizant of the kinds of desire that lead to suffering. These are termed 'cravings' (*trishna*), and the difference between craving and desire in general is that cravings are desires that involve attachment to self. One craves in the interests of trying to satisfy a self. It is this that is thought to be at the root of suffering. The Buddhist concept of suffering will be elaborated more fully in the next chapter and the notion of craving will be analysed in Chapter Five.

Both the life of luxury and ascetic poverty involve a concern with the self. In the case of luxury, this is much clearer for the desires of the self are being catered to; it is a life of self-indulgence. But the ascetic can also have a preoccupation with the self through self-denial and self-mortification. The ascetic, while physically impoverished, may remain with a strong attachment to ego. He may, for instance, be arrogant or high-minded about his ascetic accomplishments with little concern for others. Compassion and selflessness, and moral dealings with others or even just interactions with others, need not be a part of an ascetic life, but, as will be seen later, they are important aspects of the Buddha's path towards enlightenment.

The phrase 'Middle Way' or 'Middle Path' can be quite misleading, for it is not touted simply because it is in the middle, but rather for setting out a path that is different from what the extremes hold in common. The Middle Way differs in its concern with overcoming attachment to self and craving; and for its emphasis not only on bodily discipline, but also on mental and moral discipline (as set out in the Noble Eightfold Path, which will be described in Chapter Seven).

The Buddha does not deny the traditional Indian position that suffering arises from the gap between one's actual condition and one's desired state. But he does not accept it without qualification either. At the behest of his father, his princely life tried to narrow the gap between desire and actual state by trying to satisfy his desires. In his ascetic life, he sought to narrow this gap by trying to satisfy his desires as little as possible, and thereby to rid himself of desires as much as possible. The Middle Way does not fully reject this traditional view of the source of suffering. And neither does it fully reject the ascetic approach to lessening suffering by lessening desire. Rather, it seeks to refine both this view (of suffering) and this approach (of asceticism). The gap between desired and actual states is still viewed as causing suffering, but not all desires are considered problematic. Likewise, the approach to overcoming suffering still involves overcoming desire – for this is still the root cause – but again, it is just that not all desires are to be overcome. Again, it is craving – desire that is motivated by attachment to ego or self – that is to be overcome. The Buddhist approach to dealing with suffering still relies on overcoming attachment and desire, but unlike the ascetic approach which is heavy-handed, it aims to be more discerning.

To sum up, asceticism is unsuccessful because not all desires can be extinguished. We cannot overcome hunger and thirst, even if we can come to get by with very little. Second, the ascetic life is overly concerned with the body and specifically with denial of the body. The Buddha, in recognizing that overcoming suffering requires overcoming cravings and attachments to self, recognized that mental discipline is crucial for this task. And for this a well-functioning body is needed to attain to heights of mental discipline (for a malnourished body inhibits a sound and clear mind). And third, the Buddha's asceticism, as with his princely life, displayed a preoccupation with the self. The ascetic is consumed with self-denial, self-mortification, and while this may serve to overcome many desires, this does not by itself undo attachment to self. With the Middle Way we find a movement away from Indian approaches that seek to achieve liberation through extreme poverty and asceticism. The Middle Way, once again, is somewhat misnamed for it does not simply carve a path between two extremes (indulgence and deprivation), but rejects points held in common by both extremes (attachment to self and focus on the body). Viewing the Middle Way as simply a path of moderation ignores these crucial elements (for a moderate life may include as much, or more, self-attachment as a life of luxury). Calling it the "Middle Way" seems natural enough, given the extremes being rejected, but this should not be interpreted simply or literally.

A Symbolic Reading

The Buddha's life is upheld as providing an example, indeed an exemplar, of the path to enlightenment. And yet, the Buddhist adherent is not advised to do all that the Buddha did in his quest, but in fact to avoid certain steps the Buddha took. The Middle Way is traditionally read as commending the avoidance of both the paths of luxury and asceticism. In this reading, the Buddhist adherent is advised to do as the Buddha said to do, and not do all the Buddha himself did.

But there is also a symbolic reading of the Middle Way. According to this, the princely and ascetic lifestyles that the Buddha led prior to the Middle Path are not to be avoided, but rather provide a real trajectory on the path to enlightenment. This symbolic reading is not at odds with the traditional reading, but complements it by adding a further layer of meaning to the life story of the Buddha. On this symbolic reading, we are – or at least many of us are – already in the same predicament as was Gautama as a luxuriant prince. We may not have the same degree of riches, but we are alike to the extent that we seek comfort as a way of dealing with life's travails. Whether we strive for the pleasantness of riches, fame, glory, success, or prestige; whether we pine to satisfy an addiction; whether we indulge in entertainment, food, sex, sport, or chatter; or whether we just need the comfort of being with others to avoid feeling forlorn, we often seek comfort and distraction as a way of living life and dealing with its roughness and challenges, and this is widespread for rich and poor alike. Viewed in this manner, Gautama's luxuriant life signifies not literally a princely life, but a life that seeks to deal with suffering through an ignorance maintained in comfort, indulgence and escape. The palace walls – held secure for so long by Gautama's father, and which kept out the sights of old age, sickness and death and kept Gautama locked in and occupied with youthful and sensual pleasures – are interpreted in this symbolic reading as mental walls. These mental walls allow us to likewise maintain, or perhaps feign, ignorance of the realities of life; they are mental walls kept in place through comforts and indulgences.

Williams elaborates this point further:

> Gautama had been brought up radically to misperceive things. He saw things one way, when they are really another way. His story portrays in acute form the situation that the Buddhist claims all unenlightened people are in, whether they realize it or not.[1]

The supposedly analogous deception is that we generally deal with the prospects of such things as growing old and dying by turning our heads; we seek comforting distractions. Old age and death are inevitabilities, and we, for the most part, do not deal with our discomfort regarding them squarely; or perhaps because we see no way to deal with these

---

1 Williams (2000), pp. 28–29.

discomforts squarely, we avoid and evade. We may not be able to achieve the level of comforts of Gautama in his father's palace, but we often try to deal with the challenges of human existence by seeking comforts, and turn our eyes and minds away from perceived troubles through these comforts. But there is also a disanalogy here with the Buddha's life story: as noted above, Gautama was *raised to misperceive*; prior to having left the palace, he was not troubled by the inevitability of old age, sickness and death, not because he closed his eyes and mind to them, but because he did not know of them – according to legend, that is. This was an ignorance not of his own doing, but nevertheless maintained through comfort and distraction. Once Gautama witnessed the first three signs, he could not ignore them; he could not return to his previous luxuriant life. He realized that old age, sickness and death were unavoidable, despite any amount of comfort and riches. And thus, with the encouragement found with the fourth sign of one who has "gone forth" and who seemed to be at peace, he sought a different approach to dealing with suffering: one which was not evasive and mired in comforts, but which was directed at coming to terms with the root causes of suffering. The symbolic reading does not deny that the luxuriant life is to be avoided, but it adds that Gautama's starting point, symbolically construed, is also ours. We are not all princes, but according to this reading there is nonetheless a shared element: a turn to distraction and comfort that tries to keep certain realities of life out of sight and mind.

Gautama's ascetic turn can also be read symbolically as something to be enjoined in a way. Symbolically read, the ascetic turn is a turning away; it is a self-critical step that involves becoming aware of and confronting attachment to distraction and comfort as a way of dealing with the realities of life. To read asceticism symbolically is to recognize that distraction and comfort offer no real remedy for suffering, and that one must learn – through discipline and challenge – not to seek escape or solace in comfort. The ascetic turn, symbolically construed, does not foreswear all comfort or luxury. Instead it tries to confront certain motives for indulging in comfort and luxury: escape, avoidance, and neglect of suffering. It challenges a wilful ignorance, a building of mental walls, similar to Gautama's palace walls, which keep certain undesirable realities out of mind and at bay. The ascetic turn recognizes – just as Gautama recognized upon venturing outside his palace – that a real and lasting reprieve from suffering is not to be found in comfort, indulgence, or the effects of wilful ignorance. Read in this manner, the ascetic turn is asserting that the path to enlightenment – the Middle Way – has an order. Asceticism, symbolically read, is preparation for undertaking the further detachments from self of the Middle Way; it is a direct challenge to indulgence and avoidance for these must be faced if suffering is to be overcome. And just as reading the Buddha's luxuriant life symbolically did not suppose that we all live as princes, reading his ascetic life symbolically does not require extremes of poverty and discomfort.

On this symbolic reading, the ascetic turn is not another sorry alternative before the discovery of the Middle Way; it is not a step from which we would have to recoil back to the middle path for it is a step on this middle path. The symbolic reading holds that we already find ourselves on the path of luxury, analogous to the Buddha's princely life. The ascetic turn is the leaving of this luxuriant life. Again, symbolically construed, this leaving involves confronting the attachment to comfort in one's mind, and one's predilections for avoidance and ignorance. Symbolically read, it does not involve the extremes of asceticism but may yet involve much dispossession, forfeiture of comfort, and discipline. All this is a necessary step if self-oriented cravings and attachment to self are to be overcome, and enlightenment achieved. The symbolic reading does not conflict with the traditional reading, but complements it by bringing out a further lesson to be learned from the Buddha's life story. The symbolic reading does not deny that the literal extremes of luxury and asceticism are to be avoided, but finds that when looked at symbolically, these major stages in the Buddha's life highlight an order on the path to enlightenment that is applicable to all.

Concluding Remarks

Returning to the traditional reading, the Middle Way is an expedient to enlightenment, one that the Buddha himself did not see until after his life as a prince and ascetic. The Buddha himself did not take the most expeditious path to enlightenment. While the historical veracity is unclear, portraying the life and legend of the Buddha in these terms certainly has a pedagogic value: we see more clearly the virtue of the Middle Way by being shown – through the Buddha's own life story – that a life of luxury and a life of abject restraint are not sufficient for overcoming suffering. This should be more persuasive than merely being told the same through a teaching or doctrine. Furthermore, the Middle Way allows for a simple interpretation of moderation and modesty that is easier to appreciate and follow, and a more demanding interpretation that involves fully overcoming craving and attachment to self. But the Middle Way, on the traditional reading, conveys that the Buddha's own path was not the most direct. This may be because, as the story is presented, he was simply not aware of the Middle Way prior to having lived out the two extremes; or it may just be that, in the legend of the Buddha, this is an effective way of conveying the virtues of a Middle Way (and of course, it may be both). But what this also conveys is that the follower is directed to do as the Buddha said and not do all that he actually did in getting to the Middle Way.

What further complicates the matter is that the Buddha himself, repeatedly, opted to charge his own path towards enlightenment. This is in the nature of a religious pioneer, but it raises the question of how the example of the Buddha's life is to be viewed. The Buddha, in leaving his father's palace, chose to find his own path. In leaving his initial teachers in yogic practice, he chose to find his own path. In leaving his ascetic practice, and the ascetic disciples he had attracted, he chose to find his own path. In leaving the Brahmanic practices that were common during his day, he was leaving behind the traditions of the Vedas and Upanishads to find his own path. To look at the life of the Buddha, one might draw the lesson that enlightenment must be pursued through one's own path, and this raises questions about how to think about the role of the Buddha's teachings and the path they prescribe. In one view, and this would be a traditionally religious view, the Buddha's teachings are universally correct and the teachings the Buddha encountered from the various religious guides and gurus of his time were more or less incorrect. But there is also in Buddhism the position that teachings, including the Buddha's teachings, are not to be taken as statements of universal and eternal truth, but as practical guides to be left aside when no longer useful. This notion was introduced in the Preface with the famous simile that likens the Buddha's teachings to a raft that is to be left aside after being used to cross a river, rather than lugged around on one's back (this simile and the notions it raises will be elaborated in Chapter Fourteen). It is worth reminding ourselves, as we encounter Buddhist concepts and doctrines in the coming chapters, that the objective of the Buddhist path is a practical objective – the end of suffering and the gaining of enlightenment (these are considered synonymous) – and that the value of any teaching is ultimately a consequence of its role in realizing this objective.

IV

The First Noble Truth: Three Understandings of Suffering

Introduction

GAUTAMA LIVED A LIFE of luxury for twenty-nine years, and as an ascetic for six. He found each lifestyle inadequate for overcoming suffering. After leaving his ascetic practice, Gautama sat and meditated under a pipal tree and, with his mind quiet, he reflected on the nature of suffering, about its origins, causes and the means to its dissolution. He then experienced an awakening – an enlightenment experience in which he is said to have extinguished the suffering that had so long plagued him – and came to an understanding of the nature of human suffering and the means to its elimination. This understanding of suffering and the path to its elimination are encapsulated in his "First Preaching," commonly called the 'Four Noble Truths'. He spent the next forty-five years helping others understand and overcome suffering in the sense in which he himself came to understand and overcome.

In brief, the Four Noble Truths are as follows:

1. There is suffering (*duhkha*)
2. Suffering is caused.
3. Suffering can be eliminated by eliminating its causes.
4. The way to eliminate the causes of suffering is to follow the Noble Eightfold Path.

The concern of this chapter is the First Noble Truth. The Sanskrit word that is being translated as 'suffering' in this first Truth is '*duhkha*'. This is the usual translation, but it is also commonly noted that this is not a precise translation. Other translations are 'disharmony', 'unsatisfactoriness', 'ill', and 'sorrow'. All these translations retain a negative connotation. Coming to terms with the proper sense of '*duhkha*' is important, for it is not quite suffering as we usually conceive of it. We will translate '*duhkha*' as suffering, as this is most common, but it should be kept in mind that a proper understanding of suffering in the Buddhist conception is to be determined.

Pervasiveness and Eliminability

Notice that the First Noble Truth seems to say something quite obvious. It should be clear that there is suffering in life to anyone who has lived a little, and observed suffering in themselves or others. But the First Noble Truth aims to say more than just what is very obvious. While it is not stated in universal terms, so as to say all is suffering, the First Noble Truth does not merely affirm that some suffering exists in life,[1] or

---

1 Kalupahana notes that the Buddha was reluctant to present suffering as a universal or all-inclusive truth: "'All or everything is suffering' is a statement that is conspicuously absent in the early discourses attributed to the Buddha. A general statement about suffering is always concretized by the use of the relative pronoun 'this.' Thus the most general statement one can find in the discourses reads, 'All this is suffering.' This allows the Buddha to specify and elaborate on the conception of suffering." Kalupahana (1992), p. 86.

that there are some examples of suffering to be found. Instead, the First Noble Truth asserts that suffering is widespread and pervasive in life; it asserts that an unenlightened or unawakened existence is a suffered existence.

The view of life as pervaded by suffering may make Buddhism seem pessimistic. And this apparent pessimism would remain even if 'duhkha' were instead translated as 'ill', 'sorrow', or 'unsatisfactoriness'. Given this apparently pessimistic outlook, it may seem that Buddhism cannot be of universal appeal, speaking only to those who already share this pessimistic worldview, and not to those who do not. After all, if you do not believe that your life is pervaded by suffering, then the promise of a path out of pervasive suffering should be of little appeal. Indeed, while we all suffer some of the time, and some of us seem to suffer much of the time, it does not seem correct to say that the lives of all (unenlightened) people are pervaded by suffering. Thus, pervasive suffering faces a great burden of proof: pervasive suffering requires that we must be suffering even when we believe we are not. Buddhism aims to provide a general diagnosis of the unenlightened condition of all, and not just of those who already agree that life is pervaded by suffering. If this diagnosis of suffering, captured in the First Noble Truth, is correct, then this means that we can suffer, in some sense of the word, without realizing it. Being able to suffer without realizing it implies that suffering in the Buddhist conception must mean something different than the suffering we do readily recognize.

In what follows, two elements of the Buddhist conception of suffering will be elaborated. These are that suffering is pervasive and eliminable. These two elements are necessary conditions of the Buddhist conception of suffering, and will guide the analysis of this conception. First, as noted, the First Noble Truth holds that an unenlightened life is pervaded by suffering. This need not mean that all of unenlightened life, in every respect, is suffered; but it is to be read more strongly than as saying merely that some suffering is present in life. The Second Noble Truth asserts that suffering has causes and the Third Noble Truth that suffering can be eliminated by eliminating these causes. This brings us to a second key element in the Buddhist conception of suffering: suffering is eliminable. The eliminability of suffering is integral to Buddhism and the Buddhist path (which is supposed to find its end in Nirvana, the extinguishing of suffering). If suffering is not pervasive but only occasional, then there is less, or little, motivation or reason for taking up the Buddhist path. We can add that if suffering is not eliminable, then there should seem to be no motivation or reason for taking up this path (particularly when the Buddhist path is presented as finding its end in the end of suffering). Both pervasiveness and eliminability are integral for providing motivation and rationale for Buddhist practice.

In what has come to be known as the "First Preaching" (also known as the "First Turning of the Wheel of the Dharma") after his awakening, the Buddha – now that he is supposed to be enlightened we can call him 'Buddha', and not just 'Gautama' – presented the Four Noble Truths and their account of suffering. Below is a fuller presentation of these Truths compared with the bare-bones version presented earlier. Of particular interest for the concern of this chapter is the First Noble Truth, which elaborates upon suffering.

(1) Now this, O monks, is the noble truth of suffering: birth is suffering, old age is suffering, sickness is suffering, death is suffering, pain, sorrow, lamentation, dejection, and despair are suffering. Contact with unpleasant things is suffering, not getting what one wishes is suffering. In short the five aggregates of grasping are suffering.

(2) Now this, O monks, is the noble truth of the cause of suffering: that craving, which leads to rebirth, combined with pleasure and lust, finding pleasure here and there, namely the craving for passion, the craving for existence, the craving for non-existence.

(3) Now this, O monks, is the noble truth of the cessation of pain: the cessation without a remainder of that craving, abandonment, forsaking, release, non-attachment.

(4) Now this, O monks, is the noble truth of the way that leads to the cessation of suffering: this is the noble Eightfold Path, namely, right views, right intention, right speech, right action, right livelihood, right effort, right mindfulness, right concentration.[1]

In the First Noble Truth above, the Buddha offers several examples of suffering. It is common to find three groupings here.[2] These three groupings indicate three perspectives or understandings of suffering, each conveying successively further insight into the nature of suffering in the Buddhist conception. We will see that the third, which involves what are called the aggregates (*skandhas* in Sanskrit, *khandhas* in Pali), provides an understanding of suffering which underlies the first two.

The First Understanding

The first set of examples in the First Noble Truth above includes birth, aging, sickness, death, pain, sorrow, lamentation, grief, and despair (this list of examples varies among renditions and translations). This is an ostensive definition – definition by reference to examples – and it is not indicated in the First Noble Truth that this is an exhaustive list. It seems clear that pain, sorrow, sickness, and despair involve suffering. Aging and death, while they need not involve suffering (if one ages and dies agreeably perhaps), they can and usually do. Birth is included in this list. A mother, through the pains of pregnancy and childbirth, suffers; likewise, the infant may suffer pain and discomfort in being born. But birth is also on this list of examples because it is the start of a suffered life; in fact, it is commonly held that birth is the start of a cycle of suffered lives or a transition between one suffered life and another.

While this list provides examples of suffering, they are inadequate for proving that life is pervaded by suffering. For occasions of grief, there

---

1 *Dhammacakkappavattana Sutta, Saccasamyutta, Samyutta Nikaya* V 421-22, p. 1844.
2 Cf. Williams (2000) pp. 42-43; Gethin (1998) p. 61; and Koller (2007) pp. 54-55.

are occasions of joy (indeed, it may be the loss of this joy, such as from the company and life of a loved one, which occasions this grief). For times of sickness there are times of health, for sickness involves the privation of health and could not be viewed as sickness without this contrast. Likewise, aging is contrasted with youth, pain with pleasure, dejection with cheerfulness, despair with ecstasy or euphoria, and so on. The list does provide examples we commonly associate with suffering, but if not for their positive counterparts, these examples would not have the connotation of suffering they carry (for each example of suffering here can be viewed as resulting from the privation of its counterpart). Hence, these examples alone do not prove that suffering is pervasive, but only that suffering is common (and perhaps no more common than the opposite of suffering).

Moreover, included in this set of examples in the First Noble Truth are examples that cannot be eliminated. If even possible, it would be very difficult to eradicate experiences of sickness and pain from life; in a coma or paralysis these are perhaps avoided, but not otherwise. Old age is impossible to eradicate without dying early, and aging is altogether impossible to eradicate. And death, so long as we remain mortal, is also impossible to eradicate. However, the Third Noble Truth holds that suffering is eliminable; Nirvana is the extinguishing of suffering. Thus, these examples – including sickness, aging and death – while they may be associated with suffering, cannot *by themselves* be examples of suffering in the Buddhist sense. Gautama, of course, knew this upon leaving the palace for he was told by his driver that sickness, aging, and death are inevitable for all.

Sickness, aging and death cannot be interpreted as examples of suffering in the Buddhist conception unless Nirvana, the extinguishing of suffering, is itself reinterpreted to involve immortality, and everlasting youth and health. This would be to transcend the human condition and, certainly, there are some legends that portray the Buddha as akin to a deity. But this is misleading insofar as the Buddha's enlightened life is to provide a human example for other humans to emulate. Also, it is held that the Buddha did get ill, feel sorrow, age and die, and this additionally implies that the examples in this first grouping are not examples of suffering in themselves, but examples we associate with suffering (and thus, overcoming the suffering associated with these examples – sickness, aging, death, etc. – requires overcoming the association, and not overcoming the experiences themselves). In sum, if Nirvana, the extinguishing of suffering, is humanly possible (as the legend of the Buddha and the Third Noble Truth attest), then this first grouping of examples cannot by itself convey the Buddhist conception of suffering. A deeper understanding of suffering is required, and this takes us to the second grouping in the First Noble Truth.

The Second Understanding

The second grouping is described in the First Noble Truth above as contact with the unpleasant, and not getting what one wants. It does seem that not getting what you desire can lead to suffering, as can contact with things that are unpleasant when they are not desired. The degree of suffering, in both cases, is a function of the degree of desire for the pleasant and the degree of desire to avoid the unpleasant (i.e., the more we desire the pleasant end that we do not attain, the more we suffer). If we cannot avoid something we dislike, or cannot have something we desire, we suffer.

This second grouping takes a further step than the first grouping in observing a relation between suffering and desire. It comments on the nature of suffering, and conveys that the examples in the first grouping – pain, illness, death, to name a few – involve suffering because we desire their opposite. For instance, this second grouping provides an analysis according to which illness is not by itself suffering but that suffering arises only when we are ill and desire not to be (after all, if one desires one's ailment, then it does not seem suffered, at least not like the suffering of one who desires to be without it). Presumably then, we can be ill, even gravely ill, and not suffer as long as we have no desire to not be ill. Thus, the first grouping gives us examples and circumstances that we usually associate with suffering. The second grouping informs us that suffering arises not solely from our circumstance, but from our desire to be in a different circumstance.

Recall that with the first grouping, sickness, old age and death are neither pervasive nor eliminable features of life (and thus do not yield an understanding of suffering under the Buddhist conception). A charitable interpretation of Buddhism and the path to enlightenment – which requires that we take seriously that suffering is pervasive and eliminable, for these provide motivation and reason for taking up the Buddhist path – requires that we reject that the first grouping of examples can, by themselves, provide an understanding of suffering in the Buddhist conception. The second grouping falters similarly. While not getting what one desires can be frustrating, this cannot be all that there is to suffering in the Buddhist conception for there are also many cases, at least for many people, of getting what one desires. This is to say that the second grouping does not yield an understanding of pervasive suffering. Moreover, the association of suffering with unsatisfied desires does not account for the eliminability of suffering in the Buddhist conception. For instance, the desire to eat, sleep or even breathe, may vary in degree from one circumstance or person to the next, and the pull of these desires may be lessened through self-discipline, but they cannot be entirely eradicated. The desires to breathe when lacking oxygen, and to sleep when one has gone long without sleep, are biologically rooted reactions to a lack of air and sleep. Desires are not fully eradicable for the embodied being. Hence, unsatisfied desire cannot be all that there is to suffering in the Buddhist conception.

Freedom from suffering in the Buddhist conception does not portend a life free from pain, sickness, sorrow, grief, despair, death, or all unsatisfied desires. Insofar as these bring unhappiness, it follows that some unhappiness will remain and be a part of a life free from suffering in the Buddhist sense. Additionally, since suffering is pervasive in the Buddhist conception – and since this implies that we can suffer even when we believe we are not – it follows that we can seem to be happy, to ourselves and to others, and yet still be suffering in the Buddhist sense.

Thus, under the Buddhist conception of suffering, we can both suffer when we feel happy, and be free from suffering while also unhappy. While freedom from suffering in the Buddhist sense of suffering may bring happiness, it is not commensurate with, or simply equivalent to, the feeling of happiness. Also, an absence of unhappiness in the presence of other people's pain and distress may compromise the ability to feel and extend compassion to others. Compassion towards others is a significant component of Mahayana Buddhism in particular, and Buddhism generally, and this further suggests that freedom from suffering is not to be simply equated with freedom from unhappiness. This will be further discussed in Chapter Fourteen.

Frustrated desires often are desires for permanence. Even if we are healthy, wealthy, and young, and even if we feel we have all that we presently desire, the thought that all this will not last is associated with suffering. Even in the vigour of youth, the prospect and thought of giving way to age can cause suffering. In the midst of any desirable and pleasant state, the prospect and thought of its impermanence can lurk. And most of all, the prospect and thought of our inevitable death can arise with any experience, pleasurable or not. Gautama, when he first ventured out of his palace, was still living a life of tremendous luxury, but all the same he became greatly troubled by thoughts of impermanence. He was told by his driver that he too would grow old, become ill, and eventually die, and all this unnerved Gautama even though he was, at the time, young, healthy, and very rich. The desire for an unachievable permanence caused him to suffer. It might seem that an appropriate course of action for overcoming this suffering is to overcome the accompanying desires. We see this thinking in the move from an understanding of suffering as per the first grouping of the First Noble Truth to that of the second grouping, and in the move from Gautama's life of luxury to his life of asceticism.

The three groupings of suffering in the First Noble Truth, and the three understandings of suffering they yield, correspond to the three main stages of the Buddha's life. The first grouping corresponds with Gautama's palace life wherein suffering was associated with specific examples (sickness, old age, death) which were kept out of sight and thereby, it was hoped, out of mind. These are examples that many of us first think of when we think of suffering. The second grouping rejects this view of suffered examples in favour of finding suffering in the desires to be free of these examples. In finding the root cause of suffering in desire, this second grouping presumes to offer a deeper understanding of the nature of suffering and its mechanism. Suffering is not pain, on this view, but the desire not to be in pain (which, as it happens, usually accompanies the experience of pain and may be difficult to distinguish from it). This second grouping thus suggests a course of action for dealing with suffering: to overcome desire. This understanding of suffering corresponds to the second main stage of the Buddha's life: asceticism.

Gautama, while an ascetic, knew there was a connection between desire and suffering. Asceticism can be seen as a response to this connection for, upon finding the root cause of suffering in desire, the ascetic tries to overcome suffering, not by satisfying desires as much as possible, but by diminishing desires as much as possible (for by continually lessening desire, the gap between one's actual state and one's desired state narrows). As an ascetic, Gautama tried to combat his desires without appropriately discriminating; he did not realize at the time what he later claimed to know, namely, that it is craving (*trishna*), a specific kind of desire, that is problematic. There are specific aspects of craving that differentiate them from other desires (and this will be attended to closely in the next chapter), but the key factor that marks a craving, and that leads to suffering in the Buddhist conception, is an attachment to self. It is this understanding of suffering that corresponds to the third stage – the enlightened stage – of the Buddha's life. It is this understanding of suffering that is given in the third grouping of the First Noble Truth.

The Third Understanding

The third grouping in the First Noble Truth, and the account of suffering it provides, is the key to understanding both the pervasiveness of

suffering as well as the potential for its elimination. Suffering is pervasive, on this understanding, because of attachment to self, something we
generally take to be independent of our ever-changing psychophysical
states. The third grouping establishes the pervasiveness of suffering by
connecting it to the entrenchment of our attachment to self. We are
aware of our desires, hopes, and fears as the desires, hopes and fears of a
self; we pursue the satisfactions of desires, hopes, and fears, not simply
out of biological compulsion, but also to satisfy this sense of self. But
it is one thing to say this attachment to self is pervasive, and another
thing to say it is suffered (for this is not clear, especially given that we
often pursue the interests of our "selves" in order to relieve or avoid
suffering; this will be discussed further below). In addition, on this third
understanding, suffering is considered eliminable because it is held that
this attachment to self can be overcome. This is not to overcome all
desires, hopes, and fears, as an ascetic may attempt, but to overcome
attachment to self in one's desires, hopes and fears. For instance, there is
a difference between the desire to breathe when lacking oxygen, and the
connected and anxious thought that there is a self who will perish if this
desire is not satisfied. The former is unavoidable – for again, some desires
arise simply in virtue of being embodied creatures with instinctive or
hard-wired reactions – but the Buddhist conception holds that the latter,
through discipline, can be overcome.

Buddhism does not promise the eradication of the examples in the
first grouping of the First Noble Truth (e.g., pain, sickness, death).
Again, these are inevitable in the human condition. Without attachment
to self, these states will still occur, but there is cause to think that they
will not matter in quite the same way. For instance, the prospect of aging
and death will be less troubling if we do not view these as involving the
demise of an enduring self. Likewise, unsatisfied desires as presented in
the second grouping will still be experienced as they are an ineradicable
part of human existence. But without a sense of self vested in the desire,
there is again cause to think that this will not matter in quite the same
way. For instance, while being without food for a long time does cause
hunger – which is a desire – being without attachment to self means that

it will not matter in quite the same way as when there is the accompanying anxious thought that the well-being, and perhaps existence, of a self or ego is at stake with the unsatisfied hunger.

In the third and last part of the First Noble Truth it is said that the five aggregates of grasping or attachment are suffering. The five aggregates are the constituents of our awareness of self. It is held that there is nothing other than these five aggregates in our awareness of self; in particular, there is no underlying and permanent entity that exists apart from these constituents. Attaching a sense of permanent selfhood to the aggregates is asserted to be the root cause of suffering, and hence the aggregates are known as aggregates of attachment. The lack of a permanent and independent self is the claim of the doctrine of No Self. An argument for the doctrine of No Self can be developed from an examination of the five aggregates, and this will follow below (the doctrine will be further discussed in Chapter Eight).

The Five Aggregates

The Buddha, after the First Preaching of the Four Noble Truths, preached of the non-existence of self and soul. It is the existence of a self in a substantive sense – as an entity existing separately from the ever-changing aggregates – that is repudiated. This is held to be an entity we identify with. It is an entity that seems to stand separately as agent or author, and preside over and issue directives over our thoughts and behaviours; an entity that stands as the subject of what happens to our bodies and the viewer of what occurs in our minds; an entity that seems to remain intact and, in some essential respect unchanged, through all the changes that occur to our minds and bodies. Careful attention to the five aggregates yields an argument for No Self that repudiates the notion of self in these sorts of considerations.

The primary method for the Buddha, in determining that there is no substantial self or soul, was empiricist: the judgement was based on careful observation. Observing the states of his body, and the contents of his mind, he observed that there is nothing that remains constant in his awareness. There is no entity observed with the qualities listed in the paragraph above. The body changes through the processes it undergoes, and the contents of the mind are observed to be in constant flux. Through observation, the Buddha finds no underlying and unchanging self that stands behind his mental and physical processes; rather, he observes only the processes. He calls these processes the five aggregates of attachment (*skandhas* in Sanskrit, and *khandhas* in Pali). The aggregates refer to the different sorts of things the Buddha encountered in carrying out this careful inward investigation. These five aggregates are bodily processes, sensations, perceptions, mental formations, and consciousness, and our false sense of being a self is said to be built from attachment to these aggregates.

1. Bodily Processes

The first aggregate is standardly interpreted to refer to our body and its different physical states and processes. The idea here is that our sense of self – what we take to be our self – is no more than a composite of this body and its states, together with the mental states and processes identified in the other aggregates. In looking to my body and its processes, there is nothing that I find that is my self. True enough, there are bodily parts, states and processes that I associate with myself and as belonging to myself, but the thought is that I do not take these to be the same as my self. For instance, I can speak of *my* eyes, *my* stomach, *my* indigestion, or *my* body. The body and its states, at least in our way of speaking, are possessed by the self. The self is presumed to be that which directs and moves the body, experiences the things that happen to the body, but to not be the same thing as the body.

With this first aggregate, two interpretations will be considered. The first, just noted, is that the first aggregate refers to the physical body and its physical processes (*rupa*). This is the standard interpretation. A second, nonstandard interpretation is that this first aggregate involves, not the actual body and its physical processes, but the awareness of the body and its processes. The remaining four aggregates all involve mental states and contents that we can observe introspectively. The second interpretation of this first aggregate involves viewing it in the same manner as these other aggregates.

As just noted, the standard view favours interpreting the first aggregate as referring to our actual bodily states and processes (*rupa skandha*). But this view faces some difficulties. First, it renders the first aggregate dissimilar from the rest, for it speaks of physical states and processes whereas the other aggregates all speak of mental states and processes. On this standard interpretation, the physical components of this first aggregate could not be objects encountered in the mind's eye through an act of introspection or meditation, as the other aggregates are able to be encountered. The other aggregates, as we will soon see, are all introspectible mental states, and thus the Buddha's empiricism – his methodology of observation – would be differently employed for this first aggregate than for the others (note that speaking of mental states in contrast to physical states involves using terms that refer to the contents of our minds as we observe them from a first person point of view, and does not imply that the mental states are non-physical or immaterial). In a similar vein, the doctrine of Impermanence applies to the aggregates and asserts that the aggregates arise and pass. But this sense of impermanence as involving arising and passing is more clearly applicable to mental states than to physical states (for while physical states do change ceaselessly, their manner of change is categorically unlike the quick arising and passing of mental states from the mind's awareness). Being able to apply the doctrine of Impermanence univocally and consistently is again a reason for reading the first aggregate in a manner similar to the others (this sense of impermanence as involving arising and passing will be discussed in Chapter Nine).

The standard interpretation of the first aggregate, as referring to the physical body and its processes, is additionally challenged by the following question, which at first may not seem obvious: why stop at these physical boundaries? To elaborate, the aggregates are supposed to include all that we can encounter and associate with our sense of self. We certainly do associate our bodies with our self-concept, and this is accommodated in the first aggregate. But the question arises as to whether other physical entities that are closely identified with one's sense of self should also be included as aggregates. For instance, if I have a keepsake that has been handed down in my family for generations, and if this keepsake has a story and special meaning and contributes significantly to my sense of self, and to my sense of being an abiding or continuing entity over time, then for the sake of consistency and completeness, it seems that this keepsake should be listed as an aggregate (for it is also a possible constituent of my sense of being a continuous self). Furthermore, why not include a person's wardrobe, or house, or car, if these physical items also contribute to a person's identity and sense of being a continuing self? Or why not abstract items such as principles or causes or careers, for these might also be similarly associated and identified? Or what of other entities that may be judged to exist and that may be closely associated with one's sense of being an enduring self over time, such as a ghost or a spirit or a god? The monist, for instance, may want to include all physical (and non-physical) reality in his conception of self (i.e., his True Self or Atman), and thus, all reality should presumably be included as an aggregate (for again, the aggregates are to include all constituents that may be attached to or identified with one's sense of self). Once we view the first aggregate as pertaining to the physical body and its states, we run the danger of treading into absurdity, for then other things (physical and non-physical, concrete and abstract, earthly and divine) that may also exist separately from our sensations, perceptions, and other mental aggregates, and that we may associate or identify with our sense of self or self-concept, should also be listed as aggregates. Once again, if the conclusion to be drawn is that nothing among the aggregates can account for our self-concept as an enduring entity over time, then the categories of the aggregates should include all that can be encountered and associated with this self-concept. But once we venture beyond the contents of the mind in accounting for this self-concept, then there is no reason to stop with just the physical body. Anything can then be an aggregate if it is identified with our sense of self.

The aggregates catalogue the building blocks of our self-concept. Based on the observations of the aggregates, the Buddha concludes that none of these, singularly or collectively, justify the substantive self-concept to which we are attached. In light of the above discussion, it seems that a charitable reading of the 'Argument from the Aggregates' (which is what this argument for no self will be called), warrants interpreting this first aggregate as not referring to the body and its processes themselves, but to the awareness of the body and its processes. This interpretation does not question the existence of the physical body, or of physical substance generally; but it does convey that the argument for no self that is based on the observation of the aggregates runs into difficulty when the aggregates include the physical body. Admittedly though, this is not the standard interpretation. The standard interpretation is clearly exegetically supported, but the other interpretation given here seems to serve argumentative consistency better (and that is why it is raised). For our purposes though, it is enough to draw attention to and elucidate the different approaches to this first aggregate, and to critically consider them, without having to render a verdict.

2. Sensations

It is held that there are six kinds of sensations, and they are each either pleasurable, painful, or neutral. The first five kinds of sensations are a product of the contact between our bodies – our sense organs in particular – and the external world. These include sensations gained through contact of the eyes with visible forms, the ears with sounds, the nose with odours, the tongue with tastes, and tactile sensations involving contact with the body's surface. The sixth kind are internal sensations involving the contact of the mind with mental objects. The mind is considered here as akin to a sixth sense faculty; as providing a sixth basis for sensation, on par with the other five (but not a mysterious or paranormal sixth sense faculty). Unlike the other five, mind sensations are gained introspectively. The difference between mind and eye sensations, for instance, is not the nature of the sensation (for both may be a sensation of redness, for instance), but their source. The eye comes into contact with external visible forms, and this produces sensations. But similar sensations may also arise inwardly in introspective observation, perhaps through imagining or recollecting. Since these are not directly caused by contact with external visible forms, or involve the outer sense modalities, a sixth faculty – an inner sense faculty – is needed to account for these. To be clear, the only difference between mind sensations and the others is their proximate or immediate cause: if the immediate cause of a sensation is your recollecting, imagining, or hallucinating it, that is, if the proximate or immediate cause is your own mind, then it is called a mind sensation; if the proximate or immediate cause is your sensory organs being affected by something external, then it is not a mind sensation but one of the others.

3. Perceptions

Perception is different from sensation in that it incorporates conceptualization. Thus, I might have a visual sensation of something small reddish and round, but when I see it with immediacy as a red apple, then that is a perception. A perception involves seeing something *as* something, subsuming sense data under a concept; it involves recognizing something as being the cause of our sensations. A sensation, in contrast, imparts only raw sensory data without interpretation or conceptualization. Thus, a perception is different from a sensation due to its cognitive and conceptual content. Thus, when I see a pen, or book, or chair, this is regarded as a perception because it involves not just being affected by sense data but the application of a concept or category in experiencing that sense data. Like sensations, perceptions are of six kinds: five corresponding to the different sense faculties plus mind perceptions. For example, if I hear words spoken on the radio, then this involves auditory perceptions. If I later recall and hear those words in my mind's ear, then the immediate cause is not my ear coming into contact with sound waves, but recollection in my mind, which renders it a mind perception.

4. Mental Formations – Intentional and Volitional Activity

This aggregate involves our responses to perceptions and includes instances of our will, intentions, and dispositions or inclinations. For instance, I may see a scrumptious chocolate cake (a perception) and be led to a desire for cake (an intention, or intentional state). This aggregate includes states such as desires, fears, hopes, likes, dislikes, loves, hatreds, expectations, etc. These are intentional states, to use a philosophical term. Intentional states are so called because they have an object towards which they intend; that is, they are mental states that are directed at or about something, be it a person, place or thing (e.g., a particular desire is always a desire *for* something, a fear is a fear *of* or *about* something). The connection between an intentional state and the object towards which it intends can involve an attachment to self, that is, an egoistic concern for one's self. In so doing, the connection is said to be karmic, or generate karma, and cause suffering. The attachment to self or ego within intentional states will be elaborated in the next chapter in its discussion of cravings. The Buddhist understanding of karma will be discussed later in Chapter Eleven.

5. Consciousness

The last aggregate – consciousness – includes states of awareness, including the awareness of the other aggregates. There is a difference between having perceptions and desires, and being aware of having perceptions and desires. The latter is not itself a perception or desire, and the aggregate of consciousness includes these states of awareness. To elaborate, there is a difference between perceiving a tree, and my being aware of perceiving a tree. Both are introspectible contents of my mind. I can notice the perception as a content in my mind, and I can notice that I am aware of the perception as a content in my mind. The awareness of other mental states is a mental state itself and one of which we can be introspectively aware. These states of awareness are included in the aggregate of consciousness. It is in the aggregate of consciousness that reflection and higher-order awareness (i.e., being aware of being aware) are included.

The Buddha and David Hume

These aggregates are the sorting categories for the contents of our minds. They are supposed to encompass all that we encounter in our conscious minds and that we associate with our sense of self. The Buddha contends that our sense of self is no more than a composite product of these aggregates. Whenever we are aware of ourselves, whenever we look within and observe, we find only one or more of these aggregates at work; one or more of bodily states and processes, sensations, perceptions, volitions or intentions, or instances of conscious awareness. We observe that these aggregates are in constant flux, and we observe nothing else – nothing enduring and stable – outside of or underlying these aggregates. There is no agent or owner or subject or soul encountered as existing apart from these aggregates. There is, in other words, nothing to ground a belief in and attachment to a permanent self. Whether or not the classification of mental content in terms of the five aggregates is exhaustive of all possible mental content, or whether or not it fits well with contemporary classifications of mental content, is beside the point of this argument for No Self. What matters for the argument is whether anything that can be observed or experienced can serve to justify a belief in, and attachment to, a permanent self or soul. The Buddha, carefully carrying out these observations, concluded not.

This line of argument is empiricist. It is making a judgement about what can be known to exist based on what is or can be observed, and the line of argument is very similar to that of another empiricist, David Hume. Hume stated:

For my part, when I enter most intimately into what I call *myself*, I always stumble on some particular perception or other, of heat or cold, light or shade, love or hatred, pain or pleasure. I never can catch *myself* at any time without a perception, and never can observe any thing but the perception. When my perceptions are removed for any time, as by sound sleep, so long am I insensible of *myself*, and may truly be said not to exist. And were all my perceptions removed by death, and could I neither think, nor feel, nor see, nor love, nor hate, after the dissolution of my body, I should be entirely annihilated, nor do I conceive what is farther requisite to make me a perfect non-entity. If any one, upon serious and unprejudiced reflection, thinks he has a different notion of *himself*, I must confess I can reason no longer with him. All I can allow him is, that he may be in the right as well as I, and that we are essentially different in this particular. He may, perhaps, perceive something simple and continued, which he calls *himself*; though I am certain there is no such principle in me.[1]

Hume noted that in introspective awareness, we observe nothing other than various mental states: beliefs, thoughts, emotions, feelings, memories, etc., all of which he grouped under the term 'perceptions'; we observe nothing that stands as owner or agent to these mental states. We do not encounter the believer behind a belief, the thinker behind a thought, the viewer of an inner image, etc. Even when we recall a memory, or conjure an image of ourselves, that is just to encounter another thought, another mental object or image, and not a self that stands behind the thought or image. Descartes contended that so long as I am thinking I can know that I exist, for it seemed to him that thought is impossible without a thing having the thought. Hume, relying on an empiricist methodology, attested that we do not encounter or experience any such "thinking thing." Basing his judgement of what exists on what can be observed or experienced, he argued that the sense of self we have, and are familiar with, is simply a composite or bundle of various mental states, without a permanent self or "owner" standing behind this bundle and its states. This has since been known as the "bundle" or "no owner" theory of self.

The Buddha argued in a similar empiricist fashion to Hume (although this is not the only Buddhist line of argument for the doctrine of No Self, as will be seen in Chapter Eight). It is an argument realized in

---

1 Hume's *Treatise of Human Nature* 1.4.6. Italics are Hume's.

the course of mindful, inward awareness or meditation. The Buddha, as Hume, also noted that these observed processes are always in flux. Hence, not only is there no agent observed behind any given mental state – no thinker observed behind the thought – but also, there is no justification for the claim of a permanent entity if all that is observed or experienced is impermanent. If everything experienced comes and goes from the mind's awareness, then there is no empiricist basis for the judgement of a permanent or abiding self. This connects the doctrines of No Self and Impermanence, which will be discussed more fully in Chapter Nine.

Importantly, the Buddha, and here he differs from Hume, held that the realization of No Self had practical consequences. He advocated that his followers realize fully, which is to do more than just to come to believe, the lack of the existence of a permanent and independent self. It is held that for all of us who are unenlightened, the sense of being a self, in the substantive sense indicated, is strong and entrenched. It is part and parcel of how we see the world; how we interact with others; and how we think of our own ambitions, desires, plans, etc. Overcoming the suffering that is said to come with this attachment to self involves significant psychological change. The Buddha famously asserted: "If a man should conquer in battle a thousand and a thousand more, and another man should conquer himself, his would be the greater victory, because the greatest of victories is victory over oneself."[1] In the Buddhist conception, the pervasiveness of this attachment to self – its presence throughout our thoughts and behaviours, cravings and aversions, accounts for the pervasiveness of suffering. But suffering is also held to be eliminable because it is held that this attachment can be overcome, since it involves identifying with a non-existent entity. Fully realizing that this abiding self does not exist involves not just a change in belief, but a wholesale reform of thoughts, intentions, desires, behaviours, and more.

As discussed, we cannot escape suffering as understood in the first two groupings of the First Noble Truth without escaping our mortality

---

1 *Dhammapada*, Ch. 8, 103.

and our embodied existences. However, we can overcome suffering as understood in the third grouping because attachment to a sense of self (as being something that exists separately from the ever-in-flux psychophysical aggregates) is alleged to be an unnecessary and eliminable attachment. That is, suffering according to the third grouping is not caused by our embodied and mortal natures, but by psychological attachments and cravings that keep this sense of self in place. The undoing of these attachments and cravings thus serves to undo the cause of this suffering. This is to undo a delusion for which we are ourselves ultimately responsible and to which we are closely attached. To overcome this, careful and honest self-examination is advocated in Buddhism. It is asserted that if we look carefully at our psychophysical states, we will find no self that stands independent from these states. But again, the objective is not simply to amend this belief. In the Buddhist view, even upon amending the belief in self, the attachment to self may persist in our desires, hopes, aversions, behaviours, and more (this is to speak to the affective component – as opposed to solely the cognitive component – of our attachment to self, and it is the harder component to dislodge). That we can explicitly hold a belief in no self but, quite easily, demonstrate the contrary attachment in our behaviour and intentional states is telling and important for Buddhism. It means that an attachment to self can be much more entrenched than we recognize, and can persist even after the belief in a permanent self is explicitly rejected. In the Buddhist view, our attachments to self – and thus the roots of suffering in the Buddhist conception – run very deep.

Concluding Remarks

Serious questions can be raised concerning why attachment to self should be construed as suffering, particularly because it seems that such an attachment can bring many apparent benefits. For starters, attachment to self can bring about pleasures that would not otherwise be experienced, for often we will pursue and indulge in comforts, not simply for the pleasant feelings they arouse, but for the pleasantness they arouse to our sense of self. Chocolate has a very nice taste, but the pleasure I gain from eating chocolate is not just the taste to the palate, but the pleasure of satisfying a self through the palate.

Also, the attachment to self carries survival advantages for an individual. For instance, a person may avoid the prospect of bodily harm not only out of a desire to avoid the accompanying pain, or out of instinct, but also out of conscious thoughts of self-preservation. With an attachment to self, the conscious aversion to pain is not simply an aversion to the sensation, but an aversion to causing *oneself* pain and harm, and this adds impetus to averting pain and harm. We can readily conceive of attachment to self as being an adaptive mechanism which is naturally selected, for it provides further incentive for self-preservation. Another example: worrying over a school grade can be worrying *for one's self*, and display attachment to self. Presumably, suffering in the form of worrying over a grade can be eliminated by stopping the worrying. This may be difficult, but Buddhism offers techniques for mental discipline that can be used for this. But to eliminate the worrying is to eliminate something that can be seen to have value: the worrying for one's self may lead one to work harder, to be more careful, and thereby it can lead one to succeed. The concern for self and furthering self-interest can, in other ways as well, lead individuals to strive and succeed. The elimination of attachment to self may eliminate suffering in the Buddhist conception, but it is not without consequence and the loss of much that we at present value. While Buddhism does not advocate for abandoning a sense of self, it does prescribe overcoming *attachment* to self in the specific sense of something permanent and independent of the ever-changing aggregates. But as just described, this attachment can be a source of pleasure, benefit and survival advantage.

The first grouping of the First Noble Truth gave us examples, such as sickness, old age and death, which we readily associate with suffering. The second grouping was also in line with an intuitive understanding of suffering for it is clear that unsatisfied desires are often frustrating. With the third grouping, we arrive at a conception of suffering that is supposed to lie deeper, and that can account for both the necessary elements of the pervasiveness and eliminability of suffering in the Buddhist conception (and thus the third grouping yields the only understanding of suffering among the three groupings that fits the Buddhist conception; it is, to emphasize, the only potentially eliminable suffering). But in doing so we have also veered further away from an intuitive and obvious understanding of suffering (and even if we look to the other connotations of 'duhkha', involving unsatisfactoriness or sorrow, it is still far from clear that attachment to self must imply the pervasiveness of these qualities). If we begin to question whether the Buddhist conception of suffering is really suffered, we question whether there really is motivation for, or benefit to, taking up the Buddhist path (which is described as having its point and purpose in the end of suffering). The Buddhist conception of suffering, involving an attachment of self to the ever-changing aggregates, may be better described as a spiritual suffering (and this may be a suffering that we do not readily recognize as such without being of the appropriate mindset and preparation, and perhaps it is only really recognized as suffering upon its alleviation). Indeed, the very pervasiveness of suffering in the Buddhist conception may explain why we may not recognize it as suffering: we lack the experience of being without this sort of suffering, and so may not recognize that we suffer in this way because we lack a contrasting perspective. Still, if we are to call it a kind of suffering – spiritual or not – there should be a recognizable reason for calling it so. This concern will be further attended to in the next two chapters, on suffering and craving and the end of suffering respectively.

V

The Second Noble Truth:
An Analysis of Craving

Introduction

As discussed in the last chapter, the three groupings of suffering in the First Noble Truth correspond to the three stages of the Buddha's life. The first grouping, with its examples, conveys how suffering is usually conceived: pain, sickness, aging, etc. Thus, the way to avoid suffering is to not be in pain, not get sick, old and die, and ideally these should not be brought into mind either. This is what Gautama's palatial life tried to bestow (by keeping all signs of sickness, old age, and death outside the walls). The second grouping shows an understanding of suffering that corresponds to the Buddha's ascetic life. The second grouping observes that the root cause of suffering is desire, and specifically unsatisfied desire. Thus, pain need not be suffered as long as one is disciplined enough to not be bothered by the pain. In his ascetic life, the Buddha underwent severe conditioning and impoverishment in order to lessen his desires and to overcome the temptations of his desires. The third grouping corresponds to the Buddha's enlightened life as he realized that it was not just any desire that instigated suffering, but desires that involve an attachment to self (specifically, to the sense of being an enduring self that is independent of the ever-in-flux aggregates). This specific kind of desire is called 'craving' (*trishna*, which translates literally as thirst). The Second Noble Truth asserts that cravings are the cause of suffering. This chapter will analyse the notion of craving and its connection to suffering, and the distinction between cravings and other desires that are not cravings.

Craving is a kind of desire that involves attachment to self. To illustrate, hunger is a natural response to an empty stomach. It is an evolved reaction to a need for sustenance and nutrition, and cannot be eliminated entirely (and as hunger also manifests as a kind of pain, the pains of hunger cannot be eliminated entirely either). For the adept ascetic who is habituated to living off very little food, it is nevertheless unavoidable to feel some hunger – to desire some food – when the stomach is empty (particularly so when it has been without food for a long time). The ascetic may be disciplined enough to deal easily with this hunger, but the desire itself is biologically rooted and will still arise. But in the Buddhist conception, the desire for food need not be suffered, even when it is unsatisfied. Suffering in the Buddhist conception arises when we have a *craving* for food; when the desire involves trying to satisfy a self who yearns for food. This craving for food – this trying to satisfy a self over and above trying to meet a biological requirement – is held to be eliminable. Without an invested sense of self in the hunger, the hunger may remain but it will not be a craving. Likewise, one may be in pain, or grief, but these need not be suffered according to the Buddha. Suffering arises when we crave, in order to assuage a sense of self, to not be in pain or grief. According to the Buddha, cravings can – with training and discipline – be uprooted. They involve attachment to an entity that is held to not exist. This is the sense of suffering to be overcome and, unlike the pang of an empty stomach and the biologically rooted response of desiring food, it is the only suffering that can potentially be overcome.

Once we divorce pain, sorrow, etc., from attachment to self, then an important dimension of these experiences is removed. Again, there will still be pain (for instance, there will still be specific neuronal responses resulting from exterior tissue damage due to a cut or lesion). But there will not be the associated anxiety and trepidation that comes with thinking of a "me" that is in pain. Without this dimension, states such as grief and sorrow may remain, but presumably would be very different, and perhaps diminished, without a sense of a *me* that is in grief, or of *my* sorrow. Investing a sense of self in one's hunger or pain can cause suffering that is over and above the feelings of hunger and pain. The experiences are exacerbated when it is thought that there is a self who will suffer from the hunger and pain, and who will benefit from their alleviation. It is this dimension that is held to be eliminable by the Buddha.

An attachment to self may add to the need for expediency in resolving a feeling such as hunger. It may lead to the thought or fear or anxiety that one's well-being, and perhaps one's very self, is at stake with the unsatisfied hunger, and this may add impetus to finding food to satisfy the hunger.[1] But in the Buddhist view, while it may add urgency to our desires, and press us to bring about their satisfaction, attachment to self is also held to be suffered.

Craving and Permanence

According to Buddhist doctrine, impermanence is an aspect of our world that is closely linked to suffering. It might seem that a desire for permanence must cause suffering, for, in an impermanent world, it must end in frustration. The desire for immortality is an example. However, this thinking is too quick: suffering in the Buddhist conception is not simply a matter of a *desire* for permanence in an impermanent world; it must be a *craving* to be suffered.

Consider that some desires for permanent states of affairs – such as a desire for a lasting world peace – need not cause suffering in the Buddhist sense. An unsatisfied desire for a lasting world peace may be upsetting. But there are many unsatisfied desires that can be upsetting and painful

---

1 See the closing section of the previous chapter for further discussion of this.

(such as continuing thirst, hunger, etc.). As already explained, unsatisfied desires need not be suffered under the Buddhist conception of suffering (for if they were, suffering could not be eliminated for not all desires can either be entirely satisfied or eliminated). Therefore, while a desire for permanence (such as for permanent world peace) may remain unsatisfied, this does not by itself imply that it must be a suffered desire. The mere inclusion of permanence in an unsatisfied desire does not alone make the difference between suffering and not suffering. Only if the desire for permanence is a craving – only if it involves a concern for an enduring or permanent self – does the desire for permanence involve suffering in the Buddhist conception.

A craving is a special kind of desire; one that entails the existence of the desirer's continuing self. To illustrate this, consider a desire for the fleeting experience of sexual gratification. The lack of this gratification might indeed be distressing, but this is not by itself suffering in the Buddhist sense. But suppose that what's desired is that *I be a person* who experiences sexual gratification – that is, that a continuing "I" be the subject of this experience – that this continuing subject be in one state rather than another (even though that state may be fleeting). This is the kind of desire that is being called a craving, and this is what Buddhism aims to free one from. Not, in this case, by providing sexual gratification, but rather by removing the desirer's concern about his continuing self. Having at least some unsatisfied desires is an inevitability in life and the Buddha's unsuccessful experience with asceticism is supposed to show this. We can't expect the world to conform to all our desires, and we can't make all our desires conform to the world. What we can do though, according to the Buddha, is eliminate cravings.

As discussed, the Buddha, in the third grouping of the First Noble Truth, links suffering to the five aggregates (which are referred to as the 'aggregates of attachment'). These aggregates are the constituents we associate with our sense of self. These are called 'aggregates of attachment' because we readily attach a sense of self to these aggregates (as when we think along the lines of *my* body, *my* desires, *my* sensations, *my* feelings, etc.). While the aggregates are ever-changing, the sense of self we attach to the aggregates is thought to remain the same through these changes. It is the subject or experiencer of the changing aggregates that, in some essential capacity, is presumed to remain the same or permanent over time. It is held that we attach a sense of permanent selfhood to the ever-changing aggregates and in this way suffering is connected to permanence. Our concept of self does seem to presume permanence, that is, a continuing existence as the same entity over time. This is evident in the way we speak for we use the same word, 'I', to refer to ourselves at different times in our lives despite the many changes we have undergone and continue to undergo. This attachment to permanence may involve the presumption of being an undying and unchanging soul, or it may just be the sense of being the same self through the changes experienced through one's lifetime. But again, it is attachment to a sense of permanence – of being the same self in some essential respect over time – that is involved with cravings and is the source of suffering in the Buddhist conception (the notion of remaining the same self over time will be discussed again in Chapters Nine and Eleven).

Craving and Wanting – A Difference in Kind

In order to clarify terminology, we will stipulate a difference between cravings and wants as different *kinds* of desires: cravings are desires vested with a sense of self and pursued in the interest of satisfying this self, and wants are desires that are not vested with a sense of self, and are not pursued in the interests of satisfying a sense of self.[1] The former lead to suffering in the Buddhist conception while the latter do not. And thus the end of suffering – Nirvana or Enlightenment – involves the elimination of cravings but not of wants. Wanting, after all, cannot be entirely eliminated anyway; many of the activities we do, from getting up, to brushing our teeth, to making turns while driving a car, to doing our daily chores and tasks, may not get done without there being wants

---

1 See also Williams (2000), p. 44.

leading the way. When I get up to brush my teeth I need not explicitly tell myself that I want to do so, but there may still be a want leading the way (without which I may skip brushing). Furthermore, there is no contradiction in saying that enlightenment involves the elimination of cravings and also saying that it is an objective that can be wanted (and thus desired) for these are different in kind. Cravings for enlightenment must end if enlightenment is to be achieved, but wanting enlightenment — which is equivalent to wanting to end cravings — is not only possible but necessary for leading to practices for reaching enlightenment.[1]

When we crave we do not just want with more emphasis, or with greater intensity. Again, craving involves attachment to self; it involves the feeling or sense that something is at stake for oneself in one's desires (we might say that it involves the sense of being a stakeholder in one's desires). Cravings are pursued in the interest of satisfying one's sense of self and unsatisfied cravings are felt as suffered by this sense of self. The difference between cravings and wants is one of kind, and not just of degree, and this underlies why cravings cause Buddhist suffering while wants do not.

In order to see this more clearly, let us suppose the converse is true, namely, that cravings and wants do not differ in kind but only in degree (i.e., suppose that cravings are strong or burning desires and wants are weak desires with no other relevant difference). There are a number of difficulties with this view. For one, a strong desire, without attachment to self, need not be problematic in the Buddhist view. An example is a strong, but selfless, desire for world peace. If a strong desire is unsatisfied,

---

1 Williams elaborates upon this distinction: "... it does not follow from wanting something that one has a craving for it. The Buddha's alms-round was
   not the result of craving ... Thus it was not considered faulty, and certainly
   not contradictory (as people sometimes tell me) for a Buddhist to want
   enlightenment. A Buddhist wants enlightenment in the sense that wanting
   something is a condition of freely and intentionally engaging in practices
   to bring it about. It is indeed faulty to have craving for enlightenment and,
   since the Buddhist path is precisely designed to bring craving to an end, to
   want enlightenment is to want practices which will eliminate among other
   things craving after enlightenment itself. There is no contradiction in any of
   this." Williams (2000), p. 44.

frustration may ensue (and presumably more frustration than for a weakly felt desire). But merely being an unsatisfied desire is not sufficient for constituting suffering in the Buddhist conception. As explained in the previous chapter, unsatisfied desires are unavoidable in life while suffering in the Buddhist sense is held to be eliminable. Some desires – weak and strong – are just unavoidable consequences of being embodied creatures (e.g., the desire for sleep is unavoidable given a length of time without sleep, and fittingly, a strong desire for sleep is unavoidable given a very long time without sleep). The eliminability of suffering means that cravings cannot simply be strong desires.

In addition, we can observe that many desires become stronger the longer they remain unsatisfied (as is the case with the above-mentioned desire for sleep). If the difference between wanting and craving is solely one of degree, then at some point the want for sleep becomes a craving merely in virtue of becoming sleepier. A difficulty with this is that it is not clear at what point this turn is made (for again, we are supposing, for the sake of consideration, that there is no difference of kind that could mark the turn). Moreover, saying that only strong desires cause suffering under the Buddhist conception suggests that we should aim to satisfy desires while they are still weak and before they become strong. Thus, to avoid incurring suffering, we should give in to desires for food, sex, ill will, vengeance, wrath, etc., while they are weak, and before they have a chance to grow strong. This, however, promotes a licentiousness that is at odds with the Buddhist emphasis on discipline and compassion on the path to enlightenment. Strength of desire may usually or often be part of craving; cravings, for instance, may often be felt as burning desires, and this for reason of being wound up with trying to satisfy a sense of self. But merely being a strong desire is not sufficient for being a craving. Simply characterizing the difference between craving and wanting in terms of a difference in degree – a difference in strength of desire – does not bring out the character of craving. There is a difference in kind that must be accounted for, and the following two sections will elaborate this.

The Character of Craving – Qualitative Observations

The Buddha, upon enlightenment, is held to have overcome attachment to self, and with this a whole set, but not all, of his desires were extinguished. These desires have been called 'cravings'. Clearly, we associate pain, sorrow, sickness, and many unsatisfied desires with suffering; this is true now just as it was in the Buddha's time. That these need not involve suffering under the Buddhist conception tells us that there is something special about this conception of suffering; something that, once overcome, does not stop pain, sickness and unsatisfied desires from being experienced, but does stop them from being suffered in some way (or from being unsatisfactory in some way, to use another connotation of *duhkha*). And hence there is something special about the nature of craving, and something special about the investment of a sense of self in a craving, that makes it suffered. There is a difference between feeling pain or sickness, and feeling pain or sickness with attachment to self; there is, in other words, a difference in kind between mere wanting and craving. This section will elaborate upon this difference in kind, and the special characteristics of craving.

To begin, it is important to note that attachment to self may usually, but need not always, involve selfishness. It is the attachment to being a self in the sense of something permanent and independent of the ever-changing aggregates that is problematic in the Buddhist view, and this can be present in even unselfish people. As noted, a presumption of the Buddhist conception of suffering is that suffering is pervasive. If attachment to self simply meant selfishness, then suffering would not be pervasive – for many of us are not predominantly selfish, and a few of us are rarely selfish. Again, it is the attachment to the sense of being a permanent self, separate from the ever-changing aggregates, that explains the pervasiveness of suffering in Buddhism (and unselfish persons can still believe and feel themselves to be a self in this sense, and be attached to this self, while still being generally unselfish). Unselfishness, or selflessness, certainly plays an important role in overcoming attachment to self, but it is not sufficient. The Noble Eightfold Path, to be discussed in

Chapter Seven, delineates steps that involve unselfish action and thought, but also steps that require other disciplining measures as well.

The attachment to self in a craving is not to an actual self, for this is held to be nonexistent. Instead, it is to what we feel or sense to be a self. This is a more visceral attachment than the mere belief in a self. The attachment is emotive and affective. For instance, we pursue the satisfaction of many desires in the interest of satisfying not simply the desire, but a self or subject that feels the pangs of the desire; we feel unsatisfied desires not merely as feelings of being unsatisfied or hungry or frustrated, but as a self that is unsatisfied, hungry and frustrated. Attachment to self adds a dimension to the pursuit of desire, and to the experience of unsatisfied desires. This is an affective addition that makes a difference to the experience of the desire. And it is an introspectively observable difference. The involvement of attachment to self makes craving feel qualitatively different than mere wanting (to use a contemporary philosophical term, we can say that there is a difference in *qualia* with craving). For instance, there is an inwardly observable difference between just feeling hungry, and feeling myself to be hungry (the latter, for instance, may involve a feeling that there is something more – something of myself perhaps – at stake in feeling hungry). The introspectible difference involves a sense of *someone* suffering with the unsatisfied craving. Suffering in the Buddhist conception involves this added affective dimension to desire. And thus the elimination of suffering should remove this added affective dimension while perhaps leaving other aspects of the desire in place.

Introspectively appreciating this qualitative difference between wants and cravings may not be easy. For instance, I may have a craving for food, but may not be aware of it as a craving. That is, I may not be aware of the attachment to self in the desire; I may be thinking only of the food and not of the self that is to be satisfied with the food. This does not mean that attachment to self is not present, for it need not be consciously registered for it to be present. Attachment to self may not lie on the surface, and it may not lie near the surface either. And so introspectively observing attachment to self may need very close attention. Also, it is worth noting that the act of introspection may add a concern for self, or attachment to self, that may not have been present in the original experience (i.e., introspecting or reflecting may unwittingly change a want into a craving). For instance, in introspectively observing or reflecting on feeling sleepy I may notice that *I* am sleepy. But the thought and attachment to I or self may not have been present in the original desire for sleep; it may have just been a want for sleep that became a craving – that is, came to involve an ego–conscious concern for self – in the act of self-examination. Clearly, self-examination for the Buddhist needs to be done with care.

There is a difference between feeling hungry and feeling *my* self to be hungry: the former is a want and the latter is a craving. Merely recognizing that I am hungry need not turn the hunger from a want to a craving. Even recognizing the hunger as being in my body, or in my stomach, need not turn the hunger into a craving (for locating the hunger in my body, or in my stomach, may be just to give it a location, or associate it with an individual, and need not involve attachment to self). But recognizing the feeling of hunger as the feeling of a hungry self can transform the hunger into a craving. This is because the feeling of being the hungry *me* is different from the feeling of just being hungry. Wants may become cravings, not simply by being observed as wants, but by being observed, and felt, as *my* wants. Also, note that a craving is not simply a conjoined state formed from two separable components: the feeling of being hungry *and* the feeling of myself, for it involves the feeling of hunger as *my* hunger. The addition of an attachment to self to a want is not simply an addition on top of the want; rather, it transforms the want. Since Buddhism holds that suffering can be eliminated, this means that cravings can be transformed into wants, or uprooted entirely. The next section will offer some further elucidation of this difference in kind between wants and cravings with observations on the formal complexity or structure of cravings.

The Character of Craving – Formal Observations

One way to explain the difference in kind between wants and cravings is to say they differ in their attitude. To illustrate, a hope and fear may be directed at the same object but they differ in their attitude towards that object. For example, a hope for rain is quite different in its attitude towards rain than a fear of rain. They can both be said to involve desire but in different ways: to hope involves desiring for something to come about and to fear involves desiring that something not come about. Likewise with craving and wanting. They are similar for neither is indifferent to the end attained; both involve desiring or preferring. But they can be said to differ in their attitude towards this end. One way to explain this difference in attitude is to say that craving involves an attitude of desirousness or covetousness whereas wanting does not. Bahm makes just this point.[1] Craving involves desirousness, but wanting i⌐ desiring without being desirous. There is something appropriate about this characterization, and it works with cravings involving an attachment to self. That is, we are more likely to be desirous, or covet, when we are trying to satisfy a sense of self than when we are only following through on a brute biological desire without concerns for self. One can be hungry without being desirous or coveting; but to be desirous in one's hunger goes beyond just being hungry.

Bahm takes this analysis of desire further with a discussion of differently ordered states. He observes that desires occur at different levels or orders. This is not a novel observation, but his application of it in thinking through Buddhist suffering is noteworthy. Hunger or the desire for food is an example of a first-order desire. A second-order desire is a desire about a first-order desire, such as the desire to not give into the desire for food (as someone on a diet may have). A third-order desire is a desire about a desire about a desire (such as a desire to not be so strict about one's desire to stay on a diet, which itself is a desire to abstain from indulging one's desire for food). More generally,

---

1 See Bahm (1959), pp. 60-61.

we may say a third-order desire is a desire about an intentional state about another intentional state. Intentional states include desires, fears, hopes, expectations, likes, dislikes, loves, hatreds, etc. They are called intentional states because they are all directed at or about something, be it a person or object or feeling. For example, a fear of snakes is a fear *of* something; a desire for chocolate is also *directed* at something. A desire for chocolate can be a desire for a sensation, that of experiencing the taste of chocolate; the desire is an intentional state but the sensation of tasting chocolate is not, for it is not directed at or about anything but is merely a sensation. Simply put, intentional states intend at something (and they are appropriately grouped under the aggregate of intentional and volitional activity). Hence, a desire to overcome one's fear of heights would be a second-order desire; it is second-order because it has another intentional state, in this case a fear of heights, as its object. Fourth, fifth, and *n*th order desires and intentional states would continue on in like manner (although one might raise a doubt about the existence of high orders). Gautama, during his palace life, is portrayed as having all his first-order desires satisfied (be they for food, drink, or other comforts). When he left the palace, he was no longer satisfied with the satisfaction of these desires. At this point Gautama had an unsatisfied second-order desire. Gautama the ascetic tried to undo the pull of first-order desires in the pursuit of satisfying this second-order desire: the desire to be without first-order desires. This movement of concern from first-order to second-order desires involves operating at a higher order of concern, and can involve reflecting on first-order desires.

In Bahm's view, the Buddha proclaimed a very simple but profound truth. He states, "Gotama's philosophy may be summed up in a simple, clear and obvious principle, which immediately compels belief once it is understood. The principle: Desire for what will not be attained ends in frustration; therefore, to avoid frustration, avoid desiring what will not be attained."[1] Gautama the prince could not satisfy all his desires (particularly when he encountered the inevitable realities of old age,

---

1 Bahm (1959), p. 15.

sickness and death, for the desire to evade these cannot be satisfied). He consequently suffered. Gautama the ascetic could not satisfy the second-order desire to be without first-order desires for, as discussed, not all first-order desires can be eliminated (e.g., hunger). And consequently he also suffered. The Buddha's Middle Way, in Bahm's view, involves being satisfied at a higher order with unsatisfied lower-order desires. This involves some dialectical repositioning, and warrants explaining.

An unsatisfied desire for food is a first-order desire, with a first-order frustration due to its being unsatisfied. And if we desire that our desire for food be satisfied – that is, if we have a second-order desire seeking the satisfaction of our first-order desire – then there will be a compounding effect in frustration (for the desire for food will be unsatisfied *and* the desire to satisfy this desire will be unsatisfied). A second-order desire that seeks the satisfaction of an unsatisfied first-order desire adds to the pull of this desire, and thus to the frustration of it being unsatisfied. However, if we can manage, at a second-order, to be satisfied with an unsatisfied first-order desire, then this can work to quell the frustration of the unsatisfied first-order desire. For instance, suppose we are hungry. If we have a second-order desire that desires the satisfaction of our hunger, then the frustration of being hungry will grow. But if, at a second-order, we can be satisfied with being hungry, then the frustration of being hungry will diminish. We will still be hungry, but at this second order we will be okay with our first-order hunger. The idea is that while first-order desires such as hunger may not be eliminable, they can be mitigated or alleviated through our attitude towards the first-order desire at a second or higher order. If we can find peace or satisfaction at a higher order with unsatisfied lower-order desires, then suffering, according to Bahm's interpretation, can be eliminated.

On Bahm's understanding, suffering results from unsatisfied desires, be these first-order, second-order or nth order-desires. However, he adds that the suffered effects of an unsatisfied desire can be mitigated and even eliminated if at a higher-order we are okay with an unsatisfied lower-order desire. Again, the pain of hunger will not go away merely by being okay with being hungry at a higher-order of reflection. But still, something may be said to go away and, according to Bahm, this is the suffering of which the Buddha speaks.

Cravings can be said to work conversely: they are higher-order desires that are *not* okay with unsatisfied lower-order desires; to the contrary, they desire the satisfaction of unsatisfied lower-order desires. Cravings, thus, exacerbate unsatisfied lower-order desires and cause a suffering that would not otherwise be present. They compound the frustration of unsatisfied lower-order desires. Consider the example of hunger again. A first-order hunger is not a craving (and good thing as hunger is not an eliminable desire). A craving for food is a second-order desire that seeks the satisfaction of a first-order hunger. More specifically, a craving for food involves trying to satisfy a self by way of satisfying a desire for food. This is a second-order desire because it involves desiring the satisfaction of a desire for food *for* the satisfaction of a self. Thus, in addition to the involvement of attachment to self, we may draw a further distinction between cravings and wants: first-order wants are possible (as are second-order wants, third-order, and so on), but first order cravings are not possible. Cravings only arise with second or higher order desires. This is a necessary condition, but not a sufficient condition (as not all second or higher order states are cravings; for instance, one may want to satisfy a want without a craving being involved). In short, cravings involve second or higher-order desires that seek to satisfy a self by way of satisfying first or lower-order desires. Bahm does not speak specifically of cravings or attachment to self in his analysis of Buddhist suffering; nevertheless, his analysis in terms of ordered desires allows us to further characterize the difference in kind between cravings and wants.

Many first-order states are biologically ingrained and, depending on the desire, may not be entirely eliminable (e.g., hunger). Higher-order desires and states, though, seem less liable to being biologically ingrained and more open to control. For instance, the first-order desire of hunger may not be eliminable, but whether we have a second-order desire that seeks to satisfy our hunger, or whether we are unperturbed or even satisfied at a second-order with being hungry, does seem to be more susceptible to control and disciplining. The Buddha's Middle Way, in

Bahm's view, involves this kind of dialectical repositioning. It requires being constantly aware of our desires – first-order, second-order, and so on – and it requires being able to position our concerns at a higher order than the unsatisfied desires and, further to this, coming to be satisfied at this higher order with unsatisfied lower-order desires. And this is to say that it involves the diametric opposite of craving the satisfaction of lower-order desires. In sum, if we cannot satisfy our desires then, in Bahm's view, overcoming suffering requires the considered effort of placing our attention at a higher order and, furthermore, coming to feel entirely satisfied at this higher order with unsatisfied lower-order states. Maintaining this effort requires vigilance, significant self-discipline and control.

Criticism of Bahm

There is much to commend in Bahm's dialectical analysis of desires. In particular, it allows for an analysis of cravings in terms of second or higher-order desires. However, his description of the Buddhist understanding of suffering as simply unsatisfied desires is flawed. In this view, overcoming the suffering of an unsatisfied desire would require either satisfying the unsatisfied desire, or moving one's attention to a higher-order state where one does not desire the satisfaction of the unsatisfied desire. There are difficulties here. For one, it does not distinguish among desires. It would hold a desire for murder on par with a desire for food, for both are desires and are prone to cause suffering if left unsatisfied. On Bahm's view, a desire to murder should not cause suffering if the desire can be satisfied; it will only cause suffering to oneself if left unsatisfied. Only if the desire cannot be satisfied are we required, to overcome the suffering of this unsatisfied desire, to shift our conscious concern to a higher-order state where we can, through discipline, come to be satisfied with this unsatisfied desire. Thus the presence of any desire, no matter how insalubrious, need not incur suffering if we can either satisfy it or make ourselves satisfied with its remaining unsatisfied from the perspective of a higher-order state. But a desire to murder or steal or hurt, even if satisfied (or even if we are satisfied at a higher order with its being unsatisfied), would involve suffering in the Buddhist conception if it involves attachment to self. And this is the key difficulty with Bahm's view: it does not distinguish cravings from other desires. More specifically, it does not distinguish between desires that involve attachment to self, and that are pursued in the interests of this self, from those that do not. In this respect, Bahm makes the same error as the ascetic by not distinguishing between desires that are suffering-inducing (cravings) from those that are not (wants).

A desire for the suffering of humankind to end, even though the desire remains unfulfilled, need not incur suffering in the Buddhist sense. The response to this unsatisfied desire should not require becoming satisfied with its being unfulfilled because this will deter efforts to fulfill it. To be satisfied with one's unfulfilled desire to alleviate humanity's suffering is to be at ease with not doing anything about it; it is to quell one's desire to end humanity's suffering. It may be in order to respond to a feeling of hunger this way, but it is something very different to respond to one's concerns for humanity's suffering this way. It promotes apathy, and this is clearly contrary to the Buddha's motives and efforts. He spent the latter forty-five years of his life trying to eradicate humanity's suffering. The Buddha is alleged to have overcome suffering, but he was not someone who was satisfied with his unfulfilled desire to alleviate humanity's suffering. The story of the latter part of his life gives evidence to the contrary. The Buddha is said to have overcome suffering and craving, which means that while his desire to alleviate humanity's suffering was never fully satisfied, it was not for him a suffering-inducing craving.

Bahm's interpretation is also at odds with the moral conduct required in following the Noble Eightfold Path. The Noble Eightfold Path, as will be elaborated in Chapter Seven, requires that certain moral precepts be followed in order that freedom from suffering be realized. Not killing, stealing and hurting fall under these precepts (under what is called Right Action and Right Livelihood). But Bahm's interpretation gives license to do any of these things without causing oneself any suffering.

As long as the desire is satisfied (i.e., as long as one is successful in steal-ing and murdering), or as long as one is satisfied at a higher order with the desire being unsatisfied, then suffering does not result. But stealing and killing are clearly in conflict with following the Noble Eightfold Path. Satisfying the desire to steal does not mean that one has escaped the suffering associated with the desire. In fact, as long as the desire to steal is pursued in the interests of satisfying one's self, as it generally is, it will incur suffering in the Buddhist conception even if it is satisfied. The Noble Truths and the Noble Eightfold Path are directed, and provide precepts and steps, towards overcoming suffering. Bahm's reading admits stark violations of these precepts and this raises a significant difficulty with its being an adequate interpretation and analysis of the Buddhist conception of suffering.

Bahm's reading of suffering is in line with the understanding of suf-fering in the second grouping of the First Noble Truth (which links suffering to unsatisfied desire) but with some added dialectical complex-ity. The ascetic who tries to become indifferent to the pull of his desires fits Bahm's picture of what it is to overcome suffering. But Bahm's view neglects the understanding of suffering that arises in the third grouping of the First Noble Truth (which links suffering to the aggregates and attachment to self). Notwithstanding, Bahm's discrimination of levels of desire does allow us to better elaborate and analyse craving, and so make better sense of the concept of Buddhist suffering and the importance of higher-order awareness in overcoming suffering. Buddhist suffering arises with craving, and this involves a second or higher-order desire that seeks to satisfy a first or lower-order desire in order to satisfy a sense of self.

We will consider two more related points before proceeding to the next section. One, a higher-order state that is satisfied with an unsatis-fied lower-order state can alleviate much of the unsatisfactoriness of this lower-order state. But there is a presumption here, and that is that we are more concerned with the higher-order state than the lower-order state. That is, one may have both a lower-order state of hunger and a higher-order state that is unbothered by the hunger. The higher-order state offers alleviation only if it holds sway over one's attention. If one is still more moved by the lower-order hunger, one will still be bothered by the hunger. One way to describe this is to say that one's feeling of self-concern must not rest heavily with the lower-order hunger if the higher-order state is to have an alleviating effect. Simply having an appropriate higher-order state is not sufficient; one must be able to direct and focus one's attention and concern to this higher-order state and away from the unsatisfied lower-order state, and this requires mental discipline and concentration. The methods of mindfulness and meditation are, at least partially, directed at achieving this level of remove to a higher-order state from where lower-order states can be observed with dispassion; Chapter Seven will offer more detail on Buddhist mindfulness.

And two, since suffering is identified with having cravings, and cravings involve attachment to self and the capacity to have higher-order states, it follows that creatures that do not have a sense of self (as being independent of the ever-changing aggregates), or that cannot experience higher-order states, cannot experience suffering in the Buddhist sense of the term. They will still experience pain, but not suffer in the Buddha's sense. It is interesting to note that Peter Singer uses the capacity for experiencing selfhood as a guide in determining a creature's capacity for suffering. A fish, for example, can feel pain – insofar as it has a nervous system that enables feeling it – but as long as it lacks a sense of self, it lacks a point of reference from which this pain can be reflected upon; it lacks a basis for feeling the pain as painful to *it* (similar to how I can experience pain as painful to *me*). For this fish, the feeling may just be a brute, painful sensation and no more. If it is lacking a sense of self with which it may associate its sensation of pain then, argues Singer, it is deserving of less (but not zero) moral consideration (for the implication is that its suffering is not as weighty without its being felt to bear on a self).[1] In some respects, a similar point is made here: the Buddhist conception of suffering is a primarily human affair (but presumably not an exclusively human affair, although it is unclear to what extent other animals can

---

1 Singer (1993), Chapters Four and Five.

have an attachment to self in their desires, or experience higher-order states which are necessary for having cravings).

Self and Suffering

We may wonder why the attachment to a sense of self in a desire is held to incur suffering in the Buddhist conception, even when the desire in question is satisfied. One answer to this is that, in the Buddhist view, the self to which we are attached does not exist, and consequently any desire that involves this attachment can never really be satisfied. Such a desire has been called a craving. And a craving that seeks to satisfy a self cannot be satisfied given that the self it seeks to satisfy does not exist (see Chapter Eight for further discussion of the doctrine of No Self). This can be explained better by again distinguishing between orders of desires. A craving involves a higher-order desire that seeks to satisfy a lower-order desire in order to satisfy a self. For instance, a craving for food involves a desire to satisfy a self through satisfying a desire for food. While the lower-order desire (for food) is satisfiable, the craving is not. The higher-order desire cannot be satisfied if there is no such self (as something existing apart from the ever-changing aggregates) to be satisfied. In short, it would seem that no cravings are satisfiable, and so they cannot but be suffering-inducing. Thus, overcoming the suffering associated with a craving must involve, not satisfying, but overcoming the craving. As discussed, overcoming suffering in the Buddhist conception cannot undo or eliminate pain (or sickness, aging, etc.). But it can, allegedly, overcome the anxieties and distresses associated with the pain being *my* pain. Craving to be without pain – that is, desiring to satisfy a self by satisfying the desire to be without pain – adds a dimension to the experience of pain. Indeed, it should seem to exacerbate the experience of pain (for I am concerned not merely with the feeling of pain, but with its feeling to *me*). Insofar as cravings can be overcome, then this added dimension – and exacerbation – can be removed. My pain is able to be eliminated, not by eliminating the pain *per se*, but through eliminating the "my," that is, through eliminating the attachment to self in the pain.

As discussed in the previous chapter, the pervasiveness of suffering in the Buddhist conception implies that we must be able to suffer even when we believe or feel ourselves to not be suffering (for if not, we could easily judge that suffering is not pervasive for there are patently many moments, at least for many of us, during which we do not feel ourselves to be suffering). The pervasiveness of suffering means that suffering can be experienced without its being recognized. In this respect, Buddhist suffering is unlike a belly-ache which is difficult to overlook when one is experiencing it. And so suffering in the Buddhist sense may only be clearly recognized upon its alleviation (perhaps analogous, if only in this respect, to a muscle knot that may only be clearly noticed when it is unknotted). This means that we may not fully, or even adequately, realize the suffering of attachment to self until it is overcome. And since overcoming suffering is the motivation for Buddhist practice, a difficulty with recognizing our suffering presents a challenge to motivating Buddhist practice.

We will end this chapter with a further consideration about the end of suffering and its role as the motivation for pursuing the Buddhist path. As described, ending suffering in the Buddhist conception involves overcoming craving and attachment to self. This raises the question of the viability of a self-interested motivation. Consider that if suffering in the Buddhist conception was correctly described by the examples of the first grouping in the First Noble Truth, then a self-interested motivation for taking on Buddhist practice would be clear (for we would be gaining freedom from pain, sorrow, old age, sickness, and death). Likewise, if suffering in the Buddhist conception was correctly diagnosed as simply involving the frustration of unsatisfied desires, then again there would be a clear self-serving benefit for taking on Buddhist practice (for we would gain from being without the frustration of unsatisfied desires). But if the end of suffering is construed in terms of liberation from attachment to self then this presents a difficulty with having a self-interested motivation in overcoming suffering. It would seem that, at some point on the path to freedom from suffering, the self-interested motive or reason must be dropped (either that or the path will not meet with success). A self-interested motivation must come to be recognized as itself suffered and to be overcome. But if we know, ahead of time, that a self-interested motivation must eventually be dropped, we might wonder why we should be motivated even to begin pursuing the Buddhist path. And we might wonder how the end of suffering can even be correctly conceived of as a goal if it is not to be a goal reached by *my* self or for *my* self (for associating goals with our future selves is part of how we generally understand goals). Understanding suffering in terms of the third grouping, as opposed to the first two groupings, allows us to conceive of why suffering is held to be pervasive and eliminable, and at first sight these two points do seem to provide a good reason for taking up the Buddhist path (i.e., the elimination of a pervasive suffering). However, if the end of suffering involves overcoming attachment to self, then a personal and self-interested motivation, to the extent that this involves attachment to self or a craving for enlightenment, becomes an obstacle. The first two groupings in the First Noble Truth present understandings of suffering that are not eliminable. This raises a problem of motivation for taking up Buddhist practice (for such practice cannot eliminate these sufferings). But the third grouping raises a different problem for motivation: a self-interested motivation (in the form of a craving) will be an obstacle to what Buddhist practice aims to achieve. Perhaps a motivation for Buddhist practice need not be a self-interested motivation. In Chapter Fourteen, on Mahayana Buddhism, we will discuss the idea that if the end of suffering is to be achieved, it must come to be pursued for the benefit of all, with an altruistic or genuinely compassionate motivation, rather than for oneself. The issue of the end of suffering and the motivation this provides will also be revisited in the next chapter in its discussion of Nirvana.

VI

The Third Noble Truth: Nirvana, the Cessation of Suffering

Introduction

AS DISCUSSED, THE BUDDHA'S First Preaching upon enlightenment involved what are commonly called the "Four Noble Truths." These are the signature truths of the Buddha, the Noble or Enlightened One. The Buddha is proclaiming truths, but the primary intent is not to offer a true description of reality but rather an account of how to overcome a predicament in the human condition. In speaking of the Four Noble Truths as 'truths', the Buddha is not trying to be a metaphysician or a scientist. The Buddha's agenda is a practical one. The Four Noble Truths have been described as involving a diagnosis that tells us that there is a problem or malady (pervasive suffering), describes its causes (cravings involving an attachment to self), prescribes a cure (to eliminate suffering we must eliminate these cravings), and offers a specific means for realizing and practising this cure (the Noble Eightfold Path). Buddhaghosa, an important Theravadin[1] commentator from the 5th Century (and whose name translates as "voice of the Buddha" in Pali), states: "The truth of suffering is like a disease, the truth of origin is like the cause of the disease, the truth of cessation is like the cure of the disease, and the truth of the path is like the medicine."[2] The Buddha is regarded more as a physician than a metaphysician, but his concerns with suffering are not quite the same as is the ordinary physician's (indeed, from the discussion of the previous two chapters, it should be evident that the Buddhist conception of suffering differs substantially from the ordinary physician's).

As described in the previous chapter, suffering results from cravings. These cravings are second or higher-order desires; they are desires about desires that seek to satisfy first or lower-order desires, not just for their own sake, but in order to satisfy a self. And in so doing these cravings further entrench attachment to the sense of being a self that exists separately from the five aggregates. The Buddha, as seen in Chapter Four and as we will see again in Chapter Eight, argues that no such entity exists; and that all that can be said to exist (with respect to our "selves") is what can be experienced or encountered in the five ever-changing aggregates.

From the perspective of Western religious traditions, this may be perplexing: what, it may be wondered, is the merit of a religious practice if it does not benefit a self (be it our own self or other selves)? There can be no personal salvation, or eternal life for a soul, or heaven it seems, if there is no self in the form of an enduring independent entity that can reap these rewards. But with Buddhism, there is a set of beliefs and practices that are held to be of spiritual significance, and yet this path is godless, soulless, and without benefit to a substantial self. Buddhism is often regarded as polytheistic, but as with Jainism, appeal to gods or deities is not integral for following the Buddhist path; the end of suffering does not depend on a god or gods as salvation may in other religious traditions. Indeed, attaining enlightenment and the end of suffering

---

1 Theravada is the oldest school of Buddhism. It declined in India, but is the main religion today in several South-East Asian countries.
2 *Visuddhimagga of Buddhaghosa.* XVI 87.11., p. 520.

involves the very realization that there is no substantive self. As noted, the First Noble Truth speaks of the nature of suffering, and the Second of its cause, which is craving. The Third Noble Truth speaks of the cessation of suffering, and thus of the overcoming of attachment to self. This is the realization of Nirvana, and this will be the focus of this chapter.

Samsara

'Samsara' is a term used to signify the unenlightened existence in which we – that is, the unenlightened amongst us – find ourselves. It is described in terms opposite to Nirvana. It is described as the cycle of birth and rebirth, and as being permeated by suffering, cravings for permanence, sensation, and self. In the *Dhammapada*, it is described as involving impermanence, suffering and illusion: "'All is transient.' ... 'All is sorrow.' ... 'All is unreal.'"[1]

Nirvana, the extinguishing of suffering, is the release from Samsara or Samsaric existence. If Samsara is our suffered earthly existence, it might seem that Nirvana should be conceived of as an unearthly or other-worldly existence. That is, the contrary terms in which Samsara and Nirvana are portrayed may convey that Nirvana is a heavenly world or transcendent realm. However, this view of Nirvana conflicts with the Buddhist conception of suffering. If suffering is construed in terms of the first grouping of the First Noble Truth – that is, as involving pain, sickness, aging and death – then liberation from suffering should then involve reaching a heavenly or transcendent existence marked by immortality and freedom from physical discomfort and degeneration. But this understanding of suffering has been shown to not be suffering in the Buddhist sense, and thus Nirvana – the extinguishing of suffering – is not to be understood in these terms either. Likewise, if suffering is understood in terms of the second grouping of the First Noble Truth, then realizing Nirvana would again involve becoming something more than human

---

1 *Dhammapada*, Ch. 20, Sections 277-79.

Wheel of Becoming

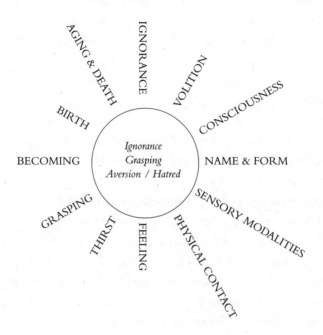

(for it would involve overcoming the desires of human embodiment). The Buddha's life is instructive for a correct understanding of suffering: he is alleged to have overcome suffering, but he did not overcome sickness, aging, death, or all desires, and so these cannot be the suffering to be overcome in Buddhism. The understanding of suffering as per the third grouping of the First Noble Truth – that is, as involving craving and attachment to self – has implications for understanding Samsara and Nirvana: namely, Samsara involves craving and attachment to self and Nirvana a release from these.

Samsara is popularly characterized by what is called the 'Wheel of Becoming'.[1] Along the outer edge of this wheel are twelve points depicting characteristics of suffering and human existence. These include

---

1 Also called the 'Wheel of Life'.

ignorance, volition, consciousness, name and form, sensory modalities, physical contact, feeling, thirst, grasping, becoming, birth, and aging and death. The twelve elements of the wheel are taken to characterize our unenlightened existence, and include elements from each of the three groupings of suffering from the First Noble Truth. To be in Samsara is to be caught in the cycle of these elements; and to be released from Samsara to Nirvana is to escape attachment to these elements and the cycle of this wheel. Escaping Samsara requires stopping the underlying forces that keep this wheel in motion. These forces are ignorance, grasping and aversion or hatred. These are regarded as the Three Root Evils or Poisons. These forces arise within the aggregate of intentional and volitional activity and involve reactions to that which is perceived as pleasing (through grasping) and displeasing (through aversion and hatred). That which is perceived as neutral, as neither pleasing nor displeasing, can result in confusion as no clear reaction may present itself. These three forces are pictured as lying in the interior core of the wheel. These are called root evils because they propagate suffering and maintain the cycle of suffering. They are aspects of our attachment to self. Overcoming suffering, and thus stopping the motion of this wheel, requires counteracting the three root forces of ignorance, grasping and aversion or hatred with their opposites: wisdom, generosity and compassion. This is implemented through the practices of the Noble Eightfold Path (which will be described in the next chapter). There is thus a causal understanding of suffering displayed in the Wheel of Becoming. The twelve elements of the wheel causally affect each other and the three root forces cause the wheel to turn and cause the unenlightened to be bound to its motion and bound within its elements. A similar causal understanding is, of course, displayed in the Four Noble Truths (i.e., suffering is described as caused, and the elimination of suffering is described as involving the elimination of its causes). The understanding of causal interconnectivity is further refined in the Buddhist doctrine of Dependent Origination and this will be discussed in Chapter Ten.

Understanding and Describing Nirvana

The Third Noble Truth asserts that suffering can be eliminated by eliminating its causes, namely cravings. The elimination of suffering, 'Nirvana', translates as "extinguished" or "extinguishing," as in putting out a flame. Referring to the extinguishing of craving and the realization of no self, Nirvana is sometimes construed as involving the annihilation of self. But this is not accurate. The self is not an entity to be extinguished. Instead, it is overcoming attachment to this illusory self that is required. This involves realizing that there is no self, in the sense of an entity existing independently of the aggregates, to begin with. If we are to speak of annihilation at all, it is the annihilation of the fiction or delusion of self, and of the attachment to this fiction.

As noted, Nirvana is not a transcendent place or realm. It is not the Buddhist word for god or heaven. And there is no absolute or monistic reality, such as Atman or Brahman, which is realized with Nirvana. The realization of Brahman is described as involving a realization of the True Self (Atman). Nirvana, in contrast, involves the realization that there is no self in any substantive sense. This is not to deny the utility of the concept of a self, for this allows us to organize thoughts, memories, etc., around the notion of a central agent. Rather, it is to assert that attachment to self extends beyond these and other uses.

This attachment to self is displayed in how we think and speak about experiences, including Nirvana. Consider the question: if there is no self who exists apart from the aggregates, then who experiences the aggregates? And who experiences Nirvana? It seems that suffering must be felt by a self, and so should the experience of the cessation of suffering. If there is suffering, there must be a sufferer. For Descartes, this reasoning was certain. If there is thinking, doubting, perceiving, as there assuredly are, then, he concluded, there must exist a self or soul who is doing the thinking, doubting and perceiving. Descartes famously concluded *cogito ergo sum*: thinking implies existence (or, as more commonly translated, "I think therefore I am"). Descartes reasoned that, even if he was incorrect and deceived about the content of his perceptions and thoughts, he must exist to have these deceived perceptions and thoughts; every perception – veridical or not – requires a perceiver, and every thought necessitates a thinker. As long as I am currently perceiving or thinking, for that time I can be certain that I exist.[1] Thus, for Descartes, knowledge of the existence of self is indubitable.

Note that the self, on this reasoning, must exist independently of the aggregates. This self is independent of sensations, perceptions, thoughts, and consciousness for it is that thing which *has* sensations, perceptions, thoughts, and is conscious. It is the experiencer of the aggregates, and so the self must exist independently of the aggregates. It is, for Descartes, the "thinking thing" and exists independently of the thoughts it thinks. According to Descartes, the self must also not be the body for we can, with some imaginative work, entertain doubts about the existence of the body, but not the self (i.e., my awareness of my body relies on sensations and perceptions and I may be deceived about these, perhaps by an evil demon, but again, according to Descartes I cannot be deceived by anyone about my own existence for I must exist to be deceived). The self, on this Cartesian view, exists necessarily and independently of the aggregates. Critics, however, objected that it does not follow from the existence of thoughts to the existence of a thinker; it might be that there are just the thoughts. Likewise with perceptions, beliefs, doubts, hopes, etc. We saw a similar response expressed by Hume in Chapter Four. The Buddha, as also discussed in Chapter Four, held a comparable view two millennia earlier. According to the Buddha, the existence of this self is not only dubitable, it is denied. In marked contrast to Descartes' famous conclusion, the Buddha asserted: "action exists, but no doer."[2]

It does seem that thinking requires a thinker, perceiving a perceiver, suffering a sufferer, and the cessation of suffering one for whom suffering has ceased. This is certainly in line with how we speak. It is a feature of our grammar that every predicate requires a subject for a predicate is

---

1 See *Meditations One* and *Two* in Descartes (1993).
2 As quoted in Collins (1982), p. 105. Collins also states here: "The Sanskrit form also implies a deed needs a doer, and this is contested directly by the Buddha."

what is asserted of a subject. Our grammar (and this applies in English as well as in Sanskrit) implies that there cannot be a predicate, such as suffering, without a subject – the sufferer. However, to say what is grammatically necessary must be necessary in actuality is to say what is necessary of a linguistic description of the world must be necessary of the world. This is fallacious (we may describe this as the fallacy of moving from *de dicto* necessity to *de re* necessity).[1] Descartes' inference was, arguably, not a logical necessity but a grammatical one (and given the close connection between rules of grammar and the way we think, his inference was not without cause). Once again, this inference from predicate to subject – from action to doer – is explicitly denied by the Buddha. It is noteworthy that the First Noble Truth presents the truth of suffering as simply: "there is suffering." It speaks to the predicate but does not overtly ascribe a subject; it does not say "we all suffer," or "all who are unenlightened suffer." We might think that if there is suffering, then there must be someone who is undergoing the suffering (and that this someone must exist independently of the suffering he experiences, and independently of other experiences). But the First Noble Truth is careful not to assert the truth of suffering in these terms, since it is the self – or specifically, attachment to self as present in cravings – that is at the root of suffering in the Buddhist conception.

The use of indexical words such as 'I' and 'me', or proper names, can suggest the existence of selves (for the grammatical role of such terms is to refer, and so it can seem that there must exist a referent to whom they refer). However, in the Buddhist view, a grammatical role should not be confused for existence. The indexical 'I' is used in assertions that describe one's self (e.g., 'I am hungry' or 'I am going out'); and phrases such as 'my body', 'my pain' and 'my idea' function, respectively, to express the possession of a body by a self, the feeling of a pain by a self, and authorship of an idea by a self. This is why, in the third grouping of

---

1 It is a *de dicto* necessity that anyone who is your sister is your sibling; this merely follows from the words. But (it's sometimes argued) the fact that 7 + 5 = 12 is not merely a matter of words: it would be necessarily true (*de re*) even if there were no words to talk about it.

the First Noble Truth, suffering is summed up in terms of the aggregates of attachment: we attach a notion of I or self to the aggregates, as the possessor and experiencer of the aggregates, while presuming the I or self nevertheless exists independently of the aggregates. These are linguistic usages that allow us to express ourselves to others as well as reflect on our own states. However, in the Buddhist view, these useful ways of speaking should not be taken to refer to a separate and underlying self. Again, the grammar of our speech, and the grammar that underlies our linguistic thinking, may posit or presume a grammatical subject, but the thinking is that this should not be taken to imply the existence of a metaphysical subject. The main difficulty, from the Buddhist point of view, is that even if we have not made this implication explicitly, our attachments – as betrayed in our desires and hopes and fears – suggest we have done so implicitly.

As noted, while we may associate an experience with an experiencer, or an action with a doer, this need not be taken to mean that there is a self who is doing the experiencing and acting. Consider the following: we may say a pet goldfish is hungry, or that it is swimming in circles, but these associations of a subject with a predicate need not imply that the goldfish has a self. Similarly, we can give the goldfish a name, and while the name refers to the goldfish, it need not be taken to refer to the goldfish's self. Likewise, a dog might respond to a name, but that does not mean that the dog has a sense of self, in the sense of being something that exists separately from its ever-changing psychophysical aggregates, and that this self is what is responding upon being called. Again, this is not to say that the concept of self is without use or value, or that it should be abandoned. My experiences, memories and more are associated with and organized around a self-concept. My thoughts of others and interactions with them, and theirs with me, also deal with this self-concept. All this is useful and presumably necessary for living in the world, for having dealings with others and making sense of ourselves. But in the Buddhist view, this does not imply the existence of a self as an entity that exists separately from the collection of psychophysical states or aggregates of which we are comprised.

To return to the discussion of Nirvana, it is noteworthy that Nirvana is not usually described in positive terms. If it is described at all, it is usually described negatively (i.e., it is described in terms of what it is not, or by what it lacks). A negative description is still a description; it still conveys information, just as a positive description. For instance, if I say that I am not sleepy then this says something about me. Though it may not say as much, or have as much determinate content, as a positive description of my state, such as saying that I am feeling alert. Another example: directions which tell me not to head West tell me something, but not as much as a positive description of which way I should go (i.e., it does not specifically tell me to head North or South or East, and so may leave me standing where I am, but all the same, I have gained some information). A negative description does provide some information or content; an indeterminate description is not the same as no description. However, negative descriptions convey without pinning down. They leave us, not with nothing, but also without a clear picture of Nirvana. For instance, saying Nirvana is without suffering tells us something important, something that may motivate its pursuit, but can also leave us without a clear appreciation of what the experience of Nirvana is like.

Negative descriptions are consistent with the Buddhist emphasis on detachment, and undoing craving, by directing our minds to reject associations of qualities with Nirvana. Hence, negative descriptions may be viewed as rejecting the attachments that may come with positive descriptions of Nirvana. Still, defining Nirvana in negative terms as the extinguishing of suffering does provide an outcome which may be pursued with craving and attachment. But note that a craving for Nirvana would be more likely with the portrayals of suffering in the first and second groupings in the First Noble Truth than with the third: an end to pain, sickness, old age, death and frustrated desires provides a greater basis for craving than does overcoming attachment to self. As discussed in the previous chapter, craving Nirvana is an obstacle to its realization (for the cessation of suffering requires the cessation of self-attachment and craving). Negative descriptions, because they do not pin down a determinate content, may be less susceptible to attachment and craving than positive descriptions, and thus provide less of a hindrance to the realization of Nirvana while still offering some useful description. This is one reason for using negative descriptions in speaking of Nirvana.

The *Vinaya Pitaka* describes Nirvana as "difficult to understand ... beyond abstract reasoning, subtle ..."[1] Very subtle, perhaps, for Nirvana is often not described at all: the Buddha is renowned for remaining silent on such matters. Gethin explains this silence: "... ultimately whatever one says will be misleading; the last resort must be the 'silence of the Aryas', the silence of the ones who have directly known the ultimate truth, for ultimately in such matters syllables, words, and concepts are of no use."[2] Nevertheless, Nirvana is still described, and again, this usually involves negative terms and descriptions. The following passage is a key example of such a negative description, and the passage itself is described as an 'inspired utterance':

> There is, monks, a domain where there is no earth, no water, no fire, no wind, no sphere of infinite space, no sphere of nothing-ness, no sphere of infinite consciousness, no sphere of neither awareness nor non-awareness; there is not this world, there is not another world, there is no sun or moon. I do not call this coming or going, nor standing nor dying, nor being reborn; it is without support, without occurrence, without object. Just this is the end of suffering.[3]

Notice, first, that this "inspired utterance" describes using only negative terms. Notice, second, that much of the description is contradictory. Nirvana is described as not something (i.e., it is not composed of what were presumed to be the basic elements of earth, water, fire or wind), but also not nothing ("no sphere of nothingness"). We are told that there is no awareness, but also no non-awareness. It is neither coming nor

---

1 *Vinaya Pitaka* I 4, as quoted in Harvey (1990), p. 62.
2 Gethin (1998), p. 79.
3 *Udana* 80, as quoted in Gethin (1998), pp. 76-77; and also in Williams (2000), pp. 49-50.

going. It is neither standing and living, nor dying. What then is it? The use of not only negative descriptions but contradictory terms conveys that there is no content – positive or negative, affirming or nihilistic – that we can assert of Nirvana. Contradictions cannot be true, and thus the use of contradictory descriptions repudiates any informational content as ascribable to Nirvana. Contradictory descriptions convey that Nirvana is beyond conception, for it seems we cannot conceive of how a contradiction can be true or make sense. The indescribability of Nirvana in linguistic terms, and its incomprehensibility through concepts, is thus indirectly conveyed with the use of contradictory descriptions. Using negative descriptions can yield some informational content, without pinning down a determinate content to Nirvana. But using contradictory negative descriptions goes further for it suggests no content – determinate or indeterminate – can be accurately associated with Nirvana. Contradictory descriptions do not directly yield any informational content. Of course, contradictory descriptions may also be interpreted differently: not as suggesting that Nirvana is indescribable, but rather that it is impossible. However, insofar as realizing Nirvana is possible, as the Third Noble Truth asserts, then the appropriate way of reading these contradictory descriptions is that they are an indirect way of saying that Nirvana is ultimately indescribable. Merely saying "Nirvana is indescribable" would be a self-refuting description. Employing contradictory negative descriptions conveys this indescribability and inconceivability emphatically, but without saying specifically of Nirvana that it is indescribable. Nirvana, insofar as it is realizable, is clearly unlike other experiences that can be described and conceived.

Moreover, this very consideration – that Nirvana is beyond linguistic description and conception – conveys something more about what is needed to realize an end to suffering. To explain, in the above "inspired utterance," Nirvana is negatively described as not being constituted of the basic elements of earth, water, fire or wind but also described as not being nothing. Nirvana is neither of the self (since it involves overcoming attachment to self) nor of the world (as these negative descriptions convey). These and other negative descriptions convey that Nirvana is neither a something nor a nothing. But these distinctions, between is and is not, or existence and non-existence, are basic distinctions of dualistic thought. Indeed, any description of Nirvana, positive or negative, must involve asserting what Nirvana is or is not and thus must employ a dualistic framework. The categories and distinctions denied of Nirvana in the "inspired utterance" convey that Nirvana is not concrete, not infinite, not of awareness, not of non-awareness, not of this world, not of another world, not coming, not going, not occurring, not standing, not living, not being born, and not dying. The conclusion to draw from all this is not that Nirvana is nothing (i.e., that a nihilistic interpretation is appropriate), for this too is specifically denied in the above "utterance." Rather, the conclusion to draw is that the basic categories of dualistic conception do not apply to Nirvana. This suggests that realizing Nirvana – again, assuming that it is realizable, as the Third Noble Truth asserts – cannot be achieved solely through a dualistic perspective and awareness. That is, the negation of these dualistic categories suggests, elliptically, that realizing Nirvana must involve a release from dualistic thinking.

In sum, the contradictory negative descriptions convey, not just that Nirvana is beyond accurate linguistic conception, but also that a proper appreciation of Nirvana must involve a role for non-dualistic awareness or experience (for the contradictoriness of the negative descriptions implies a rejection of basic dualistic categories as being appropriate to the understanding and realization of Nirvana). To be sure, saying that experiencing Nirvana involves overcoming dualistic attachment and awareness is saying something about Nirvana (and saying it dualistically at that). But this description is limited as it does not effectively communicate the nature of the experience of non-dualism – convey what it is like from a first-person perspective – to an understanding and perspective that is dualistic. Issues involving the indescribability of Nirvana, and its connection to non-dualism, will be revisited in Chapter Thirteen.

VII

The Fourth Noble Truth: Walking the Noble Eightfold Path

Introduction

SOON AFTER LEAVING HIS palace, Gautama encountered yogis from whom he learned meditation techniques. He first encountered Alara Kalama who taught Gautama how to enter into the "sphere of nothingness." Harvey describes this as "a mystical trance attained by yogic concentration, in which the mind goes beyond any apparent object and dwells on the thought of nothingness."[1] Gautama was a quick study, but found this state insufficient for overcoming suffering. As Harvey describes, Gautama "felt that, while he had attained a refined inner calmness, he had not yet attained enlightenment and the end of suffering."[2]

---

1 Harvey (1990), p. 18.
2 Harvey (1990), p. 18.

The sphere of nothingness was thus not the enlightenment he sought. Next, Gautama encountered Uddaka Ramaputra who taught him how to enter into a state or trance described as the "sphere of neither cognition nor non-cognition." Harvey adds: "This went beyond the previous state to a level of mental stilling where consciousness is so attenuated as to hardly exist. In response, Uddaka acknowledged him as able to be his own teacher, for only his dead father had previously attained this state. Again Gotama passed up a chance of leadership and influence on the grounds that he had not yet reached his goal."[1] This story was recounted in Chapter Two. These encounters are mentioned here again because they help to convey how Nirvana – the end of suffering that Gautama was seeking – is not to be conceived. Nirvana is not an awareness of nothingness or nihilism (for Gautama allegedly attained such a state of mind soon after leaving his palace, with Alara Kalama, but was not satisfied for he did not find this conducive to ending suffering). The 'sphere of neither cognition nor non-cognition' seems better, for it seems to be a state that is non-dualistic. That Gautama turns away from this also indicates that he is not interested in a transient state of mind; overcoming suffering is not simply a matter of experiencing non-dualism. While an experience of non-dualism may be a necessary aspect of the realization of Nirvana, as the "inspired utterance" discussed in the previous chapter suggests, the encounter with Uddaka Ramaputra and the meditational state he learned from him suggests it is not sufficient.

As described in Chapter Two, Gautama was not interested in merely the "comfortable abidings" of these meditational states. He was after a more substantial and lasting change. Gautama realized that his desires and attachments could remain unabated after these meditational states ended. These desires and attachments needed more attention, and for this discipline was required. The ascetic path, to which he turned next, certainly involved a heavy dose of discipline. But this path too was ultimately found wanting: as described in Chapters Two and Three, the discipline practices were, among other things, too extreme in their asceticism; too focussed on bodily discipline; and while other desires

---

1 Harvey (1990), p. 18.

and attachments were being conditioned, attachment to self remained entrenched through the ascetic practice. He left behind this ascetic path, but the importance of discipline on the path to enlightenment remained. What was needed, he realized, was a better understanding of the kinds of disciplines needed on the path to enlightenment. This understanding involves what is called the Buddha's "Middle Way," and the necessary steps and disciplining measures for following this Way are presented in the Noble Eightfold Path. The Fourth Noble Truth asserts that the way to Nirvana, the cessation of suffering, lies in successfully treading the Noble Eightfold Path. This path and its steps are the focus of this chapter.

The Noble Eightfold Path, as compared to its destination – Nirvana – is described in clear, concrete terms.[1] This is interesting, for it conveys that while the path may be clearly understood, the end to which the path is directed is less open to clear presentation. It seems that the path to the end of suffering is to be followed without a clear picture in mind of its destination, Nirvana.

The Noble Eightfold Path

The path to Nirvana involves following the Noble Eightfold Path. This is the path of the noble or enlightened one, i.e., the Buddha. The eight elements of this path are Right View, Right Intention, Right Speech, Right Action, Right Livelihood, Right Effort, Right Mindfulness and Right Concentration. According to a traditional demarcation, the Eightfold Path can be divided into three categories: Right View and Right Intention fall under the general category of Wisdom (*prajna*). Right Speech, Right Action and Right Livelihood fall under the general category of Moral Conduct (*shila*). Right Effort, Right Mindfulness, and Right Concentration fall under Mental Discipline or Meditation (*samadhi/bhavana*).

---

1 As Harvey relates: "In general, Buddhism sees it as more appropriate to describe this Path than to try and precisely describe its goal." Harvey (1990), p. 63.

The objective of this path is the end of suffering. Since suffering involves attachment to self, the objective of the Noble Eightfold path thus involves overcoming attachment to self. Overcoming attachment to anything involves discipline. For instance, a child attached to a favourite toy may grudgingly acquiesce to a request to give it up. But the child will likely not overcome his attachment by simply making the decision to give away the toy. To overcome his attachment, the child must deal with his desires and cravings for the toy. This requires discipline. The same is true for attachment to self, except much more so. Attachment to self manifests in our beliefs and desires, hopes and fears, likes and dislikes, affections and aversions, loves and hatreds (it manifests with the aggregates, and once again this is why attachment to the aggregates is summed up as the source of suffering in the First Noble Truth). To remove attachment to self thus requires a wholesale change in our natures. For this, much discipline is needed. The Noble Eightfold Path, presented and elaborated below, speaks to the different elements of the discipline required. The steps in the Noble Eightfold path are presented as separate steps but, as will be noted, they are not exclusive; there is overlap between various steps on the path, as well as between the groupings. The steps in the Noble Eightfold Path are not to be pursued successively, but more or less collectively. But, having said this, there is still some semblance of succession, and some measure of dependence, among some steps.

1. Right View

Having Right Views involves understanding and accepting the Buddha's teachings, the Dharma. This includes seeing the truth of the Four Noble Truths and the doctrines of the Buddha. It involves believing what is true, and not believing what is false, particularly as this concerns knowledge of what is necessary for overcoming suffering. This includes knowledge of the nature of suffering, and the nature of one's attachment to self. Right View also involves not craving right views or true beliefs, for knowledge, as with anything, can become an object of craving and selfish pursuit. The gaining of Right Views without craving or attachment to self requires discipline, for not only is one pressed to correctly understand, but to not be desirous for understanding or knowledge, or to pursue understanding in a way that entrenches attachment to self (as through feelings of pride, or the prestige that may be gained through intellectual accomplishment). The admonition here involves not being greedy for Right Views.

Right Views about the Noble Truths and doctrines of the Buddha involve seeing how they apply to oneself. This involves seeing the sources of attachment in oneself. Knowing oneself, and not being deluded about one's motives and desires, requires being sincere with oneself. In this respect, Right Views connects to Right Mindfulness, which is described below. Coming to the Right Views about the teachings of the Buddha and how they apply to oneself requires that one carefully observe one's motives, desires and how one is moved to act.

Obtaining Right View involves a certain amount of intellectual attainment (for a correct understanding of the Noble Truths, and the teachings of the Buddha in general, involves not simply coming to accept their truth, but coming to understand why they are true). Having said this, it is not asserted that great intelligence or cleverness is needed for obtaining Right Views. Coming to an understanding of what is true involves intelligence, but in addition to this, Right View stresses the discipline needed to approach knowledge with the right attitude and without attachment, and sincerity so that one does not mislead oneself. Discipline, as we will see, is an important element of every step on the Noble Eightfold Path.

2. Right Intention

Having Right Intentions involves being free of selfishness, possessiveness and acquisitiveness. It involves, as one might expect, acting with what are considered to be wholesome intentions. Examples of Right Intention include not acting bravely for reason of craving a reward, or being kind for reason of fostering a good public image. Right Intentions, particularly in examples such as these, involve a moral aspect. The Buddhist is charged not only to act appropriately but also to have the morally right intentions in acting appropriately. In this respect, while it is customarily placed in the category of Wisdom, Right Intention also pertains to the category of Moral Conduct.

Right Intention, along with Right View, falls under the category of Wisdom in the Noble Eightfold Path. Accordingly, having Right Intentions should further wisdom, and be a mark of the wise. To this end, having Right Intentions involves having the right reasons or motives for one's actions. Having the right reasons for actions, or doing things with proper motives, requires knowing what the right reasons are, and knowing one's motives. Knowing one's motives, recognizing proper from improper motives, and amending one's motives as need be involves wisdom. Having Right Intentions certainly involves not having wrong or corrupt or self-focussed intentions, and this requires mastery over one's intentions and inclinations. Thus Right Intention requires self-discipline and mastery. One must be able to set the course for one's thoughts and intentions, and amend them if they are wrongly directed towards self or craving (and this connects Right Intention to Right Effort, which is described below); it requires that one know what to think about, or desire or fear, and how to direct one's thoughts appropriately. This mastery over self and thought is a mark of wisdom. Right Intention also works with Right Speech and Right Action (the next two steps), for these follow upon having the Right Intentions.

3. Right Speech

Right Speech involves not speaking in ways that are misleading, hurtful, idle, slanderous and, importantly, self-creating (and this listing is not exhaustive). Attachment to self may become entrenched through the use of language, and in particular through the unmindful use of names and words like 'I' or 'me' or 'mine'. Right Speech involves being mindful of such usage so that it does not propagate attachment to self.

Speech is not only carried out externally, but internally insofar as we think in words. As with one's outward presentations in words, one's inward thoughts should also not be hurtful (to others or to oneself – e.g., one should not have self-denigrating thoughts). One's thoughts and words should involve care so as to avoid hurtful thoughts and words, and one should notice the encroachment of attachment to self in thought and speech. Right Speech connects closely to Right Intentions, and involves discipline in our public as well as private utterances.

4. Right Action

Right Action involves refraining from harming others, stealing, lying, killing, sexual misconduct (for monks, this would generally be extended to any sexual activity) and more that is considered unwholesome. As mental actions are also actions, Right Action extends to internal actions or mental events (such as thoughts, desires, feelings, etc.). In this respect, Right Action overlaps with Right Intention. Clearly, the categories are not exclusive, and can be interpreted widely, but they are nevertheless intended to cover particular areas of discipline, and Right Action pertains primarily to our outward behaviours.

5. Right Livelihood

Right Livelihood involves making a living in ways that do not infringe on the other elements of the Noble Eightfold Path, particularly those that prescribe moral conduct (such as Right Action and Right Speech). Again, this would include not killing, stealing, lying, etc. Right Livelihood can be regarded narrowly, as pertaining to how we make a living, or more broadly, as pertaining to how we should live in general. In this respect, Right Livelihood requires practising Right Intention, Right Speech, Right Action, and other steps, through one's day and over the course of one's life.

6. Right Effort

Right Effort involves the effort that needs to be put forth for following the Noble Eightfold path. It includes making the effort to prevent unwholesome mental states from arising. As noted, it overlaps with Right Intention, and is needed in order to enable one to have the Right Intentions. Right Effort, in preventing selfish, hurtful, hateful or otherwise unwholesome thoughts from arising, clearly involves discipline.

This disciplining can take the form of keeping one's attention on contrary states of mind such as compassion and kindness.

Right Effort is included in the grouping of mental discipline. It includes the discipline involved in moving one's attention from one thought or state to another (as from an unwholesome thought to a wholesome thought, as noted above, or from a first-order desire to a second-order state that does not desire the satisfaction of the first-order desire). This kind of detachment, and control over the course of one's thoughts and desires and locating one's attention appropriately, requires the mental discipline of Right Effort (as well as other steps on the Noble Eightfold Path, in particular the next two).

7. Right Mindfulness

Right Mindfulness involves being continually aware of one's thoughts, motives, and actions. It involves being aware of when a sense of self intrudes and begins to lead one's behaviour or thoughts. In order to exercise the self-control of Right Effort, and be able to prevent unwholesome states of mind and actions from coming to pass, it is important to be closely self-aware, and Right Mindfulness involves this constant vigilance and self-awareness. Right Mindfulness involves paying close attention, watching the elements of the aggregates (sensations, perceptions, volitions, etc.) to see whether there is craving and attachment. The idea is that by watching closely one will be less prone to falling prey to cravings and attachments, for one will be aware of these states as they arise. By astutely observing the impermanence of the aggregates, the mindful practitioner will see that there is nothing permanent to which to attach.

In being mindful, a distance is created in the mind wherein one steps back in order to observe mental processes, rather than just be embroiled in them. Being mindful is important for not being subsumed in one's thoughts and desires. To elaborate, mindfulness requires a degree of detachment or remove in order to stand back and be aware of thoughts, desires, and other mental states as they occur. This standing back and being aware, or being mindful, involves occupying a higher-order state in relation to the lower-order state of which one is being aware. In contrast to cravings, which are higher-order states that seek the satisfaction of lower-order states in order to satisfy a self, being mindful involves being aware of lower-order states from the vantage of higher-order states without being desirous of their satisfaction. Mindfulness, it is important to note, is not passive awareness. It involves the (Right) effort of *moving* one's thoughts and attention to a perspective or vantage from which one may be aware of lower-order thoughts and desires. In being mindful one takes one's attention to a step remove. Mindfulness involves detachment, and placing attention in a detached state requires concentration and mental discipline. Notice that if, for instance, someone is mindful of being angry, then he is not fully invested in his anger; he is stepping back in his mind's attention in order to be aware of being angry, and this is consequently to become at least a little less angry than he might otherwise be. Thus mindfulness also has an important role to play in cultivating moral conduct in the Noble Eightfold Path.

By being mindful a person may shift from being fully invested in following through on a desire to concomitantly being aware of himself as following through on the desire. In doing so, he moves his attention, or divides his attention, away from the desire. And the better the powers of his concentration, the better he can redirect and focus his attentions. Thus, Right Mindfulness involves and draws upon Right Concentration.

8. Right Concentration

Right Concentration involves cultivating focussed awareness. As described, all the steps on the Noble Eightfold path involve discipline. And discipline requires concentration and focus. Right Concentration pairs up well with Right Mindfulness and Right Effort, particularly as these apply to mental cultivation. It is important to be mindful – aware and removed – in order to put forth the Right Effort to prevent unwholesome states from coming about, or to help overcome them once they have come about. But being mindful requires concentrating. Thus, it is not enough to be aware without focussed awareness. Likewise, it is not enough to put forth effort without focussed effort. Without Right Concentration, Right Effort and Right Mindfulness can fall into disrepair and idleness. In a sense, Right Concentration speaks to the *Rightness* in Right Effort and Right Mindfulness (for to put forth Right Effort and Right Mindfulness *rightly* involves concentration and focus). Right Concentration is not only important for cultivating Right Mindfulness, but can also be described as extending or building upon Right Mindfulness, for in Right Concentration one is not just called on to be aware from a step remove, but to concentrate in being aware; to wilfully be aware not of many things, but of few or one. It involves focussing or channelling one's powers of attention and mindful ability, just as a magnifying glass can focus the sun's rays. This capacity for Right Concentration is especially important for meditation.

More on Mindfulness

Mindfulness is meant to be a constant or fairly constant state of mind. In being mindful one is to be ever vigilant, rather than occasionally or intermittently mindful (for this intermittence may not notice, let alone prevent, the rising of unwholesome thoughts and cravings – the preventiveness of mindfulness requires exercising it without such gaps). This constant employment does not seem to be required, at least not to the same extent, of other steps on the Noble Eightfold Path. For instance, Right Speech and Right Action pertain to moments when speech and action are performed or are called for. But again, Right Mindfulness (although perhaps not only Right Mindfulness) is required as a constant state of mind. This constant mindfulness means that the Buddhist is always supposed to keep a mindful distance and detachment in his mind. This means never getting fully embroiled in a mental state (be this hate or love, anger or joy, or any other state) for reason of always occupying a mindful remove. A Buddhist adept cannot be mindfully aware of an episode in his mind if he is fully preoccupied with it. To be mindfully aware of his mental states, an adept must remain partly removed from them. Mindfulness requires that he keep at least part of his power of attention occupied with being an ever watchful eye. Right Concentration, it is worth recalling, involves being effectively mindful and even more fully allocating and concentrating one's attention to this watchful eye (as with concentrated awareness of the movement of one's breath in breathing meditation).

As described, being mindful of being angry involves relocating attention away from being angry, or away from other concerns, to being mindful. As a consequence, being mindful of being angry entails being at least a little less angry than one might otherwise be; it involves being partially removed from the feeling of anger so that one can be mindfully aware of it. But it is not only unwholesome states of which the Buddhist is charged to be mindful. As noted, Right Mindfulness requires that the follower be ever-mindful. And thus, the follower is to be mindful of happiness or joy as well. This is to say that, in the experience of happiness, one is not to indulge fully in the feeling, but to concurrently be mindful of the feeling. Again, in being mindful, the Buddhist adept removes part of his attention to a point from which he may concurrently be aware of being happy. But this should mean that being mindful leads him to be less happy than he might otherwise be (just as being mindful of his anger should lead him to be less angry than he might otherwise be due to the detachment involved). Thus, the mindful person may be less angry, less happy, less sad and less joyful, than he might otherwise be for reason of being mindful and the detachment this involves. The mindful person should be less attached to extremes (good or bad), and more detached and more dispassionate in general.

Perhaps this is at a cost: a moderation with fewer extremes of happiness and joy than otherwise might be available. However, the end of suffering and the attainment of happiness are not univocal in Buddhism (not unless happiness is reinterpreted so that it is not merely a pleasant psychological feeling, or the result of desire satisfaction, just as suffering has been reinterpreted away from being merely an unpleasant feeling or the result of unsatisfied desire in the movement away from the first and second groupings to the third grouping of the First Noble Truth). The end of suffering involves overcoming attachment to self. This may lead to happiness, but, as we all know, a feeling of happiness can also be gained through satisfying the desires and pleasing the senses of a self. These experiences, while not bad in themselves, lead to suffering in the Buddhist sense if pursued with attachment and craving. Indeed, attachment to happiness is also suffering-inducing, and so maintaining a mindful remove from an experience of happiness is a good thing from the Buddhist perspective (even if there is some cost in happiness). Mindfulness, for instance, can help one realize that happiness is transient. But this realization involves detachment from the experience of happiness (so that one may stand back and observe the transience of this happiness), and this involves some cost in the happiness being experienced. A lowered potential for feeling extremes of happiness or pleasure seems to come with the detachment and dispassion involved in the disciplines of the Noble Eightfold Path, and in particular the exercise of Right Mindfulness. However, there is arguably a compensatory benefit, not only in the end of suffering, but in the greater awareness, and in the greater repose and equanimity, that may come with detachment and dispassion.

In being mindful of one's thoughts there is no literal looking going on, for there are no literal eyes directed inwards to the contents of one's mind (and no literal things to be seen even if there were eyes). The attentiveness of mindfulness may be described as involving a metaphorical looking. It is introspecting with attention and discernment. The Argument from the Aggregates (which was described in Chapter Four and which will be revisited in the next chapter) involves mindfulness of the aggregates; it involves looking carefully and with discernment at the play and movement of the aggregates and observing that there is no permanent self or entity to be found. More than this, and as already described, the process of being mindful helps in the process of overcoming attachment to self. This is because in being mindful one detaches, at least somewhat, from the state being experienced so that one can be observant and mindful of the state. The detachment that comes with a mindful and dispassionate observation of one's mind is part of overcoming attachment to self in one's mind.

VIII

The Doctrine of No Self

Introduction

THE BUDDHA FAMOUSLY STATES: "If a man should conquer in battle a thousand and a thousand more, and another man should conquer himself, his would be the greater victory, because the greatest of victories is victory over oneself."[1] In this chapter, the doctrine of No Self will be discussed. In the following two chapters, the doctrines of Impermanence and Dependent Origination will be presented. These, along with the Noble Truths, are basic doctrines and truths of Buddhism. The doctrine of No Self will be derived primarily from what is being called the 'Argument from the Aggregates'. This argument was first presented in Chapter Four. In this chapter it will be described further, developed with two textual analogies and additional aspects and consequences will be discussed.

No Self is a translation of the Sanskrit *anatman* (*anatta* in Pali). *Anatman* is a literal denial of *Atman*. It is a rejection of self as being any sort of entity that is permanent or enduring and that stands apart

---

1 *Dhammapada* Ch. 8, 103.

from the ever-changing aggregates. The doctrine of No Self denies an essence or substance underlying the aggregates. When it comes to the self, there are just the changing aggregates. The Buddha, after his "First Preaching" of the Four Noble Truths, preached of the non-existence of the self and soul. As described in Chapter Two, the Buddha, while meditating under a pipal tree prior to his awakening, carried out a careful and patient observation. Observing the states of his body, and the contents of his mind, he observed that there is nothing that was constant. The body changes through the processes it undergoes, and the contents of the mind are in flux. He found no underlying and unchanging self that stands behind his mental and physical processes; rather, he observed only the processes. He called these processes the five aggregates (*skandhas* in Sanskrit, *khandhas* in Pali). These were described in Chapter Four. They are called "aggregates of attachment" because it is held that we readily attach a sense of an unchanging self or ego to the aggregates. According to the Buddha, the self is really no more than a composite of the five continually changing aggregates with no permanent core. The Argument from the Aggregates repudiates the notion of a permanent, substantive self that is independent of the aggregates but, in doing so, it admits a notion of a changing self that is composed of the aggregates. This rejection of a substantive self, while admitting the possibility of a composite self, will be discussed later in this chapter.

The Argument from the Aggregates

The Argument from the Aggregates for the doctrine of No Self, originally presented in Chapter Four, appears straightforward. It is an *a posteriori* argument based on empirical observation. The Buddha observed the movement of the aggregates, and observed nothing but these aggregates. He observed no underlying or permanent self among these aggregates. And based on these observations he concluded that there was no permanent self. To be clear, there is no self that is unchanging over the course of one's life, but also, there is no self that is unchanging for any length of time over which the aggregates are observed to arise and pass. There

is nothing that is observed not to arise and pass in our conscious awareness, and so there can be no self that stands as an exception to changing,
arising and passing. The conclusion of No Self in this argument is based
on observation, and thus the argument is empiricist in its methodology.
According to this methodology, our belief in self – our sense of self –
should be based on nothing more than what is observed. If our sense of
self involves a permanence that is not observed in the arising and passing
of the aggregates, it is ungrounded.

This is the Argument from the Aggregates. It repudiates the notion
of a permanent self. Its methodology affirms that if anything is judged
to exist it must be open to empirical observation. However, if the self
is unobservable, then the method of empirical observation cannot be
applied. Such a concept of self arises with Atman in the Upanishads.
This is the True Self. Atman is described in the Upanishads as pure subject. This is taken to mean that it is pure consciousness without object or
content; awareness without an object of awareness. On this view, Atman
does not exist as an object, and so it is not an observable object. The
Argument from the Aggregates faces a challenge with this concept of
self, and this is worth elaborating.

The aggregates – our sensations, desires, intentions, bodily processes,
etc. – are objects of our awareness (be this introspective awareness of
the contents of our minds or, in the case of bodily processes, also outward sensory awareness). We can only observe what can be an object of
awareness. No unchanging subject is observed among these aggregates.
But then the subject of awareness – the subject that is aware and that is
doing the observing – cannot be observed *qua* subject. The experiencer
cannot be observed *as an experiencer*, but only as an object of experience.
Thus, the conclusion that there is no pure subject to be found among the
aggregates does not rely on observation for it is not the sort of thing that
could be observed. It can be concluded *a priori*, without observation, that
no pure subject will be observed among the aggregates, for the subject
that is aware cannot be observed without being rendered as an object.
To further illustrate, an image of oneself in a mirror (or an image of
oneself in one's mind's eye) is an object of observation. To observe this
image is to observe an object and not the subject who is observing. The

observer *as a subject* is not observed. To recall a memory of oneself is to encounter a memory, and not to encounter the subject who is recalling. Since observation can only observe what can be an object of observation (or experience can only encounter what is an object of experience), it follows *a priori* that the subject of experience *qua subject* will not be observed. No actual observation need be conducted to know that a pure subject will not be encountered in an observation. This is not to say that such a subject exists, as the Upanishads purport, but only that the Argument from the Aggregates appears restricted by its empiricist methodology from arguing against the Upanishadic Self or Atman.

The method of observation of the Argument from the Aggregates does not apply to Atman as pure subject. Thus, if the appropriateness of this method is not independently justified, then its use against Atman is question-begging. To elaborate further, the applicability of the Argument from the Aggregates depends on the concept of self under scrutiny. If the self is understood to be a permanent entity that exists as an object in the world, then the method of observation can yield that no such entity is found. But if the self is considered to be a pure subject – something that is not an object in the world and is thus unable to be observed as an object or entity – then the method of observation cannot be applied and yields no conclusion. Of course, to say that the self exists but is not an observable or encounterable entity or object in the world is a tall order. Perhaps unjustifiable. But the Upanishads did assert such a view of Atman. Consider the following passage from the *Brhadarankyaka Upanishad*:

> You cannot see the seer of seeing, you cannot hear the hearer of hearing, you cannot think the thinker of thinking, you cannot understand the understander of understanding. He is your self [Atman] which is in all things.[1]

---

[1] *Brhadarankyaka Upanishad* III.4.2, p. 220. See also III.7.23, p. 230: "He is never seen but is the seer, he is never heard but is the hearer. He is never perceived, but is the perceiver. He is never thought but is the thinker. There is no other seer but he, there is no other hearer but he, there is no other perceiver but he, there is no other thinker but he. He is your self [Atman], the inner controller, the immortal. Everything else is evil."

In the early Upanishads, the self is the mysterious subject: the self is the seer, the hearer, the thinker and knower. The self – and it is Atman that is meant here – is not the seen, the heard, the thought or the known. It is pure subject, or pure consciousness, and because of this, it is mysterious (for it cannot be known as an *object* of knowledge). Atman cannot be observed or known as an object. That is why Atman is held to only be knowable through a direct, unmediated, inward experience – an experience of pure consciousness (for this is thought to be able to know Atman as pure subject). Again, the method of observation employed in the Argument from the Aggregates does not apply to this self. The method of observation does not discover that the Upanishadic Self is not found; its method precludes its being found. Later in this chapter, another argument, that does not appear to beg the question, will be applied to Atman; it is called the 'Argument from Lack of Control'.

The Argument from the Aggregates has another related weakness. The method of observation presumes a dualism between the observing subject and the object observed. But Atman, by way of its identity with Brahman, is not dualistic; it is monistic. Thus, an argument that presumes a dualistic framework in arguing against Atman – as does the Argument from the Aggregates – again seems to beg the question. Buddhism, as discussed, does not subscribe to the monism of the Upanishads. It does, though, uphold the possibility of non-dualistic experience (and like the Upanishads, it connects non-dualistic experience to the ending of suffering – this connection was considered in Chapter Six in the discussion of Nirvana and will be revisited in the discussion of Emptiness in Chapter Thirteen). The point here is that non-dualistic experience – such as the realization of Atman – presents an exception to the dualistic empiricist methodology of the Argument from the Aggregates.

Still, the primary aim of an argument for No Self is not simply to render a conclusion about what does or does not exist, but to be of service in the practical objective of overcoming suffering. The Buddha lived at a time when the heights of spiritual realization were described as involving a realization of True Self. The Upanishads hold that the True Self is to be known through a direct inward experience, and that this enables a monistic experience of reality in which suffering is overcome. The Buddha, in rejecting this, presumably felt that this approach was not an effective way of obtaining release from suffering and hence enlightenment. The Buddha's disagreement with this traditional approach is quite pronounced, for the Buddha's approach involves overcoming, rather than a realization of, an independent and permanent self. For the Buddha there is no True Self. Anatman is a repudiation of Atman. But we might still wonder why the pursuit of No Self is preferable to True Self as the practical means to ending suffering? After all, both approaches involve overcoming attachment to the ego-self.

This question may be answered by considering which approach is more useful for overcoming craving (which is, according to the Second Noble Truth, the source of suffering). Arguably, the objective of True Self, as opposed to No Self, provides a positive end or goal that may be more readily pursued with craving and attachment. In contrast, the doctrine of No Self tells us that there is no self to attach to; no self in whose interests we may crave. In this respect, No Self is similar to negative descriptions of Nirvana: both serve to repudiate any positive content upon which one may focus one's cravings. This is not to say that No Self cannot itself be construed as a goal that one may crave; rather, because it is framed negatively and without positive content, it may provide a goal that is less amenable to attachment and craving. No Self, unlike True Self, involves a denial rather than an assertion of self and thus seems to provide less of a target for craving and attachment. Since craving involves attachment to self, and seeks to satisfy a sense of self, it is arguably more effective for overcoming craving to focus on realizing that there is no self rather than focusing on attaining to a greater, universal conception of self. As explained earlier, overcoming suffering involves, not overcoming desire in general, but overcoming attachment to self in desire. This realization was central to the Buddha's enlightenment and Middle Way. Attaching a sense of permanent selfhood to the ever-changing aggregates is summed up to be the source of suffering in the First Noble Truth. Given this understanding of suffering, No Self may be better suited for leading the aspirant away from suffering than the pursuit of an unchanging True

Self (for to put it plainly, with No Self there is no self to attach to the aggregates). These are practical considerations, and not metaphysical considerations, in favour of No Self over True Self.

The Argument from the Aggregates adopts an uncomplicated empiricist methodology: that which is not observed cannot be said to exist. Likewise, we will presume, that which is observed can be said to exist.[1] A permanent or enduring self is not observed. But the aggregates are. The Argument from the Aggregates – in concluding that there exists no permanent self based on an empirical observation of the ever-changing aggregates – admits the existence of the aggregates. This means that a self that is a composite of these aggregates is admissible under the doctrine of No Self. Since the aggregates are ever-changing, a self that is composed of the aggregates would also be ever-changing. In short, in rejecting the concept of a permanent self that exists independently of the ever-changing aggregates, a concept of self that is a composite of the impermanent aggregates is admitted.

A self that is a composite of its aggregate parts, we might think, cannot be more than the sum of its parts. After all, a physical object such as a toaster cannot weigh more (or less, for that matter) than the sum of the weight of its parts. Notwithstanding, a whole need not be the *mere* sum of its parts for the ordering and organization of these parts makes a difference. This can be illustrated with the example of a computer. To say a computer is more than just the sum of its parts is not, if conceived in the right way, to say that a computer contains a hidden or mysterious or immeasurable component. Rather, it is just to assert that the operation of the computer is not to be found in the operation of any of its parts considered separately, but in all the parts considered jointly, in the right assembly and properly functioning. If these parts are disassembled and separated, the parts remain but the computer does not. The same

---

1 The concept of emptiness in Mahayana Buddhism, while it repudiates the independent existence of the aggregates, admits the dependent existence of the aggregates. Consequently, emptiness need not be taken to undermine the observational claims that underlie the doctrine of No Self. The concept of emptiness and these points will be elaborated and discussed in Chapter Thirteen.

point applies to the notion of self permitted under the Argument from the Aggregates. This self is a composite entity, composed of aggregates and, in a sense similar to a computer, can be a whole that is more than the mere sum of its parts. That is, while a self that is a permanent entity existing independently of the aggregates is denied, a self that is more than just the mere sum of the aggregates – in the sense just described – is not denied by the Argument from the Aggregates. The sense in which a whole can be more than the mere sum of its parts may lead to the misapprehension that there is something hidden, something unwavering and underlying the parts. It may lead to a belief in Atman, or soul, or permanent self. But this appeal to something special is not needed to account for why a whole is more than the sum of its parts while still being, in another sense, no more than the sum of its parts. Two traditional analogies will be presented to further illustrate this, and to bring out further aspects of the doctrine of No Self and the Argument from the Aggregates. The first involves a lute, and the second a chariot; they both involve kings.

A Lute, a Chariot and the Composite Self

In the lute analogy, a king is moved but mystified by the sound of a lute. He wants to know where the sound comes from and investigates. He does not find the sound upon looking at the lute, and so proceeds to see if he can find it among the parts. He breaks the lute into pieces but still does not find the beautiful sound among them.[1] The beautiful sound only emerges when the parts are together, under a certain assembly, and then only when played well. The instrument is more than the mere sum of its parts for a mere sum – without specific order and assembly – is not sufficient for being a lute that can be played to produce a beautiful sound.

---

1 *Salayatanavagga, Samyutta Nikaya* IV 196-98, p. 1254. As Collins notes, the lute image recurs in the *Milinda Panha* 53, p. 84 and a similar analogy is made using a conch-shell or trumpet in the *Digha Nikaya* II 337-38, p. 360. See Collins (1982), p 279, ff. 20.

By analogy, the parts of the lute are the aggregates, and the sound of the lute is the self. It is worth further considering this, for there may seem to be some ambiguity in the example between whether the self is analogous to a well-functioning *lute* (i.e., one that can produce a beautiful sound), or whether the self is analogous to the *sound* of a well-functioning lute. That is, there may seem to be some scope for ambiguity in this analogy between whether the self is taken to be analogous to the object (the lute), or to the emergent property (the beautiful sound emerging from playing the lute). Given that the king investigates the lute and its disassembled parts looking for the beautiful sound, this suggests that the self is being analogized with the sound – the emergent property – of the lute rather than with the lute itself. The association of self with the sound of the lute, rather than with the lute itself, suggests what in contemporary terms would be called a functionalist view of self (for what matters for producing the sound is that the parts be organized and work collectively, i.e., what matters is the function being carried out, and not the particular parts themselves).[1]

In the chariot analogy, a king named 'Milinda' is asking questions of a monk named 'Nagasena'.[2] The monk, standing before the king, tells the king that although he is called 'Nagasena', there is no permanent self or ego to be found. The king is puzzled by this response. Nagasena elaborates with an analogy. He asks King Milinda how he managed to arrive at his present location. The king replies that it was by his chariot. Nagesena asks whether by 'chariot' the king refers to the wheels. King Milinda answers "No." Nagasena asks if he means the frame, and the king again answers "No." Nagasena continues in this vein and asks if 'chariot' then refers to the axles, the spokes, the reins, and so on. For each part the king responds "No," admitting that the chariot is none of these. Rather, he says, 'chariot' is what we call all of these parts put together. In the same manner, the monk responds, 'Nagasena' or 'self' is just a label

---

1 For a further explanation of functionalism see Kim (2011), Chapters 5 and 6. An analogy for the self with the harmoniousness or attunement of a stringed instrument is, interestingly enough, raised by Simmias and rejected by Socrates in the *Phaedo*.

2 *Milinda Panha* 25-27. See also pp. 129-33 in Warren (1987).

we attach to a sum of parts working together, and there is no underlying entity, separate from these aggregated parts, named 'Nagasena'. There is no permanent referent of the name 'Nagasena'. That is, just as the word 'chariot' does not refer to something that exists separately from the appropriately ordered aggregate of chariot parts, likewise, the name 'Nagasena' does not refer to an entity or self separate from the ever-changing composing parts or aggregates. In this respect, "Nagasena is a mere empty sound."[1]

A chariot, in a certain sense, is more than the mere sum of its parts. A chariot is not more because it weighs more than the sum of its parts, or because it contains some extra *thing* other than its parts, whatever that may be; that's not the right sense of *more*. Rather, it is more than the sum of its parts in the sense that it can do something that the parts by themselves, taken separately or severally, cannot do. The chariot is the parts put together in a certain way, and is a chariot insofar as it carries out certain functions. The self, likewise, is more than just the sum of its parts. But this is more apt to be confused. Similar to the chariot, the self is more than the sum of its aggregate parts in the sense that the parts must be organized appropriately to function as a self. The self is *not* more than the sum of its aggregate parts in the sense that there is some extra ingredient – some unchanging essence or core or permanent spirit or soul, conveys Nagasena. From the first-person or inside point of view, however, it may seem we are more than the sum of our psychophysical states in *this* sense. The analogy with the chariot asserts that the self is properly viewed as a composite; it is a composite of the aggregates. The

---

1 *Milinda Panha* 26. See also p. 131 in Warren (1987). Collins provides an adapted translation of a passage from the *Visuddhimagga of Buddhaghosa* XVIII 32, which expresses a similar thought: "The mental and the material are really here, but here there is no human being to be found. For it is void and merely fashioned like a doll, just suffering piled up like grass and sticks." From Collins (1982) p. 133. And in the *Sagathavagga, Samyutta Nikaya* I 135, p. 230, a nun named Vajira responds to Mara, the "Evil One," by saying: "Why now do you assume 'a being'? Mara, is that your speculative view? This is a heap of sheer formations: Here is no being found. Just as with an assemblage of parts, the word 'chariot' is used, so, when the aggregates exist, there is the convention 'a being'."

analogy is limited, though, as the aggregates are ever-changing while the composite parts of a chariot need not be.[1] The analogy is similar to David Hume's so-called "Bundle Theory" of self, in which the self is regarded as a composite or bundle of perceptions, and not as something underlying and independent of these perceptions (see Chapter Four for the discussion and comparison of Hume and the Buddha).

In the lute example, the king looks for the sound in the lute; he breaks it apart and looks for the sound amongst its pieces. This indicates that the self is not analogous to the lute itself, for the king does not look for the lute, which he breaks up, but for the beautiful sound of the lute. By analogy then, the self is not the composite of the appropriately ordered aggregates but an emergent property of the composite of the appropriately ordered aggregates. In contrast, in the chariot example, this reading is not a possibility. The chariot *is* the well-ordered and well-functioning composite of chariot parts. The example does not suggest that the chariot is a property of this composite of parts. Indeed, it would not work well as an example if it did for this is not how we normally speak of a chariot (that is, we would not say a chariot is a property of a composite of chariot parts but would say a chariot is a composite object made of parts). By analogy then, the self is a well-ordered and well-functioning composite of aggregates, and not a property of this well-ordered and well-functioning composite of aggregates. The two examples thus raise differing analogies. There is a difference between comparing the self to the sound of a lute (and not the lute itself) versus comparing the self to a chariot. Nonetheless, both analogies help illustrate the Argument from the Aggregates. Both analogies convey that the self is not a permanent entity underlying the aggregates for no such self is to be found. In both analogies, the self is dependent upon the aggregates being well-ordered and well-functioning for not any ordering or organization of aggregates will do. In what follows, this concept of self will be referred to as a 'composite self', composed of the ever-changing aggregates (even though, strictly speaking, this phrasing

---

1 The impermanence of the aggregates will be discussed further in the next chapter. The Buddhist understanding of the continuity over time of objects with changing parts will be more fully discussed in Chapter Eleven.

suits the chariot analogy better than the lute analogy). While a chariot is an aggregate of physically described parts, the composite self would include psychologically described states or factors. Our composing parts are different – psychological or psychophysical states and events – but we are nonetheless held to be composite creatures.

We may admit that, when we inwardly observe, we only encounter the ever-changing aggregates. However, our sense of self may still convey that we are more than this. We may look to the aggregates and find them to be insufficient – individually, severally, and collectively – to account for this sense of self. We can see this, for instance, in our self-ascriptions. When I say "I am hungry," I speak of an aggregate: the feeling of hunger. I also speak of a self that is distinct from the aggregate. That is, in speaking this way I usually do not just mean that there is a body that is hungry, or that there is a stomach that is empty, or that the aggregates are collectively hungry (how odd that sounds!). Rather, I mean that *I* am hungry; that there is a self that is feeling the body's hunger; and that is feeling the emptiness not just of *a* stomach but of *its* stomach. I register the hunger as the hunger of a self – *my* self – that exists in some manner apart from the hunger it feels and apart from the aggregates in general. The Argument from the Aggregates asserts that this is mistaken. It asserts that this belief and sense of self is unfounded and involves thinking of the self as more than the sum of its parts in the wrong sense of 'more', as described earlier. The doctrine of No Self admits no more than that the self is a composite of the aggregates. Thus, the relation between the self and an aggregate such as hunger needs to be appreciated differently. Note that it is not just my belief about my hunger, but the affective *quality* of my hunger – which is experienced and felt as the hunger *of a self* – that needs to be appreciated differently. The doctrine of No Self conveys that our sense of self – our sense of what we are – as evidenced in our desires, hopes, fears, and other psychological states, widely overreaches the truth of what we are. And that this needs, through the disciplinary measures of the Noble Eightfold Path, to be conditioned and reined in.

The aggregates that make up the composite self are ever-changing, continually arising and passing in our awareness. The composite self is thus also ever-changing. However, the self we identify with over time and believe ourselves to be is presumed not to be this composite ever-changing self. That is, it is said that for those amongst us who are unenlightened, our sense of self presumes a permanence that is not found with the ever-changing aggregates. When we crave, for instance, we presume that the self to be satisfied will be – in some essential aspect – the same as the self who presently craves. It is attachment to this self – the self that we feel endures or remains the same in some essential aspect – that is held to be the source of suffering. The Argument from the Aggregates and the doctrine of No Self repudiate this self. No unchanging, independent self is observed. Suffering in the Buddhist conception is caused by attachment to an illusory self. This is an attachment to a phenomenon of something permanent that stands behind the aggregates and moves us and compels us but that does not exist. So it is asserted in the doctrine of No Self. Our attachments to this non-existent self convey that we do not truly know our "selves." The relation between impermanence, identity and self is important and will be continued in the next chapter, on Impermanence, as well as in Chapter Eleven in its discussion of continuity and identity.

Collins points out that arguments for no self serve not simply to persuade us of the truth of the doctrine of No Self, but are a basis for meditative reflection that is to help lead to a realization of No Self. This is to view arguments for No Self as strategies for overcoming attachment to self. Collins states:

> For Buddhist specialists, considered as a general category, the doctrine is taken literally and personally, and thus anatta represents a determinate pattern of self-perception and psychological analysis, which is at once the true description of reality – in Buddhist terms it 'sees things as they really are' – and the instrument by which the aspirant to Nirvana progresses towards and achieves his goal.[1]

---

1 Collins (1982), p. 12. Collins provides a nice rendering of a relevant passage from the *Samyutta Nikaya* III 155-56, p. 114: "when a monk lives with a mind familiar with the practice of seeing impermanence ... (*continued*)

The Argument from the Aggregates has a practical role. This argument does not merely argue against the concept of self as a permanent entity standing apart from the aggregates, but provides a means for overcoming the cravings and attachments that bind us to this concept of self. The Argument from the Aggregates is empiricist in method. Following the argument requires that we actively look at the aggregates so as to discover that there is no self to be found among them. This looking is an exercise in mindfulness. In looking, we are supposed to come to realize that our attachments to a permanent or enduring self are unfounded. The argument asks us to see for ourselves, to look to all that can be observed, to all prospective candidates for what may be a self, and discover – for ourselves – that it is not the permanent self we believe and feel ourselves to be. For each thing we encounter we can ask if it is or if it supports a permanent self, and return the answer that it is not a self and does not support a permanent self. We inwardly encounter desires, hopes, beliefs, thoughts, images, memories and much more. And for each observed state we can return the answer that it is not self; that it is not the self I think I am. This is supposed to not only persuade us, intellectually, that there is no permanent self among the aggregates. More important than this, our attachment to being a permanent self will, it is thought, begin to unlatch as we assiduously and unsuccessfully look for it among the aggregates. The primary bearing of looking closely at the aggregates is to help overcome attachment to self, and only secondarily of coming to believe in No Self (for the primary objective is to overcome suffering, and it is affective attachment, not belief, that is the key impediment). An argument that relies for its persuasion on our active looking and participation has more scope for affective influence – that is, influence in overturning our psychological attachments – than an argument that proceeds strictly deductively or without need of observation.

Also, being reminded that we are comprised of the aggregates is held

familiar with the practice of seeing unsatisfactoriness in what is impermanent ... familiar with the practice of seeing not-self in what is unsatisfactory,
in his body, his consciousness, and all external objects, with a mind which is
turned away from the conceits 'I' and 'mine', he quickly reaches liberation."

to be useful in realizing No Self. This is to be reminded that we are composed of our sensations, body, etc., just as a chariot is composed of its wheels, axles, etc. These reminders are supposed to help undo attachment to the concept of a permanent self existing apart from the aggregates because if we admit that we are partly comprised of our sensations, we thereby admit that we are not an entity standing behind our sensations; or if we admit that we are partly comprised of our body, then we admit that we are not an entity that oversees or owns or otherwise stands separate from the body. This is again to assert that this argument for No Self, as with any argument for No Self, is not strictly directed at arriving at a true belief, but in helping to overcome attachment to self. One may agree with the doctrine of No Self, but that does not mean attachment to self in the sense of being a permanent entity has been overcome. The attachment may continue (in defiance or disregard of the belief), but that is why a mere argument, no matter how compelling, is not enough to overcome attachment and suffering. Belief is one thing, and the easier to change; psychological and affective attachment is another, and much harder to purge. For this discipline is needed; and specifically, it is advised, the discipline of the Noble Eightfold Path.

The Argument from Lack of Control

In this section, another argument for No Self will be discussed. This argument will be called, drawing on Steven Collins, the 'Argument from Lack of Control'.

The ascetic with little nourishment, exposure to the elements, and other material hardships over the course of years, may seem to have put himself in a much weakened state. Being powerful and being an ascetic might not strike us as complementary. However, asceticism has been described as a means of gaining great power, indeed universal power: the ascetic tries, through severe discipline, to control his body and desires; and this self-disciplining is thought to lead to a realization of Atman, the True Self, and with this Brahman or Ultimate Reality as well. This is a world conquering asceticism. The realization of True Self, and the power implied in being one with Brahman, suggests that there should be no limitations in being able to exercise power or control over oneself. There should be no limitations that come from beyond the self for the realization of Atman is a unity with Brahman. The realization of True Self seems to entail full self-control. This way of thinking, in addition to its presumption of monism, presumes that such control over self can be gained. Collins relays a line of argument in which the Buddha contends that there is no such control. The self cannot exist without limitations in control and is not independent of being causally affected. It is thus argued that there is no control as is implied with the realization of Atman, and so there is no such self. Collins states:

> ... a major motive for world-renouncing asceticism in Brahmanical thought was the desire for universal power, attained through knowledge of, and control over, the self (atman) as microcosmic reflection of the macrocosmic force of the universe (Brahman). The first way in which the Buddha attempted to deny the existence of such a self was, accordingly, to claim that no such control existed. It is found at the beginning of the 'Discourse on the [fact of things having the] Characteristic of Not-self' (Anattalakkhana Sutta), traditionally the Buddha's second discourse. Here he speaks of all five 'constituents of personality' – I take body as an example: 'body, monks, is not self. Were it self, the body would suffer affliction, and one could have of body (what one wished, saying) "let my body be this, let my body be that."' Elsewhere, the Buddha asks an interlocutor 'do you have power over this body' to change it at will?[1]

As Collins notes, the Buddha responded to the view that the body is the self [i.e., Atman] by saying: "Were it self, the body would suffer affliction, and one could have of body (what one wished, saying) 'let

---

1 Collins (1982), p. 97.

my body be this, let my body be that.'"[1] The thinking here is that if the body is the self, or part of one's self, and the self has full control, then one should be able to overcome bodily afflictions, for affliction indicates that the self does not have sufficient control to overcome affliction. That is, if we maintain that the self is a controller to the extent of having full control, then it follows that the body cannot be included with the self for otherwise the self should have control over the afflictions of the body. This line of argument is extended to other aggregates that we might associate with the self, such as thoughts, memories, perception, consciousness. The argument unfolds similarly. With each aggregate we observe a lack of full control. For instance, we do not have full control of our memories – all our memories – such that we can recall every experience perfectly, or cease to remember experiences we wish to forget. Thus, the self cannot both have full control and include memories. Likewise, we cannot have complete control over our thoughts, desires, and beliefs; these are causally conditioned and are affected by events and circumstances beyond our control. Thus, as long as this degree of control is a requirement for being a self, then the self cannot include thoughts, desires, or beliefs either.

The argument tries to establish that the self cannot be a controller with full control, for with whatever we consider to be a self, or associate with a self, we see that there is significantly less than full control over it. Simply said, there is nothing over which a self can exert full control. The self cannot exist apart from being causally conditioned by circumstances beyond its control. That is, the argument from Lack of Control conveys that the self cannot have full control because it cannot exist apart from being causally affected. This is an argument against a self that is unconditioned, independent, and a controller to this degree. Atman, the True Self, was considered to be just such a self. Being identical with what is ultimately real – Brahman – meant that there was nothing outside of or more basic than Atman that could causally affect it; there is nothing that should be able to interfere with its extending full control.

---

1 Collins (1982), p. 97.

It was described earlier that the Argument from the Aggregates employs empirical observation. As long as this method is not separately justified, its employment against Atman seems question-begging. The Argument from Lack of Control offers another means of argument. Indeed, it seems specifically directed at Atman or True Self (for with no other view of self would we presume such full control). That is, this line of argument seems effective against ascetics and others who hold that there is a True Self (Atman) which, through its identity with Ultimate Reality (Brahman), can exert full control and not be causally affected. But it does not seem like this argument has much to offer as a general argument for No Self for such strong notions of control are generally not associated with our own sense of self. We can readily admit that we do not have full control over our bodies and mental states. Thus, this line of argument for No Self may not seem to offer any argument against the conviction that we are a self in a sense that is less substantive than Atman (i.e., a self that is independent of the aggregates but with only a limited degree of control over the aggregates).

We may not presume to have complete control, but it is still part of our sense of self that we are, to some extent, a controller (of our bodies and mental states). Indeed, part of what can make us think that our selves are independent of the aggregates is that we can exert control over them. We can it seems, through our will, initiate bodily movements and sequences of thoughts. This sense of being a controller is connected to our sense of being a free agent (for instance, in controlling the movement of my limbs I seem, to myself at least, to be doing so voluntarily). A degree of control and a degree of freedom certainly are important aspects of our sense of self. We feel free to move limbs, recall memories, make decisions, and much more, all within certain bounds. A focus on the sense of freedom in these actions, and the sense of control over these actions, can lead to the thought that we are an underlying and controlling self, and thereby entrench an attachment to self. The Buddha, with the Argument from Lack of Control, is counteracting these pulls towards self by calling attention to the other side of the ledger. That is, if feelings of control lead towards thoughts of being an independent self, then recognizing the lack of control, and recognizing that we are causally conditioned and circumstantially affected in our actions and thoughts, should lead towards thoughts of not being an independent self. It is in this respect that the Argument from Lack of Control has a wider applicability than being just an argument against Atman or True Self.

To further elaborate, the Buddha, in drawing attention to the issue of control, brings to light how little control we actually have. We believe we have control over our bodies, for instance, for we can move our limbs as we please, move our mouths to utter words as we please, and much more. But there is a great deal over which we do not have control. Affliction, as seen above, is an example raised by the Buddha. We may begin to ask why it is that, given we can control our bodies and minds in certain ways, and even improve in our ability to control with training, there are still so many limitations in the control we can exercise. For instance, why is it that, if I can move a limb freely, I cannot wilfully speed up the clotting process if I suffer a gash on that limb? Or, if I can wilfully control certain patterns of neurons, and thereby set in motion a causal sequence that leads to the movement of a limb, then why is it that I cannot control other sets of neurons to set in motion other causal sequences (such as those that would result in quicker healing, or in overcoming fears and hatreds and other deep-set psychological traits, all with a moment's will). Why is it that I can wilfully improve my eyesight temporarily by squinting, but I cannot improve it permanently by commanding the structure of my eyes to correct themselves to perfect vision? That is, why can I not wilfully reorganize the cells on the surface of my eye so as to correct my vision; why do I have control only of neurons, and only limited control at that, and not over other cells in my brain and body? Why do such problems with control or will appear in some cases but not others that are otherwise similar? Why is it that I can recall many memories at will, but there are many more things I cannot adequately or fully recall upon command? Why is it that I am in control over what I think in many cases but in other cases thoughts, memories, desires, temptations, images, etc., pop into my mind without being directed, move me in ways that may be contrary to my wishes, and remain in my attention after being directed to disappear? Why is it that I cannot easily bring myself to enjoy tastes I now dislike, or to like feelings I now dislike, so that events that make me upset or sad no longer do so? In general, why is it that we can control our bodies and mental activity in so many ways while there are so many other, and not so dissimilar, ways in which we are not in control?

Asking these questions draws attention to the relationship we have with the aggregates that we feel we preside over and control. These questions highlight the limited degree of control we have. They do not try to suggest that we should have more control, or that we do have more control than we do, but press us to account for the nature of the limitations in our control. There are certainly physiological reasons that explain why I cannot wilfully direct the cells on the surface of my eyes to change form so as to correct my vision. The Argument from Lack of Control does not challenge this. But it does press this question: if the self can exercise a degree of control over these aggregates, then why is it that it cannot exhibit a greater degree of control? Where do the limitations come from? We may presume that control originates in a self, and that this self stands independently from the aggregates it controls (in a relation of controller to controlled). Though once we admit this, the limitations in its control become mysterious. However, if the self is not independent of the aggregates — if, instead, it is constituted by the aggregates — then it is more understandable why there is not unlimited control. To be constituted by the aggregates means that there is no independent self who presides over the aggregates; and it means that limitations that apply to the aggregates also apply to the self. For instance, the physiology of my body and brain allow for certain events to unfold and prohibit or make difficult others; and if the self is not independent of this body and brain — if it is constituted by them — then it is also limited by this physiology. Again, if we maintain that we are entities that exist independently of the aggregates and also preside over and control these aggregates, then it is difficult to account for the actual limitations in control. It is difficult to explain why the self is under the constraint of the aggregates if it is independent of them. The presumption of being a controlling self is an important part of our sense of self. The Argument from Lack of Control gets us to question whether we are an independently existing controller, and is supposed to thereby help wean us from an important element in our attachment to self.

If thinking about what we can control, and the idea of being a controlling agent, leads us towards attachment to self, then thinking about the lack of control we have should help lead us away from attachment to self. This is to say that the Buddha offers a practical corrective with the Argument from Lack of Control. Although, to be sure, the Buddha is not denying that we have any control. After all, some control is presumed in being able to choose to follow and undertake the disciplines of the Noble Eightfold Path. The topic of being able to initiate decisions and extend causal control will be further discussed in Chapter Ten on Dependent Origination. Both the Argument from the Aggregates, considered earlier, and the Argument from Lack of Control, considered here, argue that there is no self which exists independently of the aggregates. The former argument asserts that no such self is observed. The latter argument conveys that a reason for thinking we are an independent self – that we have control over the aggregates – is undermined when we pay mind to the limitations in this control.

IX

The Doctrine of Impermanence

Introduction

THE DOCTRINE OF IMPERMANENCE (*anitya* in Sanskrit, and *anicca* in Pali) asserts that all arises and passes. It is a central doctrine of Buddhism. It is important for understanding the Buddhist conception of suffering, and the doctrine of No Self. In fact, the Buddhist doctrine of Impermanence implies the doctrine of No Self (for if there is no permanence, there can be no permanent self). As the self is no more than a composite of the ever-changing aggregates, there can be no more permanence to the self than is to be found among the aggregates. Our awareness of ourselves and our awareness of the world is comprised of states that arise and pass from the mind's attention. Nothing stays stable in the mind's awareness. To begin, it is important to consider the correct sense of impermanence. Change, as will be elaborated, can be conceived of in different ways, but with the doctrine of Impermanence there is a specific sense in mind.

Arising and Passing

The Buddha's method in arriving at his understanding of Impermanence, as with No Self, is empiricist. We observe change. The doctrine of No Self, and in particular the Argument from the Aggregates for the doctrine of No Self discussed in the previous chapter, involves careful observation of the aggregates. Gautama, having left behind his ascetic practice, took some food and sat underneath a pipal tree, vowing not to move until he understood the nature of suffering. He undertook a careful observation of himself – looking inwardly in meditation – and observed, similarly to David Hume, that there was no self that stood apart from the aggregates. Moreover, he observed that everything he encountered among the contents of his mind was in constant flux. Whatever could be associated with his sense of self was observed to be ever-changing. He realized not only that there is no self that is independent of the aggregates, but there is no self that could be permanent given that the aggregates are ever-changing. The careful observation of the impermanence of the aggregates, in addition to providing the evidentiary basis for the doctrine of No Self, is the basis for the doctrine of Impermanence.

The aggregates include the contents of our minds that we observe when we look inwardly. All our thoughts, impressions, perceptions, etc., of ourselves and of the world are to be found among these contents. They are observed to arise in the mind's attention and pass from the mind's attention unceasingly. When we consider the external world, outside the contents of our minds, we also see impermanence, or at least, we see change (for as noted the intended sense of 'impermanence' is specific and is not to be equated with just any manner of change – this will be elaborated soon). But when we look at the external world, we observe not only change but also absence of change. That is, many things are observed not to change, or not to change very much, or not to change at anything near the frequency observed with the aggregates. And often when we notice change it is against a background that is not changing. Rocks, buildings and mountains, for instance, or stainless steel cutlery and diamonds on rings, are not usually observed to change, at least to the naked eye. However, there are still changes occurring. For instance, surfaces erode, corrode, or gradually degrade. It is just that these changes are usually too slow to observe as they happen. And there is always change at a microscopic and atomic level: tiny bits fly off or are added to even the strongest and most solid objects; molecules decay and electrons move in their orbits. While these changes may not be observable to the naked eye, at an unobserved level change is ubiquitous. The doctrine of Impermanence, it might seem, is vindicated by modern science.

However, these scientific vindications are not germane for understanding the Buddha's doctrine, for they do not fall under the method used by the Buddha. The Buddha would not have known of change at a microscopic level. The Buddha's method was empiricist, and for this he relied on what he could observe for himself. For instance, the Buddha would not have observed that the mountain cave to which he retreated as an ascetic was undergoing change at a staggering rate at a microscopic or quantum level. He may have observed intermittent or gradual changes, such as rocks tumbling down every now and then, but he would also have observed the mountain not changing for long stretches of time. Consider the rock that tumbles down and sits at the bottom of the mountain: how is it changing? It may have undergone a change in tumbling down the mountain, but what about after that, when it is sitting unmoved, and undisturbed, at the bottom? No matter how hard Gautama might have stared, it would not likely have changed before his eyes (and certainly not with the regularity of the arising and passing of his mind's contents). We may say the same about a steel spoon, a diamond, and many things besides. The methods of observation available to the Buddha at the time would convey that change does not occur evenly and universally in the external, physical world. At best, observation can convey that change will eventually come to everything, but it also conveys that there may be very long stretches of time without observed changes (and in some cases, as with a diamond, a change may not be observed during one's lifetime). The naked eye observes in the external world both permanence and impermanence to varying degrees.

With this we come to the focus of the doctrine of Impermanence. It applies to the aggregates, which are observed to arise and pass from the mind's awareness. This is not to imply that the aggregates are non-physical, or that the mind and its contents are immaterial. Rather, it is to speak of the mind and its contents as they are observed introspectively, from a first-person point of view. This will be elaborated. A rock sitting at the foot of a mountain may not seem to change while being observed, but a perception of the rock is nonetheless impermanent. The perception is subject to arising and ceasing: it comes into our attention (when we are looking at the rock, for instance), and recedes from our minds (when we turn away perhaps, or when we are no longer recalling it). To say that the perception of the rock is impermanent is to say it will soon be displaced from one's attention. It is the nature of the mind that thoughts come and go; sensations, perceptions, desires, and other mental contents arise and pass. It is these observations that underlie the doctrine of Impermanence. The Buddha famously, and with good humour, compared the impermanence of the aggregates with swinging monkeys: our thoughts and other mental contents move in and out through our mind's attention as monkeys swinging rapidly along from branch to branch.[1]

The Buddha did not endeavour to empirically determine what sorts of things exist in the external world; his was not a scientific undertaking of this sort. Instead, he carried out a careful observation of himself, and specifically of what lay within his mind. He looked within – figuratively looked, for it was not with his eyes – and encountered aggregates such as perceptions. Perceptions may be of the outside world (e.g., a perception of the fallen rock), but among the contents of his mind he encounters the perceptions and not the objects perceived (i.e., no actual rocks in his head, so to speak). The perception of the rock he observes in his mind is about something outside of his mind. Our awareness of the world involves sensations and perceptions, such as of streets, cars, buildings, people and much more. Our awareness of ourselves also involves sensations and perceptions. For instance, feeling a toothache is a sensation and acknowledging it as a toothache involves a perception. I am aware of

---

1 *Nidanasamyutta, Samyutta Nikaya* II 94-95, p. 595: "Just as a monkey roaming through a forest grabs hold of one branch, lets that go and grabs another, then lets that go and grabs still another, so too that which is called 'mind' and 'mentality' and 'consciousness' arises as one thing and ceases as another by day and by night."

other states about myself that involve reactions to sensations and perceptions and I observe these also as contents of my mind. These include
desires, fears, hopes, dreads, likes, dislikes, or generally speaking, intentions and volitions. These are neither sensations nor perceptions, and so a
separate aggregate is needed to encompass them. This is the aggregate of
volitional and intentional activity. And further, I am also aware of being
conscious of the contents of my mind. For instance, I am not only aware
of perceptions and desires, but also aware that I am aware of perceptions
and desires. These items of reflective awareness are grouped under the
aggregate of conscious activity. I encounter still more among the contents of my mind: I am also aware of bodily states such as pain, hunger,
feelings of balance and imbalance, and other bodily states and feelings.
These are grouped under the aggregate of bodily processes.

As discussed in Chapter Four, the aggregate of bodily processes is
standardly read to refer to the physical processes themselves. A case was
made in that chapter for reading the aggregate to refer to the awareness or
experience of bodily processes (in which case this aggregate overlaps with
the aggregates of sensations and perceptions). Read in the latter way, the
aggregate of bodily processes includes the pain, rather than the gash on my
leg that causes the pain; it includes the feeling of hunger rather than the
empty stomach that causes the feeling; and it includes the feeling of being
imbalanced rather than the complex internal and external physiological
workings that may be causing the feeling. Read this way, the aggregate
of bodily processes is just like the other aggregates in that it refers to the
different things I may encounter among the contents of my mind (and not
the actual, physical processes themselves). The reason for raising this point
here is that it bears on the impermanence of this aggregate. If the aggregate of bodily processes referred to the actual bodily states and processes,
and not to the mind's awareness of these states and processes, then this
aggregate would differ from the others in its impermanence.

To explain, the awareness of specific bodily states and processes arises
and passes within the mind's attention with a frequency on par with the
other aggregates (e.g., I can come to feel hungry, think of something
else for a moment and lose sight of my hunger, and then quickly become

aware of my hunger again). But physical states and processes are not given to the same frequency or even kind of change. Changes my body undergoes, such as aging and decay, may be very gradual and are quite unlike the quick succession of contents in the mind. Also, the arising and passing of aggregates from the mind's attention is very different *in kind* from the changes a body undergoes over time. Generally speaking, changes a body undergoes would not be well characterized as involving arising and ceasing. My foot, for instance, undergoes gradual changes over time (e.g., as toenails grow), but it sounds odd, to say the least, to describe this as an arising and passing of the foot. My foot may change, but this change does not, I should hope, involve a passing or ending of my foot (and while we might describe the growing toenail as an arising, and the cut toenail as a passing, this too is out of place). These bodily changes are not aptly described as arisings and passings. However, it is not at all inappropriate to say that thoughts, perceptions, including those of my foot, arise and pass from my mind's attention. In short, thoughts and perceptions about my foot, as with thoughts and perceptions about any other part of my body or its states and processes, arise and pass. But the bodily parts, states and processes themselves are not given to this same kind of impermanence. Reading the doctrine of Impermanence univocally, as involving change in the sense of arising and passing, can affect how we understand the aggregate of bodily processes.

The aim of the systemization of aggregates is ultimately of a practical bearing: the aggregates include all that the Buddha could associate with his sense of self. They include all he was aware of or encountered within his mind, and yet the Buddha noticed an inward attachment to a permanent self that he could not place among the different things he encountered. He concluded that attachment to a permanent self is unjustified. More than this, the careful and regular attention to the aggregates, and their arising and passing, is an important part of undoing attachment to a permanent self.

Let us again consider the fallen rock, sitting still at the bottom of the mountain. It may seem unchanging to my eyes. Every time I turn to look at it I may judge it to be unmoved. I may stare at it, resolutely, and observe no changes. Of course, I may look at it from different angles and so the rock may look different as I move around, but I can easily discern that these different perceptions do not indicate that the rock itself is changing. Indeed, if I always look at the rock from the same place and angle, under the same lighting conditions, then my perceptions of the rock may not change (along with the rock itself not changing). But the stability of these appearances and perceptions does nothing to contravene the doctrine of Impermanence. The doctrine does not deny that I might have similar perceptions over time, but rather denies that any perception I have stays in my mind. And once again, while we do know that the rock is undergoing changes at a microscopic level, the Buddha, relying on the methods of observation available to him, would not have known this. The effort to justify the Buddha's findings scientifically is misplaced. Whether the rock can be known to change microscopically or not neither supports nor contravenes the doctrine of Impermanence. Impermanence is a doctrine focussed on the mind and its contents. This is not metaphysical idealism for the doctrine does not assert or presume that only the mind and its contents are real. To the contrary, encounters with the external world are held to cause sensations and perceptions (which in turn lead to desires and fears and other reactions within the aggregate of intentional and volitional activity). It is just that the doctrine's focus is not the nature of this external world (including the nature of the physical organism). That is the province of natural science. The Buddha's concern is human suffering as understood to occur in the mind. The doctrine of Impermanence asserts that the contents of the mind arise and pass from our awareness unceasingly. The Buddha was endeavouring to carefully observe his own mind, and thereby discern the roots of the suffering he felt therein, and Impermanence is a doctrine about these observations.

To sum up so far, the doctrine of Impermanence concerns the impermanence of the aggregates. It asserts that the elements of these aggregate groupings – the particular contents of our mind's awareness – do not stay in place; they constantly arise and recede. The focus of concern of the doctrine is not whether there is permanence in the external physical world. Instead, its focus is on our impressions of the physical world, as well as other mental occurrences, and it asserts that these are subject to arising and passing. The Buddha was not trying to be a natural scientist; his observations are psychological and bear on the mind and the human condition. Likewise, the doctrine of Impermanence does not comment on the permanence or impermanence of truths. It does not assert, for instance, that scientific or mathematical truths will not last, or that they will eventually turn from true to false. It does not say that Buddhist teachings are only true for a limited time (although it does not deny that some teachings may be less useful at some stages or for some objectives than others and so may need to be put aside; this point will be discussed in Chapter Fourteen). Rather, it says that any thoughts or beliefs about such truths or teachings will, just as with any aggregate, arise in our mind's attention and then pass from our attention. And if the belief arises in our minds again, this does not contravene that it had previously passed from our attention, and that it will pass again.

It will further help to elucidate the sense of impermanence in the doctrine of Impermanence to compare this with other, perhaps more commonplace, views of change.

Other Views of Change

One way in which we understand change is in terms of motion or loco-motion. In this sense, an object can undergo change without changes in its internal structure. For instance, everything on earth is moving just in virtue of the movement of the earth on its axis, or the movement of our solar system within the galaxy, or the motion of the Milky Way galaxy within the universe. This is a motion in which an object or person may take part while remaining otherwise unchanged except for this motion. Other examples: an object on the seat of a moving car is in motion but otherwise may be quite still. A bullet tearing through the air is also in motion, and so undergoing change, but it need not be undergoing change in its composition or structure while it is moving.

However, the impermanence of the aggregates does not involve motion. Not literally. The aggregates, witnessed introspectively as men-tal events do not literally move about in the mind's eye (although the brain events that underlie them do involve motion). Still, we use terms that signify motion figuratively. For instance, a fear may seem to rush in unannounced, or an anger to slowly creep away. Also, we may say, more generally, that these mental contents come and go, or arise and pass. These terms do figuratively connote motion, but even this connotation should not be taken too far. The aggregates are described as arising or being born in our mind's attention, and as passing or disappearing from our attention. Everything among the aggregates arises and passes, we are told, and this change is not primarily one of motion, figurative or not. It would be more apt to characterize this change as one of coming into existence in our awareness, and passing out of existence from our awareness.

Consider another view of change. We often speak of an object changing in aspect or quality but nevertheless remaining the same object through this change. For instance, suppose I paint a beige room blue. The room is not the same for it has changed colour. But we speak of it as the same room, for it is only different in a quality, and a fairly inconsequential one at that. In fact, no matter what changes the room undergoes, if I still speak of *the* room as having changed from what it was before then it is still, despite the changes, the same room in my estimation and way of speaking. That is, my identification of the room from before to after the change, using the definite article 'the', indicates a sameness of room. This way of speaking of change generally presupposes that something remains the same – some identifying feature – in virtue of which we can say *that thing*, or *it*, has changed. It is important for us, in describing changes, to be able to identify the object before and after the change (for again, if we could not, then we could not say "*it* has changed" or "*she* has changed" or "*I* have changed"). Consider another example: the changes a person undergoes over the course of twenty years. The person's body will have changed, and brain, thoughts, perhaps many beliefs and characteristics, or career, residence, relationships, etc. In these and many other ways a person can change significantly over the years. And if the span of time includes one's childhood, or infancy, the changes undergone will be more remarkable still. However, despite these changes, we still use the word 'I' or 'me' to refer to our previous self, prior to all the changes. No matter how much we change – how much we think we are a changed person – we generally still refer to ourselves before and after with the same referring expressions. We say "*I* used to be like this, and now *I* am not," or "that was *me*; look how *I* have grown." The use of the same referring expression, at least grammatically, conveys a sameness of subject over time and through the changes, no matter how dramatic or life-altering they may be.

The grammar involved in speaking of such changes warrants further discussion. Generally speaking, when we say something changes, there is a subject to which we ascribe change. Turning again to the previous example of the room, when I say "the room was once beige and is now blue," the room is the subject of the sentence. We might think that for any change, there must be a subject of whom we are speaking; for if there is no subject, then who or what is changing? Of what are we speaking? A predicate must speak of a subject it seems. In speaking of change this way we distinguish between the subject of change and the changes the subject undergoes. Distinguishing subject from predicate is part of ascribing qualities to a subject. However, the grammatical subject, in the Buddhist view, is not to be taken as a separately existing subject. Although I can use the indexical 'I' to speak of myself at different times, the use of the same word does not imply that something has remained the same through those different times. As discussed, the doctrine of Impermanence repudiates this. Likewise, I can say sentences such as 'I am happy' or 'I am hungry', but the separation of subject from predicate in these and other such sentences does not imply that a self exists separately from all the qualities that can be ascribed to it. In the Buddhist view, there is no self that exists separately from the aggregates. We ascribe bodily and psychological traits to a self, and we posit an unchanging *I* in speaking of this self over time. This has its uses, but again, for the Buddha, this should not be a cause for psychological attachment. Actions exist, says the Buddha, but no doer; not in the sense of an independent and unchanging doer.

Ordinarily, when we speak of change – especially of changes to ourselves – our way of speaking presumes that something essential remains the same. But the doctrine of Impermanence denies that there is a subject of change that remains the same through the arising and passing of the aggregates. Nothing is observed amongst the aggregates that does not arise and pass. While an aggregate may be observed to change in some aspect or quality – for instance, a desire may be observed to intensify or diminish – the aggregate is still observed to arise and pass. It may be replied that we often speak of a mental state or thought as being the same as one we had earlier. For instance, a desire for chocolate may be identified as being the same desire for chocolate as experienced earlier in the day. Thus, it might be said that aggregates can remain the same over time. But this does not contravene Impermanence. The later desire may be qualitatively similar to the earlier one, but it is still the case that the earlier one passed from our attention and the later one arose in our attention. The later desire is *another* desire for the same thing. They may be qualitatively similar desires but are nonetheless different particular desires. Whether mental states of the same type arise again or not, they and everything else among the aggregates are still observed to arise and pass. Sticking to his empiricist methodology and its reliance on observation, the Buddha steadfastly affirms the impermanence of the aggregates.

Numerical Identity and Qualitative Identity

Two notions of identity commonly used in the Western philosophical tradition are numerical identity and qualitative identity. These notions are relevant in discussing personal identity over time for the Buddha. Qualitative identity involves the idea of two things being the same in qualities or properties: there is no property one has that the other does not. Thus, two classroom chairs may be qualitatively identical if they are the same in colour, size, shape, construction, etc. Strictly speaking, they are qualitatively similar but not identical, as one will have scuffs or scratches that another does not have, and, of course, they have different locations; but nonetheless we can say they are qualitatively identical for most intents and purposes. Numerical identity involves identity in number; basically, something being one and the same as itself (and thus, two

classroom chairs may be qualitatively similar, but could not be numerically identical since they are two chairs).

At first, it might seem that numerical identity doesn't say much.
Obviously, something is the same as itself. However, statements of
numerical identity can be informative if they identify an object under
different presentations. Consider this example: Reginald Dwight is Elton
John. This is a statement of numerical identity because we are saying that
they are one and the same person. The statement is informative for us if
we are familiar with one mode of presentation but not the other (e.g., if
we are familiar with Elton John but not Reginald Dwight). And if Elton
John is giving a concert in Grand Prairie, Reginald Dwight cannot be in
Venice on a gondola ride at the same time. If they are one and the same
person, then what is true of one is true of the other. This is to say that
where there is numerical identity, there is qualitative identity.

It is numerical identity that is asserted when we speak of personal
identity over time. If I consider myself thirty or so years ago, it is clear
that there are many qualitative differences. My body has changed, my
brain has changed, my mind has changed, my life has changed. And
dramatically so. I am not qualitatively the same. In fact, we might say
that we adults are more qualitatively similar to each other, than we are to
the toddlers or infants we once were.

Despite these qualitative changes, I can and still do speak of being the
same person over time. I can hold up a baby picture of myself and say
"*this* was *me* as a baby." When I say that I am the same person as the baby
in the picture, that is a statement of numerical identity, not qualitative
(we should hope I am not qualitatively the same as a baby). Derek Parfit,
a contemporary philosopher who holds views somewhat similar to those
of Hume and the Buddha on personal identity, gives a good example of
this distinction when he states: "I may believe that, after my marriage,
I shall be a different person. But that does not make marriage death."[1] I
am different qualitatively after marriage, not numerically. We think and
make statements of numerical identity regularly in referring to ourselves

---

1 Parfit (1995), p. 293.

in the past, and in thinking about ourselves in the future. If I am thinking of my old age, the person I am thinking of is qualitatively different
from the person here now (he will be older and greyer). Nevertheless, I
presume that that person will be me; I presume numerical identity.

The Buddha, with the doctrines of No Self and Impermanence, is not
denying the usefulness of speaking in terms of a numerically identical self.
But he is saying, just as did Hume, that the judgement is unjustified by
what we observe about ourselves. There is nothing about me that can be
the referent of the word 'I' that remains unchanged over time. When I look
at myself, all I see are the ever-arising and ceasing aggregates. I see nothing
that remains the same and that is not subject to arising and ceasing. And
even if I did; even if I looked within and encountered some continuous
aggregate that remains unchanged, and that does not cease, then this *still*
would not adequately justify my judgement of numerical identity. This is
because my belief and sense of self involves not any particular aggregate,
but *something* that *experiences* the aggregates; *something* that *has* perceptions,
thoughts, and feelings, and this – it is claimed – is nowhere observed.

Speaking of a numerically identical *I*, and using the same word 'I'
to refer to myself at different times or stages of my life, is not without
usefulness. In early Buddhist schools, this is described as a conventional
truth, and its usefulness is not denied. What is denied is that there is
an entity that underlies my self-ascriptions over time. There are only
the ever-changing aggregates, says the Buddha. Usefulness may excuse
speaking in terms of a numerically identical self, but does not justify
the attachment to the sense of being a numerically identical self, which
Buddhism finds to be widespread and suffering-inducing.

As noted, the necessity of a subject in our descriptions of change does
not imply that there is in fact something that exists and remains the same
through changes. As discussed, a grammatical requirement does not
by itself imply existence. The doctrines of No Self and Impermanence
claim that there is no self that is independent of the ever-changing aggregates and that is permanent over time. We obviously undergo changes,
sometimes dramatic changes, but there is nonetheless a presumption of
being the same self through these changes. The changes we undergo are
ascribed to this same self. We speak of this same self, but the idea is that

we also feel there to be this same self. That is, we identify with and are attached to this same self. This attachment involves a sense of permanence over time, from moment to moment and from one period of life to another, and this is the source of suffering in the Buddhist conception. This sense of permanence over time is elaborated by the Buddha with the ideas of annihilationism and eternalism. These notions will be described in the next section.

Annihilationism and Eternalism

There is a story of a would-be follower who encounters the Buddha and interprets his teaching of No Self as follows: he understands the Buddha to be saying that the self is destroyed at death and is not reborn. The Buddha responds strongly, asserting that this is not what he has been teaching. He says there is no self that continues on after death, but also that there is no self that comes to an end at death. Both of these views presume a real basis for numerical identity, rather than a conventional or linguistic basis. That is, both presume that the self is something permanent: the one view holding that this permanence continues on after death, and the other holding that the permanence of self lasts for a lifetime and then comes to a prompt end at death. The Buddha asserts that he denies the common assumption of both: a permanent self of any significant duration, whether for a finite life or an everlasting life.

These are the positions of annihilationism and eternalism respectively. Annihilationism holds that there is a self, permanent and independent of the ever-changing aggregates, that comes to an end at death. Eternalism holds that there is a self, again permanent and independent of the ever-changing aggregates, that continues on after death.[1]

---

1 In the *Sabbasava Sutta, Majjhima Nikaya* I 8, p. 93, the Buddha describes eternalism: "This speculative view, bhikkhus, is called the thicket of views, the wilderness of views, the contortion of views, the vacillation of views, the fetter of views. Fettered by the fetter of views, the untaught ordinary person ... is not freed from suffering, I say." Also see the *Alagaddupama Sutta, Majjhima Nikaya* I 137-38, pp. 230-31.

At first, these two possibilities may seem exhaustive: either something comes to an end, or it doesn't. Either it dies, or it doesn't. One of these two views is held by most people: either I end at death or some part of me – something that is essential to me and is what I primarily mean by 'I', something we may perhaps call a soul – continues on after death even though my body may come to an end.

For the Buddha, however, these are not exhaustive possibilities. Something can't come to an end if it is not there to end. All that there is to the self, in the Buddhist view, are the ever-changing aggregates: bodily and psychological states. While we make statements of numerical identity, of being the same self over time, there is no actual sameness, no identity in the strict sense, in the Buddhist view. And so, if there is no sameness, there is no sameness to continue on after death or to end at death.

How we think of the self is closely tied to how we may think of death, for death raises the prospect of the end of this self. The Buddhist view of self here is supposed to affect one's attitude towards death. Non-Buddhists usually hold either annihilationism or eternalism. The Buddha's rejection of both these approaches is an example of the Buddha's treading a Middle Way. The Middle Way, in this case as it is elsewhere, is not a literal midpoint, for there can be no midpoint between a finite life and an everlasting or infinite life. It's perhaps better called a third way, rejecting what both diverging views presuppose: something unchanging or permanent – something that remains numerically identical – whether it be for a fixed duration or an unfixed duration. In the Buddhist view, death is not the kind of end we tend to think it is, but not because I will continue on after death in some essential capacity. It is because there is no I that has remained through a life and that is coming to an end. There is no self that remains constant, from moment to moment, through change after change, and so no such self whose demise is threatened. The difficulty of facing death is thus transmuted to the difficulty of facing what one is: one is not a permanent being over time, says the Buddha, but there is a strong psychological identification with being a permanent being, and it is this identification that needs to be faced and dealt with.

So what does the Buddha respond with then, if he is saying there is no permanence over time? What connects me to my past and what do I project to in thinking of my future? The Buddha's answer is that there is continuity, specifically causal continuity, and that this is different from permanence or identity over time. This will be discussed in the next chapter on Dependent Origination, and continued in the chapter following that on Karma and Rebirth.

Concluding Remarks

According to the doctrine of Impermanence, the aggregates are observed to arise and pass. But what, we might wonder, happens in between arising and passing? An aggregate may be changing in other ways while it is in the mind's attention, in-between its arising and passing, but as explained above, these other ways of undergoing change are not the sense of impermanence in the doctrine of Impermanence. The sense of impermanence in the doctrine of Impermanence involves arising and passing. An aggregate arises and passes, but in-between these it has a continuing existence. This means that the period of time in-between the arising and passing of an aggregate is a period of time with permanence. Consider, for example, a perception. A perception may arise and then pass from our attention, but it also remains for a time, even if only for a very brief time. Not to have some duration between the arising and passing of the perception is not to have time to register the occurrence of the perception; it is, in fact, not to have time for there to be a perception. And this is just what a mindful observance of the aggregates reveals: aggregates arise in our mind's awareness, they remain for some time, sometimes very briefly, and then they recede from our awareness. This period between arising and passing is a period of permanence in the specific sense that there is no arising and passing during this interim. This would seem to be permanence in the midst of the impermanence of the aggregates.

As to precisely what this duration of permanence between the arising and passing of the aggregates is, that is another matter, and not easily settled or without ambiguity. As explained, what does seem clear is that there should be some positive duration. The briefly subsisting constituents of the aggregates are called 'dharmas' (not to be confused with 'the Dharma', the truths and doctrines of the Buddha). Specific positions on dharmas and their durations were promoted by the Sarvastivadans and other Buddhist schools associated with the Abhidharma canon and tradition. The world we experience is supposed to be constituted by dharmas, and these dharmas were thought by some schools to have very brief durations (although different schools had differing views on this; the Sautrantikas, for instance, held that dharmas have no durations). The question of the duration between arising and passing will be revisited in Chapter Twelve, wherein the Abhidharma tradition, and the nature and duration of dharmas, will be discussed.

Lastly, it should be emphasized that the doctrine of Impermanence is not intended primarily for descriptive purposes, but to be of use in overcoming suffering. Reminders of impermanence are supposed to help staunch cravings for permanence. This practical application of Impermanence is to extend to whatever we may become attached to and crave, whether this be objects, feelings, persons, or even the teachings of the Buddha. Specifically, the idea is to look carefully at the aggregates and see that they are subject to arising and passing, with a succession similar in its rapidity to monkeys swinging on branches and vines. The result of this attentive looking is not only supposed to let one see that the attachment to a permanent self is unfounded, but also looking carefully at the aggregates is supposed to take some steps towards realizing this. As with the doctrine of No Self, a mindful awareness of the aggregates is supposed to lead not only to the conclusion of Impermanence, but to help sunder one's attachment to a permanent self. It is a strategy for overcoming attachment to permanence to carefully observe that whatever one may be attached to is impermanent and will not last. To observe the aggregates attentively is supposed to allow one to see the truth of Impermanence and No Self for oneself, but is also supposed to help one put in practice and realize these doctrines as well.

X

The Doctrine of Dependent Origination

Introduction

THE DOCTRINE OF IMPERMANENCE asserts that the aggregates
arise and pass. Sensations, perceptions, bodily feelings, desires, hopes,
acts of will, states of awareness, and much more, arise and pass from
our conscious minds. The doctrine of No Self builds on the doctrine
of Impermanence and asserts that among these arising and passing
aggregates, no permanent self is found. As no permanent self is found, our
psychological attachment to a permanent self is held to be ungrounded.
The doctrine of Dependent Origination, like the doctrine of No Self,
builds upon the doctrine of Impermanence and adds that the arising and
passing aggregates are caused to arise, and caused to pass. Furthermore,
events that are caused to arise – such as psychological attachments and
cravings – can be undone by undoing their causes. The doctrine of
Dependent Origination is about causality and causal interconnection.

This understanding of causality, we should recall, is also found in
the Four Noble Truths. The Four Noble Truths assert that suffering

exists; it has a cause; it can be eliminated by eliminating its cause; and the means to this elimination lie in following the Middle Way and the Noble Eightfold Path. The Four Noble Truths offer a causal analysis of suffering and in doing so are consistent with the doctrine of Dependent Origination. Since suffering is held to be caused by attachment to self, the way to overcome suffering for the Buddhist is to bring to mind and then undo the causes of this attachment by following the Middle Way and the Noble Eightfold Path. We are held to be creatures who, by and large, do not understand the causes of our suffering well: we find ourselves with attachments, in particular to the sense of being a permanent and independent self, without recognizing how this came about. An understanding of causes, which is an understanding of origins, is consequently of great importance in Buddhism. It is traditionally asserted that a direct understanding of Dependent Origination was integral to the Buddha's enlightenment. Understanding Dependent Origination is held to be essential to understanding suffering in the Buddhist sense and the means for overcoming it. It is also described as subtle, profound, and difficult to understand. An exchange between Ananda, a disciple, and the Buddha is recounted as follows:

> ... the Venerable Ananda came to the Lord, saluted him, sat down to one side, and said: 'It is wonderful, Lord, it is marvellous how profound this dependent origination is, and how profound it appears! And yet it appears to me as clear as clear!'. 'Do not say that, Ananda, do not say that! This dependent origination is profound and appears profound. It is through not understanding, not penetrating this doctrine that this generation has become like a tangled ball of string, covered with a blight, tangled like coarse grass, unable to pass beyond states of woe, the ill destiny, ruin and the round of birth-and-death.'[1]

Sariputra, a close disciple of the Buddha, in speaking of the teachings of the Buddha (the Dharma, or Dhamma in Pali) is reported to have

---

1 *Mahanidana Sutta, Digha Nikaya* II 55, p. 223.

said this: "Now this has been said by the Blessed One: 'One who sees dependent origination sees the Dhamma; one who sees the Dhamma sees dependent origination'."[1]

Dependent Origination is sometimes called 'conditioned arising' or 'interdependent arising'. Herein, we use the phrasing 'dependent origination'. As described, properly understanding Dependent Origination is important for understanding the Noble Truths and the path to freedom from suffering. This emphasis on causality and a causal understanding of suffering is also displayed with the Wheel of Becoming (which was presented in Chapter Six). On its outer rim, there is a series of causally related events that describe the cycle of birth and rebirth and the conditions of perpetual suffering. The Buddha describes the causal links between these elements: "With clinging as a condition, being; with being as a condition, birth; with birth as a condition, aging and death come to be, and also sorrow and lamentation, pain, grief and despair. That is how there is an origin to this whole aggregate mass of suffering."[2] In the interior core of the wheel there are deeper set causes that keep the whole wheel in motion: craving, volition, and aversion or hatred. This core presents a further level of causal analysis (for while birth leads to aging, which leads to sickness, etc., on the outer rim, the whole cycle is kept in motion with the forces of the core). The symbolism of the Wheel of Becoming presents not merely the cyclical nature of Samsara and suffering, but the causal and mechanical workings of the wheel. An analysis of suffering through an analysis of its causes, provided in the Four Noble Truths and the Wheel of Becoming, has a clear practical agenda. Indeed, a deeply theoretical understanding of the nature of one's suffering is not said to be needed. But an understanding of the causes of one's suffering, and of what is required to eliminate these causes, certainly is needed.

Despite seeming straightforward, the quotations given above convey that understanding Dependent Origination and the nature of causal connection is a subtle and far from simple matter. Dependent Origination, as with the doctrines of No Self and Impermanence, applies to the

---

1 *Mahahatthipadopama Sutta, Majjhima Nikaya,* I 191, p. 284.
2 From Nanamoli (1992) 251 ff., as quoted in Williams (2000), p. 65.

aggregates. However, Dependent Origination includes more than the aggregates in attending to causes. The aggregates – bodily processes, sensations, perceptions, intentional and volitional activity, and consciousness – may be caused by, and in turn cause, external events that are not themselves aggregates. For instance, a tree in one's direct line of sight may cause a perception of the tree; a physical blow may cause a bodily injury and feelings of pain. In these examples, the tree and the physical blow are not aggregates; they are external objects or events that are causally connected to aggregates (they cause the perception of the tree and the feelings of pain respectively). The causal connectivity that is the focus of Dependent Origination connects the aggregates to causes and effects that are external and not themselves aggregates. This is a dissimilarity between Dependent Origination and the doctrines of Impermanence and No Self (which concern the aggregates more exclusively). This impacts the question of how causality is to be understood in this doctrine for it allows for different possibilities to be considered. One way to conceive of causality in Dependent Origination is the way we tend to think of causal relations between external physical events; we will call this 'physical causation'. A second is the way we generally describe causal relations between mental occurrences; this will be called 'mental causation' and it will be seen to have different characteristics from physical causation.

In order to understand causality in the doctrine of Dependent Origination, what will be called 'Universal Causation' is of importance. This is the position that every event has a cause. Since a cause is itself an event, this position implies that every cause has a cause. Thus, under universal causation, there are no uncaused causes; there are no first causes that are not themselves caused. Considering whether or not the doctrine of Dependent Origination includes universal causation is vital for coming to understand the doctrine. Answering this question will involve distinguishing between the concepts of an uncaused cause versus a beginning cause. This will be discussed, and it will be shown that Dependent Origination does entail universal causation.

Altogether three different models of causation will be considered to see if they are appropriate for understanding causality in the doctrine of Dependent Origination. The first to be considered will be physical causation and this will be presumed to involve universal causation; the second will be mental causation without universal causation; and the third, mental causation with universal causation. The third model will be shown to be the most fitting for appreciating the sense of causality in Dependent Origination, and the Buddhist objectives of overcoming suffering and attachment to self. As noted, the Buddha asserts that Dependent Origination is a subtle and difficult doctrine. It is worth going carefully over the first two models so that we can appreciate their difficulties, and thereby see more clearly why the third model is favoured.

The First Model: Physical Causation

Causation between physical events is the conception of causation with which we are most familiar. Typically, physical causation does not admit uncaused events. An uncaused event in our physical surroundings would involve something coming about, spontaneously and without cause, from apparently nothing. An uncaused event would be difficult to make intelligible, with no scientific explanation (at least insofar as this involves explaining by providing causes). Physical causation, in addition to admitting universal causation, also admits causal determinism. Causal determinism is the position that an effect is fully determined by its antecedent cause(s) (together with the operation of the laws of nature). This means that if you have full knowledge of the antecedent cause(s), plus the relevant laws of nature and conditions in which those causes exist, then you could, in theory, accurately predict the effect(s). As a consequence of causal determinism, changes to causal sequences are not possible (since all effects are fully determined and thus necessitated). Universal causation, it is worth making clear, holds that all events are caused, but this does not by itself imply that causal sequences are determined and unchangeable (i.e., universal causation does not imply causal determinism).[1]

---

1 It might be thought that a challenge for both universal causation and causal determinism arises with evidence from quantum mechanics, (*continued*)

Let us now consider whether Physical Causation thus described is an appropriate model of causation for understanding Dependent Origination. Dependent Origination holds that there are causal connections between the aggregates, and that these causal connections allow us to follow our thoughts and feelings backwards to underlying causes, and also to follow forward and predict effects from their causes.

This causal reasoning is important for making the changes needed for overcoming suffering. The idea is that if we find ourselves with a suffering-inducing craving, by working back to its cause we can remove ourselves from the craving. Likewise, if we can predict that certain causes will induce suffered effects, then we know that we should avoid these causes. But as noted, physical causation presumes causal determinism, and this does not allow for changes to be made to causal sequences so that suffered effects can thereby be eliminated. To elaborate, the doctrine of Dependent Origination holds not only that our feelings and attachments and other mental states have causes, but that we can alter these mental states by changing or disrupting the underlying causes that lead to them. Changing causes so as to change the effects that follow is integral to following the Buddhist path. Since causal determinism does not allow for

---

for this suggests the possibility of randomly appearing and presumably uncaused events. Insofar as there are truly random events, this argues against causal determinism. And insofar as these events are genuinely uncaused, this argues against universal causation. Nevertheless, the controversial possibility of quantum indeterminism is not being considered in discussing physical causation here. The focus of physical causation herein is causation as it is presumed to occur in our physical macro-environment (where all events do appear to be caused and where, at least in theory, a full knowledge of causes, including relevant laws, forces, and other environmental factors, enables accurate predictions of effects). What is under consideration is whether *this* understanding of physical causation is appropriate for understanding Dependent Origination. Also, it can be said that quantum indeterminism is inappropriate for understanding the sense of causation in Dependent Origination since uncaused or random effects are not effects that can be eliminated by eliminating their causes, as the Third Noble Truth requires. And most simply, quantum indeterminism is not appropriate for understanding the intended sense of causality in Dependent Origination since the Buddha would have been unaware of this from the empiricist methods available to him.

such changes (i.e., since it holds that all effects are determined and necessitated by their causes), physical causation is not an appropriate model for
understanding causality in Dependent Origination.

The Second Noble Truth asserts that suffering is caused. The Third
Noble Truth asserts that suffering can be eliminated by eliminating its
causes. The Fourth Noble Truth asserts that these suffering-inducing
causes can be eliminated by following the Middle Way and disciplining
one's mind and conduct according to the Noble Eightfold Path. We are
supposed to be able to bring about an end to suffering through our own
efforts. These Truths presume that we can change causal sequences. They
presume that we can bring about changes to ourselves – our personalities
and attachments – through a disciplining of body, mind and conduct
so as to redirect the causal sequences that currently lead to attachment
and suffering. Eliminating underlying, suffering-inducing causes implies
that causal determinism does not hold and, once again, this conveys that
physical causation is not the appropriate model for interpreting causality
in Dependent Origination.[1]

In addition, the aggregates are described (in the Noble Truths and the
Wheel of Becoming) primarily in mental terms and not physical terms.
For instance, in asserting that cravings cause suffering and must be overcome it is not asserted that specific brain patterns must be overcome.
This is not to imply that cravings do not involve specific brain events,
but just that the description of the cause of suffering is in terms of mental
states, and not the underlying neurophysiological states. This is another
reason for saying that physical causation is not the right model for understanding causality in Dependent Origination. To further elaborate, the
objective of Dependent Origination, as with any Buddhist doctrine,
is ultimately to overcome suffering. As suffering involves craving and
attachment to self, Dependent Origination is thus at the service of overcoming craving and attachment to self. These cravings and attachments

---

1 It is presumed here that a compatibilist interpretation, according to which
one's apparently free choice to follow the Noble Eightfold Path, while
not compelled upon one, is a determined choice that could not have been
otherwise, is not appropriate for understanding the Buddha's doctrine.

are mental events, and are described as such. This gives a further reason for saying the conception of causality in Dependent Origination should not be based on the model of physical causation, extended to include mental events, but should be one whose primary focus is the causal connections between mental events. Rupert Gethin raises this very concern:

> Buddhist thought does not understand causality in terms similar to, say, Newtonian mechanics, where billiard balls rebound off each other in an entirely predictable manner once the relevant information is gathered. First, the Buddhist attempt to understand the ways of causal conditioning is concerned primarily with the workings of the mind: the way in which things we think, say, and do have an effect on both our selves and others. Second, Buddhist thought sees causal conditioning as involving the interaction of certain fixed or determined effects and certain free or unpredictable causes.[1]

Gethin raises two considerations here against physical causation, the mechanical "billiard ball" conception of causality as he phrases it. It is worth discussing both. Gethin mentions – and this is his second point in the above passage – that in the Buddhist view causes can be unpredictable. Thoughts, cravings, etc., can pop into our minds unpredictably. "Billiard Ball" causation, or causation in line with Newtonian mechanics, does not admit of unpredictability (in principle, in any case). On a Newtonian model of causation, if sufficient "relevant information" is available, then effects should be fully predictable. Oftentimes, the relevant information that must be in hand and processed is immense, and this makes prediction difficult in practice. This is the case with accurate long-range weather predictions, for instance. But the principal point remains

---

1 Gethin (1998), pp. 153–54. Also see Williams: "What marked out the Buddha's approach to this topic, in contrast to his fellow sramanas [ascetics], was his psychologising. Trsna [craving] is a matter of the mind, and therefore trsna [craving] is eliminated not by fierce asceticism, torturing the body, but by mental transformation through meditation. For the Buddhist it is the mental factor which is crucial. Liberation is all about the mind." Williams (2000), p. 45.

that were this vast amount of information in hand and well-understood and analysed, an accurate prediction could be made. Mechanical "billiard ball" causation involves causal determinism. Gethin is correct to note that causality in the Buddhist conception does not involve causal determinism, or a "billiard ball" model, and this was explained above.

However, while causal determinism is at odds with a Buddhist understanding of causation, predictable causation is still essential in Buddhism and it is important to draw this out. The value of Dependent Origination in overcoming suffering requires being able to determine which causes lead to suffered states, and the reliability of this procedure requires being able to make reliable predictions from causes to effects (and reliable judgements from effects back to their causes). Indeed, the value of causal thinking (in Dependent Origination and the Noble Truths) is directly proportional to the predictability of suffered effects given suffering-inducing causes (for it is this predictability that informs us of which causes to eliminate). Predictability is an important part of the understanding of causality in Dependent Origination, even if this is not to a Newtonian degree of necessitation. The degree of predictability is not the same, and it could not be since Dependent Origination applies to the aggregates and these are not observable and measurable in the same way as external physical objects and events are. Still, the value of Dependent Origination in overcoming suffering lies in a predictable causal connection between causes and effects. Predictable causality without determinism may be difficult to fathom, and this is one of the things that makes Dependent Origination a difficult or "subtle" doctrine. But it is worth pointing out that this is just what we see when we observe ourselves from a first person perspective: we can observe that there is a predictable, but not a necessary, relation between certain mental events and others (e.g., dwelling on a frustrating event and getting angry); and we can also observe that we can, perhaps with much effort, make changes to the underlying causes so as to overcome the predictable effects. It is always worth remembering, in coming to understand these Buddhist doctrines, that they are based on an empiricism that we are all supposed to be able to carry out by looking carefully at ourselves.

Gethin further states, in the above passage, that "causal conditioning is concerned primarily with the workings of the mind." This also is correct. Dependent Origination, just as No Self and Impermanence, is a doctrine about the aggregates. And the aggregates are primarily mental contents. As noted earlier, the aggregates can have causes and effects that are external and physical, and this means that causality in Dependent Origination cannot just include mental states. Nevertheless, it remains correct to say that Dependent Origination mainly concerns occurrences in the mind. Also, the objective is to overcome attachment to self and craving which are psychological states in the mind. As already noted, this focus on "the workings of the mind" should lead us to think that physical causation is not the right model for understanding causality in Dependent Origination.

The Second Model: Mental Causation without Universal Causation

The second model to be discussed, in order to see if it provides an appropriate understanding of causality in Dependent Origination, will be called 'mental causation without universal causation'. Mental causation is often a matter of giving reasons as causes. To illustrate, I may describe my getting up and going to the fridge for some cake as being caused by certain patterns of neuronal activity, which led to muscle movements, which led to the movement of my limbs, which led my body all the way to the fridge. This is a description in terms of physical causation. Alternatively, I may say that my desire for cake, plus my belief that it was in the fridge, plus a lack of interfering beliefs and desires (such as a desire to remain on a diet) led me to go to the fridge. Or more simply, I went to the fridge because I wanted cake. Stating my desire for cake gives a reason explaining why I went to the fridge, but it is also quite right to say this desire caused me to go to the fridge.[1] After all, if I find myself at the fridge wondering why I am there, I can easily trace back to my desire

---

1 See Donald Davidson's "Mental Events" in Davidson (2001).

for cake and this desire is both a reason and a cause for my behaviour. The point here is not that mental events are not also physical events in the brain, but rather that a causal description involving mental events, which can employ reasons as causes, can be quite unlike a description in terms of physical causes.

This type of explanation – that is, one that explains behaviour by appealing to thoughts, desires, and other psychological states – is some-times called a 'folk psychological explanation'. It is so called because it is the kind of psychological explanation that we "folk" commonly use in our attempts to understand the minds and behaviours of others as well as of ourselves. For instance, I may explain why someone screamed when he saw a tarantula by saying he was scared, and I might explain my own behaviour, to myself and to others, in the same way. Folk psychological analyses involve explaining our behaviour and minds by finding causes in our psychological states rather than in underlying physical states. In this respect, the Buddha is also thinking folk psychologically for he is asking us to find the causes of our suffering in our mental states, specifi-cally in our attachments and cravings. The Buddha's observation of the aggregates involves introspection, and this is a first-person observation of the mind's contents which are described in mental terms, and not a third-person observation of underlying neurophysiological states.

This model of mental causation, unlike the next one to be considered, does not involve universal causation. A reason for this is that looking at ourselves from a first-person view can convey that there are uncaused events. For instance, thoughts and actions that are willed can strike us as having no cause prior to their assertion in our will. That is, it seems that we can bring certain events about – for instance, decisions, bodily movements – by willing them to be and that this willing is an initiating cause that doesn't need a further cause behind it. Our acts of will can seem to us to be uncaused events, the starting points of causal sequences. Hand in hand with this is the idea that we are the authors of our inten-tions and actions and that there need be no further causes that lie behind and that fully cause our will and authorship. Our willing, it seems, can be an uncaused cause. Also, we are accustomed to thoughts and ideas popping into our minds from seemingly nowhere. This is not to say that a thought that just pops into your head does not have a physical cause (such as a neuronal event), but it is to say that, from a first-person point of view, the thought may appear to arise without a cause. Whether we are speaking of mental events that just seem to pop into our attention, or that seem willed into existence, it appears that mental events, observed *as* mental events and not in terms of their neuronal underpinnings, can be uncaused events. These are reasons for thinking mental causation does not admit universal causation.

The possibility of uncaused mental events, and the denial of universal causation this involves, presents a problem for Buddhism. Simply put, if suffering can come about uncaused, it cannot be eliminated by eliminating its causes as the Third Noble Truth requires. While uncaused causes present a problem, beginning causes do not. In fact, they are required for following the Buddhist path. This distinction between uncaused causes and beginning causes warrants close attention. Consider the example of getting angry. Suppose I determine that the cause of this was an insult, and the feelings of hurt, indignation, and damaged self-esteem this caused. Perhaps there is still more to the anger than just this. Perhaps there is more to trace back to, of which I may not be aware (and perhaps a therapist or specialist could help me trace back these causes further). But this would just be to find the beginning or precipitating causes − I will use these terms interchangeably − somewhere else, a layer or two deeper. The search for mental causes is a search for reasons (in this case, reasons for being angry), and the provision of reasons must come to an end. That is, giving reasons only works if this stops somewhere. For to trace back reasons indefinitely is not to give a satisfactory reason at all; the giving of reasons as causes has to end, which is to say it has to have a beginning point.[1] The Third Noble Truth attests that suffering can be eliminated by eliminating its causes. Eliminating causes requires that the precipitating causes of our suffering exist and be identifiable. If the

---

1   Appealing to physical causes in giving reasons must also involve coming to beginning causes (for as noted, no causal analysis that tries to find reasons can continue on indefinitely).

precipitating causes of suffering are not eliminated, then suffering can continue to arise anew. Admitting beginning or precipitating causes is important for understanding causality in Dependent Origination.

While admitting beginning or precipitating causes is important, admitting uncaused causes must be avoided. As noted above, if suffering can come about uncaused, then it cannot be eliminated by eliminating its causes. The Third Noble Truth, and thus Dependent Origination as well (for this doctrine is to be read as being in accord with the Third Noble Truth) require that there be beginning causes that are not uncaused causes. This means that a beginning cause must itself have a cause and yet still remain a beginning cause. To say the least, this shows that Dependent Origination, and the sense of causality it involves, is not a simple notion, as the Buddha himself attested. This issue – of beginning causes that are not uncaused causes – will be elaborated in the next section. What remains in this section is to draw out further the difficulty with accepting this second model – mental causation without universal causation.

One problem with denying universal causation, already noted, is that an uncaused cause violates the Third Noble Truth. An uncaused event cannot be eliminated by eliminating its cause for it has none. Indeed, it does not seem eliminable at all for if it has no cause, it can just come about again, uncaused. Another problem has to do with what would be readily presumed to be the uncaused source of our intentional behaviour and acts of will: the self. This is a self that is presumed to lie behind our will and our choices and is their ultimate source. For instance, if I am feeling envious and decide to stop feeling envious, the source of this decision to stop, to my mind, may seem to be my self. There may be good reasons to stop feeling envious, which may or may not affect my decision, but the causal impetus for the decision may still strike me as ultimately coming from my will, and thus from me. The self seems to be able to initiate causal sequences without being fully caused itself. That is, it seems to be able to be an uncaused cause. This is a further problem with this second model.

To further elaborate, following the Noble Eightfold Path to the eradication of suffering requires making personality changes. We may ask from where does the impetus for these changes arise? The power to effect personality change must, it seems, reside somewhere, or arise from somewhere, and an obvious reply is from one's will and thus, it would seem, from one's self. Initiating change requires initiating new causal sequences to replace emplaced causal sequences. The difficulty here concerns how to conceive of making changes to oneself without thinking that they are being initiated by an independent self. The idea that there exists a self that has the power to effect changes among the aggregates – such as turning unwholesome thoughts into wholesome ones – through the sheer power of its will while also remaining independent of the aggregates is the idea that there is a self who is an independent controller and causal agent. This view of self was challenged in the Argument from Lack of Control in Chapter Eight. An uncaused cause is a cause that carries its own power to effect change and control; it is causally unconditioned. A self that can initiate causal sequences through an act of will; that can cause effects without itself being causally affected; that can exert control over the aggregates while existing independently of the causal interconnections between the aggregates, is an uncaused cause. This is a concept of self that the Buddha finds at the root of suffering. The second model, because it admits uncaused causes, and allows for a self to serve in the role of uncaused cause, is inappropriate for understanding the Buddhist doctrine of Dependent Origination.

Beginning causes are required for correctly appreciating causation in Buddhism (for it is the beginning or precipitating causes that must be eliminated if suffering is to be eliminated). But uncaused causes, for reasons given, cannot be admitted. As described, this second model, because it rejects universal causation and thus admits uncaused events, is not appropriate for understanding Dependent Origination. Thinking in terms of mental causation is still appropriate and the right way to proceed, as the cravings and attachments that cause suffering are conceived in mental terms. However, mental causation must be interpreted in a way that admits universal causation; and this means that it must not admit uncaused causes, while, at the same time, it must admit beginning or precipitating causes. Beginning causes that are not uncaused causes will be explained in the next section, in its discussion of a third model. This discussion will emphasize the importance of a careful empirical observation of the aggregates which, of course, is the Buddha's prescribed methodology.

The Third Model: Mental Causation with Universal Causation

We have so far considered models for physical causation, and mental causation without universal causation, in trying to come to an understanding of causality in Dependent Origination. The physical causation model is causation as we observe between physical events.[1] This model was deemed inadequate for understanding causation in Dependent Origination for two reasons. One, the usefulness of looking to causes in overcoming suffering requires a predictable connection between causes and their effects, but not a deterministic causation (for changes must be able to be made to causal sequences if the causes of suffering are to be eliminated). Two, Dependent Origination is concerned with mental phenomena (for to speak of overcoming cravings and attachments is to speak in terms of observable contents in the mind and not of the neuronal underpinnings of these states in the brain).

The next model considered was called 'mental causation without universal causation'. This model contrasted with physical causation. Mental causation is not deterministic, and this model of mental causation rejects universal causation and admits uncaused causes. This model of causation is also not appropriate for understanding Dependent Origination. In admitting uncaused events this model is at odds with the Third Noble Truth (which requires that suffering be eliminated by eliminating its causes). Furthermore, in admitting uncaused causes it allows for the self to be the uncaused cause (i.e., this model is consistent with the view that the self can exert control over the aggregates while also being causally unaffected and independent of the aggregates).

---

1 Although note that for Hume, it is a contiguity of events, and not specifically causation between events, that is observed.

The third model of causation is an alternative approach to mental causation: mental causation *with* universal causation (and thus *without* uncaused causes). While this third model does not admit uncaused causes, it does admit beginning or precipitating causes (and again, these terms are being used synonymously). If causality in Dependent Origination is to be correctly appreciated, then it must admit beginning causes (because it is the beginning or precipitating cause of suffering that must be eliminated if suffering is to be eliminated). To illustrate, suppose I trace a feeling of anger back to a feeling of damaged self-esteem. If the anger is to be overcome, then this beginning cause must be dealt with (i.e., the feeling of damaged self-esteem must be amended so that it no longer leads to anger). However, if this beginning cause is also an uncaused cause, then this raises a problem with following the Buddhist path; following this path requires eliminating suffering-inducing causes but a cause that itself has no cause does not seem eliminable. The understanding of causality in the doctrine of Dependent Origination, and also in the Noble Truths, must admit beginning causes but not uncaused causes. This will be discussed in this section. The next section, which focusses on the importance of universal causation in understanding Dependent Origination, will offer further elaboration.

The doctrine of Dependent Origination, as with No Self and Impermanence, is based on a careful observation of the aggregates. When we carefully observe the aggregates, we observe that they do not simply arise, but that they are caused to arise. Also, our observation of the aggregates and their precipitating causes only extends back so far. That is, we always come to a beginning point when we look carefully at a causal sequence. We may, with more diligent observation, notice a further underlying cause, but we still reach a point where we discern no further. This is to observe a beginning cause but it is not, strictly speaking, to observe an uncaused cause. To illustrate how a beginning cause need not be an uncaused cause, consider this example. I observe a vase fall off a table upon being nudged by my cat. The causal sequence that ends with the broken vase begins with the nudging. But that is not to say that the nudging was an uncaused event (it had its own antecedent causes, in the cat's brain perhaps, or in the sequence of events that led the cat to be near the vase, and these had their antecedent causes, and so on). We can go back indefinitely in uncovering further antecedent causes, but this will not help in getting to a beginning cause. Indeed, going back indefinitely, uncovering cause upon cause, means that we will not arrive at a beginning cause. Instead, it is perfectly reasonable to say that the fallen vase was caused by the cat's nudging, and not attend to any further antecedent causes. The cat's nudging was a beginning cause; it is a sufficient reason, for our intents and purposes, but not an uncaused cause. Likewise, causal sequences that manifest in suffering may be found to have beginnings, but these beginning causes need not be uncaused beginnings (just as the beginning of a tree branch is not an unattached beginning). Thus, the observation of beginning causes does not indicate that these are uncaused causes, and thus does not imply that universal causation is false.

In addition, looking carefully at the aggregates, we can note that we do not observe a permanent and independent self (this observation, to remind, is the gist of the Argument from the Aggregates for No Self). If no permanent and independent self is observed, then it follows that there is no such self observed who is the source of causal sequences. We may presume, judge, or believe there to be such a self but we do not observe causal sequences beginning in a self. Insofar as we continue to believe that there is such a self, serving as an originating source of causal sequences, then Dependent Origination presses us to observe more closely and see for "ourselves" that causal connections among the aggregates do not begin in a permanent and independent self. The rejection of self as an uncaused cause of actions does not imply a rejection of free will so much as a rejection of a freely willing agent lying behind our actions. Again, sticking to what we observe, we can introspectively observe willings and intentions, but no self that is doing the willing or intending. And so the observational method employed by the Buddha does not repudiate willings, or acts of will (and in fact, these are included in the aggregate of intentional and volitional activity). If we insist that acts of will and intentions originate in a self then, in the Buddhist view, that is due to our attachment to this position, and is not based upon what is empirically observed. In addition, the observation of the aggregates and their causes does not support causal determinism. We do observe a predictable relationship between certain precipitating causes and certain effects (e.g., we may find that feelings of anger or desire are predictably set off by specific causes). But given that we also observe that changes can be made to causal sequences, a predictable relationship between causes and effects does not betoken a necessary or unchangeable relationship. A careful observation of the aggregates yields a picture of causation in which there is a predictable relationship between causes and effects, but not a deterministic one; and in which there are beginning causes, but not uncaused causes, and specifically no self that is an uncaused cause. These are all aspects of causality in Dependent Origination and are captured by this third model: mental causation with universal causation. It is worth further elaborating upon the importance of universal causation in understanding Dependent Origination, and this will be the concern of the next section.

The Importance of Universal Causation

The Second Noble Truth asserts that suffering is caused, and the Third Noble Truth that these causes can be eliminated. Jointly these convey that while universal causation is true (i.e., all events are caused), causal determinism is not (i.e., casual sequences are not determined and hence can be altered). It is notable that these Noble Truths are not stated in universal terms even though they appear to be making universal claims. The Buddha carefully avoided speaking in universal terms about causality and also in general. For instance, reminiscent of the presentation of suffering in the First Noble Truth (in which he asserts only that there is suffering and not a universal statement such as "all is suffering"), he asserts the following in the *Nidanasamyutta* (Connected Discourses on Causation): "Thus when this exists, that comes to be; with the arising of this, that arises. When this does not exist, that does not come to be; with the cessation of this, that ceases."[1] It may be thought that this phrasing

---

1 *Nidanasamyutta, Samyutta Nikaya* II 28, p. 552.

conveys that the doctrine of Dependent Origination does not hold that *every* event is caused, and thus does not claim universal causation. Indeed, we may think that the use of demonstratives in the above passage – the expressions *this* and *that* – indicates that the Buddha intends to refer to only particular events as being caused, rather than to all events or events generally. However, there are good reasons to reject this.

For starters, the Buddha does speak in general terms in describing Dependent Origination. For instance, "when this exists, that comes to be" should be read to say "*whenever* this exists, that comes to be." More than this, the value of Dependent Origination in helping to understand the underlying causes of one's intentions and actions, and in helping to overcome suffering, resides in its generality. The value of looking for underlying causes for unwholesome thoughts and actions requires that there be such underlying causes, and that we be able to expect such causes. When the Buddhist is directed to observe the workings of the aggregates, he is being directed to pay attention to the underlying causes. This means that a feeling, thought or action that appears uncaused should be viewed as a feeling, thought or action for which we have not yet been able to locate a cause. The presence of a genuine uncaused event would be a gap in the scope of Dependent Origination and, as explained, an obstacle to the implementation of the Third Noble Truth. The Second and Third Noble Truths, in saying respectively that suffering is caused by craving and can be eliminated by eliminating craving, are not saying that suffering is sometimes caused by craving, and can sometimes be eliminated by eliminating craving. Their force resides in their general-ity. That is, the Second Noble Truth, in asserting that suffering is caused by craving, asserts a universal causal claim: all suffering is caused by craving. All suffering is caused, and this is what enables its elimination according to the Third Noble Truth.

Still, we might wonder whether these causes must all have causes, and whether these further causes must have causes, and so on (for this is also the claim of universal causation: there are no uncaused events, which means there are no uncaused causes). In response we may note that if there is an uncaused cause somewhere down the line, and this cause ultimately leads to suffering, then the suffering to which it leads does not seem eliminable (for if the cause is uncaused, then it cannot be eliminated or even altered and so it can continue to lead to suffering anew). If an event can arise without a cause, it is unclear how it can be removed. And even if it is somehow removed, it should just be able to arise again without a cause (for it needed no cause to arise initially) and so once again lead to suffering. An uncaused cause that results in suffering makes impossible the application of the Third Noble Truth and raises a seemingly insuperable problem for the elimination of suffering. We can additionally question that if uncaused causes are admitted down the line somewhere, why not just admit uncaused aggregates, or uncaused cravings, as well? Once we admit the possibility of uncaused events that can result in the arising of the aggregates we would be hard pressed to explain why the aggregates themselves cannot be uncaused events. This is in defiance of the doctrine of Dependent Origination and the observations it is based on. Clearly, universal causation is integral to understanding causality in the doctrine of Dependent Origination.

The Buddha observes that suffering is caused and undertakes a causal analysis as the key to overcoming suffering. A useful causal analysis requires that causal sequences be traced back to a beginning cause. That is, an analysis in terms of causes, to be of use, requires that the analysis be able to come to an end; and this means it must come to a beginning cause. Again, this does not mean admitting uncaused causes or rejecting universal causation. To offer another illustration, suppose I observe a passing airplane frighten a group of birds off a telephone wire. In this observation and analysis, the passing of the plane (and more specifically, the sound and disturbance this causes) is the precipitating cause that led to the birds' flight. That does not mean that the chain of causes and effects cannot be taken back further (for there are causes that led the airplane to pass overhead, including time-tables and schedules, requirements for flight paths and ticket purchases, and there are physiological causes that account for why the birds were affected by the plane's noise, and more causes besides these). But the analysis of the event may not gain from tracing back further causes (e.g., tracing back to all the passengers who bought tickets which consequently led to a plane being scheduled on this flight path would add nothing to the causal analysis of the birds' flight even though it would be a way of tracing the chain of causes and effects back further). A causal analysis, as with any analysis, must have an end point, and this is a beginning cause.

The primary focus with Dependent Origination, as with No Self and Impermanence, is the aggregates. These aggregates, the Buddha observed, are caused; they are part of causal sequences that can be traced back to beginning causes. The aim of this observation is to be of practical value in overcoming suffering. As noted in the previous chapter, the Buddha was not trying to be a physicist, or provide a scientific description of the external world with the doctrine of Impermanence, but rather to describe the aggregates and the sources of suffering in the human condition. Likewise, Dependent Origination is not competing with physical causation to be a scientifically true account of causality. Instead, it is based primarily on inward observations of causal workings. Again, these observable causal workings involve predictable causal connections, but not necessary ones; they involve beginning causes, but not uncaused causes. Overcoming suffering is the objective and, as previously explained, this involves overcoming craving and attachment to self. This attachment to self involves the idea that the self is an agent who can initiate causal sequences; this is a self who can, through an act of will, cause events to happen – be this thinking thoughts, making choices, or performing actions – without there being a further cause apart from the will of this self. This self is an uncaused cause. A self provides a ready answer to the question of who initiated the causal sequence, or from where it came. The idea of a self as a controller, author or initiator of action and thought is a common aspect of our sense of self. The difficulty of conceiving of how change can be enacted without its being initiated by a self is, from the Buddhist view, a sign of the entrenchment of this view of self. It is this aspect of self – i.e., as something that exerts control over the aggregates while existing independently of the aggregates – that the Argument from Lack of Control tries to confront. The Argument from Lack of Control asserted that there was no such controlling self. Dependent Origination likewise asserts that there can be no self that is an originating source of control and causation for there are no uncaused causes of the aggregates.

The practical importance of maintaining that all events among the aggregates have causes, and that these causes have causes, is not to fall into the view that the self is the ultimate originating source of the aggregates. Even if we are unable to determine the cause of an aggregate, the affirmation of universal causation means that the self will not be appealed to as its uncaused cause. Indeed, this is something Dependent Origination directs us to see for ourselves. That is, we are to come to see for ourselves, by looking back to the causes of the aggregates, that these causes do not originate in a self. Dependent Origination is thus supposed to help in overcoming attachment to self by leading us to look for, and find, further causes for our mental states beyond our attribution to self, which is to *show* us that we can press beyond an attribution to self. We may find beliefs, desires, thoughts, memories, and concerns about or for our self, but no self that is their cause. The practice of Dependent Origination, and its careful attention to causes, is thus an exercise in Mindfulness.

In sum, we may not be able to trace the causal histories of internal mental events as far back as we can external physical events, or make predictions of mental events as accurately as we can with physical events, but this should not mean that mental events do not have causes, or that it is causation only analogically. The aggregates, the Buddha observes, have causes. And although Dependent Origination presses us to watch for precipitating or beginning causes, these are not to be construed as uncaused causes. To admit the possibility of uncaused causes is to admit a notion commonly associated with a self in the sense of a controlling and causing agent. Universal causation implies that the self is not an uncaused cause. Paying close attention to causes, as Dependent Origination advises, is supposed to allow us to observe this implication for ourselves.

Dependent Origination and Causal Continuity

As described in Chapter Eight, the doctrine of No Self allows for a notion of self that, while not a permanent entity existing apart from the aggregates, is a composite of the ever-changing aggregates. Causal connections between successive aggregates mean that this composite self can be causally continuous over time. A causally continuous composite self is not to be equated with an unchanging self over time. Causal continuity over time is not the same as sameness or identity over time. This distinction will be closely examined in the next chapter. But as the notion of causal continuity over time draws upon the doctrine of Dependent Origination, the discussion of this notion will begin here.

Consider the example of a leaf that gradually turns colour and then falls from a tree to the ground. There is a causal continuity of events conjoining the fallen, darkened and brittle leaf to the earlier supple, green leaf attached to the tree. This causal continuity need presume no singular substance or something unchanging and permanent across points in time. We might respond that the genetic code of the leaf remains unchanged from one state to another, but this genetic code describes the leaf as a kind or type, rather than as a particular leaf. In addition to not being something we overtly observe and base our judgements of sameness on, this genetic code would not provide identity conditions for the particular leaf (i.e., it would not explain why it is the same particular leaf as the one that was once on the tree). There is nothing specific to the particular leaf that remains unchanged in our observation of it as it changes colour and texture and falls to the ground. We observe only causal continuity. The causal continuity, though, may lead us to assert that the fallen leaf is the same leaf as the one that was once on the tree. We may say this rather than say the fallen leaf is continuous with the leaf that was once on the tree (and it is also less awkward than to say this). But using the word 'same' rather than 'continuous' should not imply an actual sameness over time. This is supposed to be true of ourselves as well. As noted, Dependent Origination asserts that there are causal connections between aggregates. This allows for a self that is a composite of the ever-changing aggregates to be causally continuous over time (based on the connections between successive causes and effects). On the basis of this causal continuity, we may find ourselves speaking of a sameness of self over time. But as with the leaf, this judgement of sameness, strictly speaking, is unjustified. It is a useful way of speaking that, in the case of a self, can lead to suffered implications (for attachment to a sameness of self over time – that is, to a permanent self – underlies suffering in the Buddhist conception).

We might think that attachment to a causally continuous self, composed of the ever-changing aggregates, can be a source of suffering just as can attachment to a permanent self. Both involve attachment, after all. Consider the following example. I can be attached to a treasured plant that I keep on my desk, and fret and worry and thus suffer over the demise of this treasured plant, without believing that there is some essence or something permanent in the plant which is being lost. Likewise, it seems that I should be able to fret and worry over the demise of a self without believing that there is a soul or permanent and underlying entity that is coming to its end. A continuous self, it should seem, is also subject to decay and ending (i.e., subject to sickness, aging and death). The suffering may be less with attachment to a continuous, composite self (for there may be more scope for attachment, and more scope for a sense of loss, with attachment to a more substantive view of self). But it seems that it can still be suffered as long as one can have cravings and attachments associated with this composite self.

However, it is worth thinking carefully about whether the attachment and cravings in this case still involve a permanent self. Consider the above example of the plant again. When I worry and fret over the demise of the plant on my desk, my worry is for what I presume to be the *same* plant; that is, I worry over the demise of the same plant on my desk that was once thriving. I need not believe that there is an unchanging essence or core or soul to the plant. Instead, I may view it as a composite object that is causally continuous over time with no actual sameness to be found. Nonetheless, I can quite easily be attached to the plant as being the same plant over time. My attachment to the plant is more than an attachment to continuity. We may describe it as an attachment to *its* continuity (and this locution betrays an attachment to sameness, to its being the same plant over time). That is, the attachment here is to permanence, even though this is not explicitly acknowledged (and even though all that is explicitly acknowledged with the plant is causal continuity over time). Attachment to permanence can be quite subtle. The discussion of the continuity versus identity of self will be continued and elaborated in the next chapter.

XI

Karma and Rebirth: Continuity, Not Identity

Introduction

'KARMA' LITERALLY MEANS ACTION. For the Buddha, 'karma' did not refer to any and all action, but specifically to willed or intentional action (and thus karma is to be grouped with the aggregate of volitional or intentional activity). Intentional or willed actions include not just bodily behaviours, but also speech and, importantly, mental activity. The act of desiring, fearing, or hoping, even if they do not manifest outwardly with bodily movement or verbal expression, still constitute karma in this Buddhist view.

The theory of karma also connects actions to reactions in a law-like manner. It is commonly held, in Buddhism and in the Indian tradition in general, that there are causal connections between past, present and future actions and happenings. That is, one's past deeds are held to have a determining effect on one's present state and one's present and past deeds, through the operation of karma, to have a determining effect on one's future state. This is not supposed to entail that one's present state is *fully* determined by one's past acts (or that one's future state will be *fully* determined by one's present and past deeds), but it does accept the existence of causal connections. It is held that we can affect the future through changes in our present actions, and this presumes that the present is not fully determined by the past. In other words, karmic connections admit universal causation, but not causal determinism, and this is in line with the doctrine of Dependent Origination discussed in the previous chapter. Thus, while the theory of karma asserts that there are law-like causal connections between the past, present and future, these are not taken to be fully determining causal connections. For instance, making changes in order to follow the Noble Eightfold path, so that suffering may be overcome, is presumed to be a possibility open at any time. If we are truly able to decide, in the present, for one course of action rather than another, then the past cannot be fully determining the present.

Instead of being fatalistic, karma is seen as something that should lead people to accept responsibility for their present and future lot in life. The idea is that, because of karma, people can come to see that their present lot and their present suffering is an outcome of their own previous actions over which they had control. This ability, to be in control of whether we suffer or not, is clearer when suffering is conceived in terms of the third grouping in the First Noble Truth rather than in terms of the first two groupings. We may not always be able to prevent ourselves from experiencing pain or grief, or from becoming ill. We cannot prevent aging and death at all. We cannot always remain unmoved by unsatisfied desires. But these are not by themselves suffering under the Buddhist conception. Suffering results from craving and attachment to self. Whether we crave, and to what extent we are self-attached, is a result of our own doing, and our own minds, and overcoming this attachment can likewise be a result of our own mental efforts.

The law-like connections between cause and effect in the theory of karma connect the concept of karma to the doctrine of Dependent Origination, as well as to the Noble Truths, for these also emphasize the importance of causal connectivity. Understanding karma in close connection to Dependent Origination is to understand karma consistently with

Buddhist doctrine. However, in other respects, it is difficult to understand karma in a manner consistent with basic Buddhist doctrine and principles. This is particularly the case with the concept of rebirth which is often associated with karma. This will be discussed further below and will involve elaborating upon a distinction introduced at the end of the previous chapter: continuity over time versus identity over time.

Karma and Morality

Karma should not be confused with moral justice, or reward and punishment. The theory of karma is a theory of cause and effect, of intentional action and reaction, which is not intrinsically bound up with justice. Still, good volitional actions are thought to produce good effects through the operation of karma (and bad volitional actions are thought to produce bad effects). Hateful thoughts, for instance, are thought to lead to suffering. Insofar as hateful thoughts involve cravings and further one's attachment to self, then given the understanding of suffering in the Buddhist sense, we can see how suffering can result from hateful thoughts. Likewise with covetous thoughts, etc. If we keep to the understanding of suffering as involving attachment to self, then hateful actions should not be thought to lead, by the workings of karma, to suffering in the form of public disapprobation, bodily injury, economic loss or some such travail (either in this life or another), as these are not intrinsically suffering in the Buddhist sense. That is, as long as suffering is conceived in terms of attachment and craving, then the nature of the causal mechanism is this: intentional actions that involve cravings and attachment to self will further entrench attachment to self; this is to cause suffering in the Buddhist sense.

Nevertheless, karma or karmic connections are commonly thought of as having a greater moral connotation than just this, and this warrants some discussion. Buddhism arose within a cultural and religious milieu with established ways of understanding things, and while Buddhism appropriated some of these ways in explaining itself, it also set itself apart by criticizing others.[1] As we have seen, Buddhism rejects aspects of traditional Upanishadic or Brahmanical thought, but it also appropriates aspects of this tradition. The Buddha's audience employed certain basic concepts in its understanding of the world, and the Buddha employed some of these same concepts in making himself understood to his audience. Karma is among those concepts that were appropriated – with some amendment – to express Buddhist doctrines.[2]

The notion of karma (as well as rebirth, to be discussed below) was prominent in the Vedic and Brahmanical traditions of the Buddha's time and was important for maintaining a moral order. Thomas appropriately describes karma and rebirth as among traditional Indian responses to the challenges to justice in light of the presence of suffering and evil. He states:

They are the Indian answers to the eternal problems of pain and evil. A man does wrong and suffers for it. But he may suffer when he has done no apparent wrong. Hence his wrong was done in a former life, and if he does wrong and apparently receives no retribution, he will be punished for his sin in another birth. Like all

---

1 C.f. Gombrich: "the central teachings of the Buddha came as a response to the central teachings of the old Upanisads, notably the *Brhadaranyaka*. On some points, which he perhaps took for granted, he was in agreement with the Upanisadic doctrine; on others he criticised it." Gombrich (1997), p. 31. And from Collins: "The intellectual stratum of Buddhism worked with the basic paradigm provided by Brahmanical thought, accepting the overall form, while rejecting certain features." Collins (1982), pp. 39-40.

2 Collins, for instance, states: "... the appearance in the Brahmanical great tradition of the ideas of samsara, karma, and moksa, was complete before the time of the Buddha. This was the cultural world into which he was born, and it was with these conceptual tools that he articulated his message of salvation." Collins (1982), p. 64. See also Harvey: "While teachings on karma and rebirth are an important part of Buddhist belief, they are not the most crucial, nor the most specifically Buddhist. They act, though, as the lead-up to, and motivator for the most important teachings, those on the Four Holy Truths." Harvey (1990), p. 46. It is interesting to note that when Buddhism reaches into China, and then Korea and Japan, where the cultural and moral traditions did not involve or require beliefs in karma and rebirth, the presentations of Buddhism makes less use of these concepts.

theories that accept sin and evil as positive realities, the doctrine of rebirth rests upon faith, and ultimately on the faith that sin must find its punishment.[1]

Karma and rebirth were notions that had wide currency. They provided a moral framework in which justice could be conceptualized as being meted out on a grand scale (by allowing for unpunished injustice in this life to be punished in a future life, and good acts unrewarded in this life to be rewarded in another). As Thomas explains, the common acceptance of karma and rebirth served to maintain a moral order by helping people believe that wrongful acts, while perhaps of immediate advantage, would by the effects of karma meet with negative consequences, perhaps later in this lifetime or perhaps in the next. A detrimental effect of this is that it can lead people to be accepting of their present circumstances – be it good, bad, rich or poor – by leading them to think of these circumstances as a fair inheritance of their deeds, or misdeeds, in a previous life. Historically, these ideas have undermined social mobility, and rigidified conceptions of caste and desert which have been problematic in India. Still, these concepts were valued for maintaining order in society. Rebirth also allows for the belief that if enlightenment is not achieved in this life, headway can still be made towards the achievement of enlightenment in a future life. To deny rebirth in its literal sense, and uproot the belief in karma with its moral implications, risks undermining this moral sensibility and rupturing the order which rests on it.

As Thomas goes on to say, "We do not need to question the fact that the Buddha adopted the best of the moral teaching that he found. Every system arises out of its predecessor."[2] Buddhism did not initiate this moral system, based on the notions of karma and rebirth, but it did adopt and work with them. At the same time, these notions presume that the same self who commits good or bad deeds will at some future time,

---

1 Thomas (1949), p. 175.
2 Thomas (1949), p. 175.

either in this life or a future life, benefit or suffer from the consequences of these deeds. This appears to conflict with Buddhist views on the self. This will be discussed in the next section.

Karma and Rebirth

The effects of karmic causal connections are held to occur not just between actions and events in this life, but to extend over successive lives. The karmic effects that extend over lives may include being reborn into better or worse conditions, or having good or bad events befall one in a future life, or even being reborn as a different creature. This view of karma as effective over successive lives necessitates an acceptance of rebirth or transmigration of self from one life to another. There is a looming difficulty with this view from a Buddhist perspective: how can there be rebirth, and how can karma affect one's rebirth, if there is no enduring self or soul to be reborn? The self is only a composite of the ever-changing aggregates. There is no permanence of self over time and so no permanence of self to continue on to another life. Buddhism is clear that there is no enduring self, and in fact asserts that attachment to this self is the root cause of suffering. Accordingly, the Buddha, while not denying rebirth outright, is also clear that rebirth does not involve a continuance of the same self. In the *Mahatanhasankhaya Sutra*, a monk is described as misunderstanding the Buddha on this point:

> ... there was a bhikkhu [monk] named Sati, a fisherman's son, in whom had arisen a pernicious view like this: "Thus it is that I understand the *dhamma* taught by the Exalted One: it is this same consciousness, and not another, which transmigrates, which goes through the round of death and rebirth."

Sati is then brought before the Buddha who criticizes and rebukes him:

Do you know anyone, you misguided person, to whom I have taught the *dhamma* in that way? Misguided person, have I not spoken in many ways of consciousness as dependently arisen, since without a condition there would be no arising of consciousness? But you, misguided person, have misrepresented us by your wrong grasp and have injured yourself and have accumulated much demerit. And this, misguided person, will lead to your harm and suffering for a long time.[1]

The strong tones in which the sutra portrays the Buddha's response, which are uncharacteristic of the way the Buddha is generally represented, conveys the gravity of Sati's error. The Buddha explains that consciousness is generated by causal conditions (the causally conjoined and ever-changing aggregates), and that it is not the same self or consciousness that continues on. Note that the Buddha does not deny continuity after death, or the idea of rebirth, but does deny a personal continuity. There is no personal rebirth or sameness of consciousness that continues on after death. And there could not be if there is no permanent self to be reborn. In Chapter Nine it was described that the Buddha clearly rejected both the positions of Annihilationism and Eternalism. Eternalism is the view that there is a permanent self that continues on after death. This view is presumed in the idea of a personal rebirth (for it is the same self that is reborn to another life). Annihilationism is the view that there is a permanent self that lives for a lifetime and then perishes. The Buddha's rejection of both these views is due to his position that there is no permanent self, and therefore no permanent self that can die or continue on after death. There is no permanent self who will receive the future karmic effects of good and bad deeds, either in this life, or in another life. The Buddha's rejection of a personal rebirth, as seen in his response to the monk Sati in the passage above, accords with the basic doctrines of No Self and Impermanence.

---

1 See *Mahatanhasankhaya Sutta, Majjhima Nikaya* I 256-71. From *Early Buddhist Discourses*, pp. 61-72. See also Collins (1982), p. 103.

What, then, are we to make of the common view that rebirth does involve a continuation of the same self? Collins addresses this by noting that the notions of karma and rebirth, as commonly understood to involve future effects to the same self, are held primarily by lay followers and non-specialists (i.e., those who are not adepts in Buddhist scholarship or practice). For them, the doctrine of No Self is not taken literally as repudiating the belief in a permanent self (particularly as the notion of no self is difficult to appreciate as being true of oneself). Rather the doctrine serves as a religious identification which differentiates them from the religious followers of the Vedas and Upanishads with their emphasis on Atman or True Self. *Anatman* is a means of emphasizing a religious difference for lay followers. For monks and specialists, however, No Self is supposed to be taken more literally and seriously (and this may explain why, in the example above, the Buddha is represented as strongly rebuking the monk Sati for thinking in terms of a permanent self).[1] In addition, we may note that causal relations are described as law-like in Buddhism, and this does not favour the re-accumulation, after death, of psychological and physical parts so as to lead to a continuation of self in some other form. This would be to view the causal workings of karma as geared towards self-preservation or personal continuation, rather than being impersonal causal workings. The notion of causal continuity, and the difference between this and sameness of self over time, will be elaborated further in the next section on continuity and identity.

Recall that suffering, in the Buddhist conception, cannot simply be physical injury, pain, sickness, aging or death (these are examples from the first grouping in the First Noble Truth and they are not eliminable from the human condition). Also, suffering cannot simply be a matter of having unsatisfied desires (this is suffering as described in the second grouping in the First Noble Truth, and this is also not eliminable from the human condition). Thus, being sickly cannot be a just desert for misdeeds in one's past, whether in this life or in a previous life, for being sickly is not, strictly speaking, suffering in the Buddhist conception.

---

1 See Collins (1982), p. 77.

Likewise, rebirth in a worse state, such as being reborn poor because one was greedy, ugly because one was angry, deformed because one was violent, all of which were commonly believed in the Buddha's time, are also not in themselves suffering under the Buddhist conception.[1] Being poor, ugly, or deformed are not suffering if they do not involve attachment to self; examples such as these are not the suffering that Buddhism aims to eliminate from the human condition. These depictions of the conditions of rebirth fit with the understandings of suffering described in the first and second groupings of the First Noble Truth. Also, these depictions presume the lay-person's understanding of rebirth described above because they all presume that it is the same self who will be reborn (for otherwise, being reborn sickly, poor, or deformed, cannot be thought of as punishment for one's past misdeeds).

Suffering, in the Buddhist sense, involves craving and attachment to self and not physical affliction. Being physically afflicted may involve suffering insofar as there is a craving not to be physically afflicted. But then, in the Buddhist view, it is not the physical affliction itself that is suffered. Rather, it is the attachment to self that is present in the craving not to be afflicted that is suffered. This is the suffering that is held to be eliminable and not the physical affliction. Given this understanding of suffering, if stealing is to cause suffering, then one who steals must, as a consequence, suffer from further attachment to self. Likewise with someone who lies, cheats, or kills. Further attachment to self does not seem to be much of a punishment (at least not as we would ordinarily think of punishment). But it does make sense to say that hateful, hurtful or greedy acts, which are usually committed out of selfish concern or

---

1 C.f. Harvey: "The movement of beings between rebirths is not a haphazard process but is ordered and governed by the law of karma, the principle that beings are reborn according to the nature and quality of their past actions; they are 'heir' to their actions (M.III.203) ... If bad actions are not serious enough to lead to a lower rebirth, they affect the nature of a human rebirth: stinginess leads to being poor, injuring beings leads to frequent illnesses, and anger leads to being ugly – an extension of the process whereby an angry person gradually develops ugly features during their present life (M.III.203-06)." Harvey (1990), p. 39. Harvey's references are to the *Culakammavibhanga Sutra, Majjhima Nikaya* III 203-06, pp. 1053-57.

self-attachment, will result in a further entrenchment of self-attachment. And it does make sense to say that this involves the workings of karma as this is an uncomplicated cause and effect relationship (i.e., self-centred actions entrench attachment to self). But again, this sort of effect is not punishment as we would normally think of it. However, as described above, the concept of karma is not inherently one of justice, let alone one of justly meted out punishment. It is supposed to be a concept about law-like causal connections between intentional actions and reactions that only indirectly relates to concerns of justice. It is easier to appreciate a causal connection between misdeeds such as stealing and killing and further attachment to self than it is to appreciate how these misdeeds result in future physical afflictions and deformities.

It should be emphasized that, in its basic doctrines, Buddhism does not present a moral theory for ordering a society or a framework for justice. It presents a theory – or better, a practice – for individuals to eliminate their suffering. There are moral consequences associated with these doctrines, such as with the selflessness that comes with practicing No Self; but that is not to say that these doctrines present a moral theory for managing social relations. Even the Noble Eightfold Path, which includes steps explicitly pertaining to moral conduct, is directed – as a path – towards overcoming suffering (i.e., the moral conduct it prescribes is instrumental and directed towards the objective of overcoming suffering). And the same holds for following the Middle Way. All this conveys that Buddhism, in its early and basic doctrines at least, is not as interested in presenting a moral theory or framework for ordering society as in presenting a theory of human suffering and the means for its alleviation. It is true that over-coming suffering for oneself cannot be achieved if it is motivated solely by concerns for self, for it involves overcoming attachment to self (and this has consequences for how one should appraise the suffering of others compared to one's own). It is also true that the Buddha's life displays an interest in pursuing the end of suffering for all humankind. Still, we do not see in these early doctrines a presentation of ending the suffering of others as a moral obligation (this sort of thinking, as we will see in Chapters Thirteen and Fourteen, does arise with Mahayana Buddhism).

Continuity of Self over Time, Not Identity

There is a Buddhist analogy for the self that involves a candle flame: there is no permanent entity residing in the flame from one moment to the next in virtue of which it is the same flame from one moment to the next. There is just a series of states – or series of flames perhaps – causally connected. Nevertheless there is an appearance of sameness, and a utility to speaking of the flame being the same over time. So it is with the self. As described, the doctrines of No Self and Impermanence assert that there is no permanent entity that remains from one moment to another. What we call self is no more than a composite of ever-changing aggregates. The continuity of a composite self over time is explained by the causal connections between the composing parts, the aggregates. Continuity does not require that there be an unchanging or abiding essence or core. By analogy, we may speak of a stream as being continuous throughout without there being a part or core that is the same throughout; or, a rope being continuous without a single thread running through the whole of it. Likewise, there is no unchanging essence or core that underlies a moving weather pattern, but we can nonetheless trace changes and movements in a weather pattern back through time, and to some extent, predict forward to the future. We can do so by tracing causal connections.

The same is true of the self. I am a continuous composite self between now and yesterday, or now and ten years ago, based on a line of causal continuity among the aggregates. I am a different person from a person sitting next to me on a bus, and different from who that person was five years ago, because of different lines or histories of causally connected aggregates.

The traditional Buddhist response to the question of whether someone reborn is the same or different is neither.[1] The person is not the same

---

1 Gethin states: "… when asked whether the one who is reborn is the same or different from the one who died, the Buddhist tradition replies that strictly he (or she) is neither the same nor different." Gethin (1998), p. 144. Gethin cites the *Milinda Panha* in which the monk Nagasena provides *(continued)*

because there is no sameness of self or consciousness that passes on from one life to another (this was described in the previous section). But also, the person reborn is said not to be different from the one who died if there is causal continuity. This is not a personal continuity involving sameness of self, but a causal continuity of impersonal aggregates which, it was thought, need not end with bodily death.

However, our subjective sense of self presumes an actual sameness of self over time. The belief in being the same self from one period of time to another involves the notion of numerical identity over time. This is the notion of something being one and the same thing over time (this notion, and the distinction between it and qualitative identity, was described in Chapter Nine). In the Buddhist view, a belief in the numerical identity of self over time, while useful in speaking about selves, is ungrounded (for again, there is nothing that remains unchanged over time that would justify a judgement of numerical identity). In the following discussion, the notion of causal continuity, and the contrast between this and an actual numerical identity, will be illustrated with analogies.

One of the things we do when we speak of sameness or identity is to contrast it with difference – to establish that one thing is not something else. For instance, if I take you to a copse of trees and point to a particular tree and say: "this is the same tree I planted ten years ago," what I do in speaking of it being the same tree is convey that it is this tree and not some other tree that I planted. Sameness is here contrasted with difference. What I don't mean, or more accurately, what I don't have to mean, is that the tree has remained unchanged, or that some part of it has remained unchanged over those ten years. It is plausible that there's not a single cell in this tree now that was in it when I planted it. My judgement is based on causal continuity, and this line of causal

---

an illustration of this idea of being neither the same nor entirely different: a man steals a mango from another man's orchard and, upon being seized, replies that the mango he took is different from the seed the other man planted. Nagasena replies that while this is true, the stolen mango is not entirely different from the planted seed: there is a causal connection between the seed and the mango, and this is sufficient for holding the thief morally responsible. See *Milinda Panha* 46, p. 72.

continuity establishes that it was not some other tree that I planted ten years ago. The tree has, strictly speaking, not remained the same, but my speaking of it as the same tree is not problematic in this context, as it is unlikely to be taken as meaning that the tree has remained unchanged. We might say that the sapling I planted ten years ago and the tree today are different parts or perspectives of one thing[1] (although this way of speaking is awkward). But again, this "one thing" is not the adult tree, or an essence or spirit shared by both the sapling and the tree. Rather, it is just the line of causal continuity between the sapling and the tree – they are both parts of this temporally strewn out and causally interconnected line. When I say *this* tree was the same as *that* sapling, I convey that there is a line of causal continuity in virtue of which the sapling is not identifiable with another tree, or the tree with another sapling. The assertion of sameness here has implications for what is other or different, and in virtue of this may seem like a judgement of actual identity rather than of causal continuity. But again, in the Buddhist view, there is only causal continuity over time upon which to base judgements of sameness and difference, and no actual identity or sameness over time.

Just as with the sapling and tree, the child I once was is in many respects different from the adult I now am. Despite these changes, I make statements of identity (as I just did in using the word 'I' in referring to myself as a child and adult). As noted, the doctrines of No Self and Impermanence deny that there is something essential, something unchanging or permanent, between these two times that would justify a judgement of sameness of self. We might reply that there is a sameness of genetic code between myself as a child and as an adult. However, this code is not part of my psychological attachment to self; it is not something which I can inwardly observe or introspect as a basis for attachment. The ever-changing aggregates are all we observe; the notion of a permanent self is something we attach to the aggregates (as when

---

1 Contemporary Western philosophers sometimes speak of the tree-at-this-instant as a stage, or an instantaneous time-slice, of the tree; together with all the other instantaneous time-slices of the tree, they constitute the tree-through-time.

I speak of "my body," or "my desires," etc.). But it is observed that there is no basis among these aggregates for this attachment to a permanent self (this was the Argument from the Aggregates, described in Chapters Four and Eight). Thus, the judgement of sameness of self must rely only on causal continuance. I am the same as the child only in the sense that I can draw a line of causal connection or history between myself and that child (and not to any other child). The child and the adult are the same only in virtue of being parts of the same causally continuous line of aggregates.[1]

Our thoughts and statements about ourselves in the future, such as in thinking about what we will do in the coming week or year, also generally presume a sameness of identity (for otherwise, who am I thinking about, or making plans for, if not for the *same* self?). When I crave (a delicious pasta, say, or to live another day) I presume an identity with the self who will be the beneficiary of the future I crave. The same holds for wants, hopes, fears, expectations, and more, that involve thoughts of our future self. For as the Buddhist monk Nagasena asks: "Can it be that one (person) trains in a craft, another becomes proficient?"[2] Buddhism does not deny the value or usefulness of these judgements of identity. It does not deny them a role or say that they should not be made. In Nagasena's case, clearly the training at one time has a causal influence on the proficiency at a later time. Rather, Buddhism denies that the judgements of identity or sameness over time are justified in terms of an actual identity or sameness. And it asserts that these judgements are problematic

---

1 In this respect, the child and adult are both parts of a greater whole: the line of causal continuity over time that connects the child to the adult. It is elucidating to view the composite self as a whole over time, rather than as an entity that is a whole at each moment of time and moves as a whole through each moment of time, for as described, this latter view lacks true identity criteria.

2 As translated in Collins (1982), p. 186. Nagasena raises other examples along with this one that pose the same question: "Is the mother of the embryo in the first stage different from the mother of the embryo in the second stage, or the third, or the fourth? Is the mother of the baby a different person from the mother of the grown-up man?" *Milinda Panha* 40, p. 63. Nagasena emphasizes while they are not identical, they are not entirely different persons either. Once again, while there is no identity, there is causal continuity.

if they lead to cravings and attachment to self (in which case they are suffering-inducing).

Judgements of the identity of self are said to have a conventional role or to be conventionally true (for reason of being useful), but not to be ultimately true. A distinction between two truths: conventional truth and ultimate truth, is commonly employed in Buddhism (we will see this distinction employed, albeit somewhat differently, in the next chapter on the Abhidharma, and again differently in the chapter after that on Mahayana Buddhism). No Self, as with the other basic doctrines, is an ultimate truth. Speaking of selves is useful though. It is important that we be able to identify others as being the same selves over time as well as identify ourselves as being the same over time. For the reason of being conceptually and linguistically useful, judgements of self, and specifically of being a numerically identical self over time, can be regarded as conventionally true. But in the Buddhist view, the conventional should be recognized for what it is, only conventional, which means recognizing its usefulness without attachment. It is when the conventional is treated as more than it is, as ultimately true and with attachment, that suffering arises. We can continue to talk in terms of being the same person over time, including through dramatic life changes, as long as this proceeds without attachment. Even if you live to be a hundred and ten, and suffer cognitive degradations, we may still speak of you as being the same person – and you may think of yourself as being the same person – even though you may have changed quite a lot. This judgement of sameness is not ultimately correct in the Buddhist view, but it is not suffering-inducing either as long as it proceeds without attachment.

Causal continuity also allows for judgements of moral responsibility without presuming an actual sameness of self. This is famously illustrated by the monk Nagasena. The example is given of a man who starts a fire to keep warm and negligently doesn't put it out. Later on, after he has left, the fire spreads and burns someone else's field. The man is arrested but he claims that the fire he started is not the same as the fire that burnt the field (these fires are not the same as they differ in size, intensity, materials burned, location, etc.). Nagasena points out that while there is no strict identity between the fire the man started and the fire that burned the field, there is nonetheless causal continuity. The fire he started to keep himself warm led to the fire that burned the field, and this is the basis for holding him morally responsible. That is, while the man is right that the fire that burned the field is not the same particular fire as the fire he started, it is nonetheless a fire he *caused*. Causal continuity is held to sufficiently justify a verdict of moral responsibility.

This example occurs in a series of discourses between the monk Nagasena and a king named Milinda (also known as Menander, an ancient Indo-Greek king of Bactria). In these discourses Nagasena illustrates the doctrine of No Self, and the notion of a composite self, with the analogy of a chariot. This illustration was presented in Chapter Eight, but it will be revisited here to further elaborate the Buddhist view of personal identity over time. Before that, it is worth observing how Nagasena begins the series of discussions with King Milinda. King Milinda, having heard of this wise monk, meets him and wants to talk with him. Nagasena agrees but on one condition: the king converse with him as the wise converse, and not converse with him as a king converses. This is quite a thing to say to a king, and King Milinda asks him to explain himself. Nagasena duly obliges and says:

> Your majesty, when the wise converse, whether they become entangled by their opponents' arguments or extricate themselves, whether they or their opponents are convicted of error, whether their own superiority or that of their opponents is established, nothing in all this can make them angry. Thus, your majesty, do the wise converse.[1]

Nagasena then elaborates that kings converse in opposing terms, getting angry when their views are disputed and so on. This exchange conveys not simply Nagasena's courage, or perhaps foolhardiness, in front of the king. It conveys not only that Nagasena thinks that discussions

---

1 *Milinda Panha* 28-29 as translated in Warren (1987), p. 128.

such as this should pursue truth and not self-promotion, although there is this too. The passage also conveys something of the psychological attitude that is required, and that a monk is supposed to keep and this is worth elaborating. The doctrine of No Self, which they go on to discuss, is described as a Right View (Right View, to remind, is the first step in the Noble Eightfold Path, discussed in Chapter Seven). But a monk is not supposed to be attached to anything as a Right View, including the doctrine of No Self. It can be easy to attach a sense of self to a doctrine, as when one argues with self-righteousness. Such an approach to the doctrine of No Self, though, is not productive. It is not simply holding or believing the doctrine of No Self that is the objective, but *realizing* it, and being attached to the doctrine, arguing for it with heated emotion, with self-righteousness, feeling pride in oneself in defending it well, and self-concern when not, are all contrary to this objective. Nagasena does not want to be party to that kind of exchange, but not just for himself – for presumably, if he truly is a wise monk, then his equanimity will not be easily disturbed in debate. His concern is also for the king. Nagasena is tasked to elaborate the doctrine of No Self to the king – that is what follows in their discourse – and he does not want the king to be possessed of, or attached to, a view in the discussion. Such an attachment would be disruptive of the spirit in which the doctrine of No Self is to be correctly appreciated.

Now, let us return to the analogy with the chariot. Nagasena explains that just as a chariot is made up of parts, such as rims, axle, carriage, etc., the same is true of the self; it is made up of aggregates. A chariot, in a certain sense, is more than the mere sum of its parts. As described in Chapter Eight, a chariot is not more because it weighs more than the sum of its parts, or because it contains something hidden other than its parts (whatever that might be). That is not the right sense of *more*. Rather, it is more than the sum of its parts in the sense that it can do something that the parts by themselves cannot do. The chariot is the parts put together in a certain way, and is a chariot insofar as it carries out certain functions. A self is also more than just the mere sum of its parts. But this is more likely to be misunderstood. Similar to the chariot, a self is more than the sum of its aggregate parts in the sense that the parts must be organized appropriately to function as a self. A self is *not* more than the sum of its aggregate parts in the sense that there is some extra ingredient – some unchanging essence or permanent spirit or soul, Nagasena affirms. From our inside, first-person point of view, however, it may seem we are more than the sum of our psychophysical states in *this* sense. Furthermore, like pins in a pin cushion that are not proper parts of the cushion in which they are stuck, it may seem that the aggregates (thoughts, feelings, etc.) are not proper parts of oneself; they may seem to be things that are had by the self, or experienced by the self, while the self is entirely something other than its aggregates. But this is likewise judged to be incorrect.

The analogy with the chariot asserts that the self is properly viewed as a composite. Also, the parts which make up the self, the aggregates, are different from chariot parts in that they are more like processes or events than things. When we turn within, the events we encounter be they desires or fears, thoughts or memories, feelings or images, all arise in our conscious awareness and then pass. The aggregates are characterized by this arising and passing, or impermanence. What makes these aggregates into a composite self are causal connections. The composite self does not remain the same over time – the continual arising and passing of its aggregate parts does not allow for an actual sameness – but it can nonetheless be causally continuous over time.

We might wonder why this composite self cannot remain the same composite self over time – remain numerically identical that is – even while it is continually changing. Something with parts, we might think, should be able to remain the same thing over time even while its parts are changing. Heraclitus famously asserted that one could not step twice into the same river. This is because the river is continually flowing – after you step in it once, it is no longer the same river. To respond to Heraclitus, one could say that you *can* step into the same river twice because the river, considered as a whole – a continuously flowing whole – is one river. Our understanding of something being one thing – in this case one river – can encompass changes in that one thing. A river doesn't continually become a different river as its water flows. It remains one and the same river.

However, this sort of response to Heraclitus does not speak to the sense of identity that is in question for the Buddha. True enough, different episodes in my life can be considered as belonging to one and the same life; the same causally continuous life. But this sense of same life, or one life, is not numerical identity. The Buddha, as well as David Hume, can readily admit that the collection of aggregates is one collection; the bundle of perceptions is one bundle. In fact, this is implied by Nagesena in comparing the collection of aggregates to a chariot: the aggregates come together to form a composite self just as chariot parts form a chariot. This composite self involves a line of casual continuity *over* time. However, it is not thereby identical *through* time. That is, the composite self is one thing *over* time, but not the *same* thing at each moment of time. No part of a river is, strictly speaking, identical with any other part, and yet we can speak of different parts as belonging to one and the same river, and this is due to causal continuity among parts. Likewise, the composite of aggregates that I am at one moment is not identical with the composite of aggregates that I am at any other moment, and yet we can speak of the composite of aggregates as forming one continuity over one lifetime, due to causal connections between the aggregates over time.

To be clear, judgements of being a numerically identical self over time may be conventionally true – which is to say they can be useful judgements, but are not ultimately true in the Buddhist view. Causal continuity allows us to speak of the parts of a river as parts of one and the same river. Likewise, causal continuity can support the judgement that parts of a life are parts of one and the same life. This is a judgement of sameness, in a sense, but it is not the judgement that there is something unchanging, something essential between the parts of a life and that migrates through the parts of one's life. Yet a common aspect of our sense of self, or of our attachment to self, is just this: remaining the same self, moment by moment, through time; undergoing changes in bodily and mental qualities, but in some essential aspect remaining the same; in short, remaining numerically identical while qualitatively changing. Again, this notion is repudiated by the doctrines of No Self, Impermanence and Dependent Origination. There is only causal continuity over time, and the only sameness between parts of a life is in virtue of belonging to the same causally continuous whole. Nonetheless, the *presumption* remains of being a self that *is* the same from moment to moment; the same in moments passed, and the same in moments to come. This is numerical identity over time, and in the Buddhist view, it is to *this* sense of being the same that we are strongly attached.

We will finish off this section and chapter with two illustrations of conventionality and arbitrariness in judgements of identity.

The first has been used to speak about questions of identity by many in the history of Western Philosophy: the Ship of Theseus. Theseus leaves port and, during his long voyage, each part of his ship – planks, sails, oars, masts, etc. – get steadily replaced. At the end of his voyage, *every* part of the ship has been replaced. The question is then asked whether this ship is the same as the one on which Theseus began his voyage. Some may say no, as it is completely materially different. Some may say yes as it is still *his* ship, and serves the same purpose. For some, the gradualness of the changes makes a difference: if the ship had been destroyed all at once and Theseus simply bought a new ship, then this would be different than the one he left port with; but with each replacement being piecemeal, and the changes gradual, the resulting ship is not different. To further complicate the matter, the possibility is raised of someone trailing behind Theseus, picking up all his cast off parts, fixing them, and reconstructing the ship from its original parts.[1] The question is then asked which ship, if either, is the same as that which left port: the ship with parts replaced, captained by Theseus, or the ship with original parts, captained by someone else? They can't both be, for, by definition, two cannot be numerically identical to one.

What is the right answer here? Although this particular example is not from the Buddhist canon, it would seem that the Buddhist response would be that it is a mistake to think there is an ultimately right answer.

---

1 Blackburn (1999), p. 127.

There is only the answer we arrive at, and that is conventionally useful. That is, if we judge that Theseus' ship is always the one he captains, and that this provides the criterion of identity, then it is the same ship as the one that left port. If our conventions favour materially being the same ship, then it is not the same ship (while the ship put together with cast off parts may be said to be the same ship). There is no fact of identity that can determine a right answer independent of our conventions. Although we still appeal to reasons in making judgements about the numerical identity of the ship, the results we come to will involve agreement or custom. That is to say, judgements of numerical identity are dependent upon convention, and are thus conventionally true. And of course, this is what Buddhism is saying about selves and their identity over time.

We may wonder, if we undergo so many changes, and there is no essentially same self through these changes, if any one age or time represents who we "really are." For instance, we may wonder if the age of twenty-five, or some other age, best captures who we really are. It is the Buddhist view that to choose any given time slice as being quintessentially you is to choose arbitrarily, for there is nothing about any one age over another that makes it *more* you, or *really* you. There can be no age that better captures who you "really" are, or that better captures the essential you – including the age at which you are now at – for there just is no essential you in the Buddhist view. This way of thinking and speaking, on the Buddhist view, continues to reflect an attachment to self.

It can be hard not to be attached to identity, even when you know – even when you tell yourself – that there is no identity through time. With this point in mind, let us consider one more illustration (this example was introduced at the end of the previous chapter and is being continued here). Suppose I have a plant on my desk, which I started as a cutting a year ago and that has now developed into a nice leafy plant. I know that there is nothing unchanging about the plant. The plant is continuous over time, and at each moment it is causally connected to the plant it was the previous moment. I know that although I can speak of the plant as being the same – such as when I say "this plant is the same as the one I started as a cutting a year ago" – I know that there is no actual sameness or unchangingness to the plant over time. Numerical identity, I can tell myself, is a way of speaking (and it is surely simpler than saying "this plant is causally continuous with the plant I began as a cutting last year"). But it is more than *just* a simpler way of speaking. There is often attachment as well.

This can be seen when something happens to the plant. If I accidently knock the plant over, and I fret over the damage done to the plant, my fretting is likely for what I feel to be the *same* plant as that which I had nurtured over the past year. While I may explicitly believe the plant is only causally continuous, I can still be attached to *its* continuity, and thus to *its* sameness. That is, I may not explicitly believe that there is anything that has remained the same about the plant and still be attached to *its* sameness. Or more simply, I am attached to *it*. Now a plant is one thing. Our attachment to ourselves, to our sense of being the same self over time, is much greater. The sense of remaining the same self, in some essential capacity, is part of how we think and speak, of how we conceive of and feel about ourselves as well as others. The attachment to being the *same* self is consequently that much more difficult to dislodge, if it is possible at all.

Suppose the plant, in being knocked over, was unsalvageable. I see no more plant where before I saw one. The plant, for me, has come to its end. What is the difference here between saying the causal continuity has come to an end versus saying its identity has come to an end? Well, the causal continuity does not, strictly speaking, end. It changes direction perhaps, and this can be an end for our intents and purposes. I throw the plant in the garbage, or into the compost, and the lines of causal continuity that follow from this are disconnected, in my mind, from the plant that was on my desk. I have taken a certain portion of that causal continuity, and viewed it as having identity. The same applies to the self. As described earlier, to the question of whether the reborn person is the same or different, the traditional response is neither.[1] There

---

1 King Milinda asks, "He who is born, Nagasena, does he remain the same or become another?" Nagasena responds, "Neither the same nor another." *Milinda Panha* 40, p. 63.

is no sameness of self over time and this follows from the doctrine of Impermanence. But as long as there is causal continuity, there is not complete difference either. The lines of causal continuity do not end when the plant is thrown in the garbage, even if our interest in this causal continuity has ended (the plant will, for instance, decompose in the trash and there will be further causal chains that will issue from this). Similarly, it was believed that the causal continuity of the aggregates does not end with death and this is because, in the Buddhist view, it is not in the nature of causal continuity to end. That is, while we might think that the causal continuity of psychological states comes to an abrupt end with the death of the body, it was thought that these lines could also continue on and manifest in a rebirth (but to emphasize again, the Buddha held that causal continuity does not support the rebirth of a same self). Note that nirvana involves the extinguishing of craving, and attachment to permanence or sameness of self. This is not the same as an end to the causal continuity of the aggregates, but more specifically, an end to certain aggregates: cravings, and thereby an end to attachment to the aggregates. The end of craving and attachment is an end to the illusion of being the same self over time.

The beginning of the self should be regarded similarly to the end. For many, physical birth is considered the beginning of the self; for others, the beginning is conception; for some, it is the beginning of brain activity, or sentience; and for others still, the beginning is some months after physical birth when a clear sense of selfhood begins to develop. All of these views presume a beginning to a line of permanence or sameness of self. As discussed in Chapter Nine, the Buddha rejected annihilationism, which was to reject the idea that there is a permanent self – a sameness of self over time – that has an end point at death. Implied in this is a rejection of the idea that there is a permanence or sameness of self that has a beginning point. There is only causal continuity over time, and causal continuity is not initiated at birth, and neither does it end with death (causal chains do not completely end and neither do they originate from nowhere; this would introduce uncaused causes and violate universal causation). Thus, the judgement that the self begins at birth may be conventionally true, and it may be supported by reasons as well, but it is not ultimately true in the Buddhist view (and neither is any other beginning point). Rebirth in Buddhism does not involve an identity or sameness of self before this life or after this life. It is instead based on the continuity of causal chains. Whether or not we accept rebirth of the self (and whether or not there remains much to accept once it is denied that it is the same self that is reborn), it is important to appreciate the Buddhist rejection of identity in favour of causal continuity in thinking of rebirth and, more generally, in thinking of the self over time.

Coming back to the illustration of the plant: I see the causal continuity of the plant on my desk as having an identity through time: an identity that starts when the cutting is planted, and ends when the plant topples (even though lines of causal continuity precede its planting, and proceed on after its toppling). I might even give it a name, as people sometimes do for plants. We even sometimes do this for storms and weather patterns, in order to identify particular ones, even though we clearly know these are ever-changing. And fair enough. Granting and speaking of identity over periods of time has clear uses, and this is nowhere denied. Thinking and speaking in terms of the sameness of self over time, whether this is our self or other selves, is clearly useful. But as described above, these useful judgements of personal identity can have only a conventional truth. There is no permanence or sameness of self over time in the Buddhist view. When we make judgements about sameness or permanence of self over time, we overstep what can be empirically justified by observations of the ever-changing aggregates. Now these judgements have their uses. But when we do so with *attachment* – that is, when we become attached to our identity over and above mere continuity – we treat the conventional as something more than it is; we treat it as ultimately true. In the Buddhist view, it is with this attachment that suffering begins.

XII

The Concept of Dharmas in the Abhidharma

The Abhidharma, the Dharma, and Dharmas

'DHARMA', IN BUDDHIST USAGE, refers primarily to the doctrines of the Buddha. They are the truths of Buddhism, and in particular, the Four Noble Truths, and the doctrines of No Self, Impermanence and Dependent Origination. The word 'Abhidharma' means the higher teachings of the Buddha, and thus the higher truths of Buddhism also. But the Abhidharma is not quite a set of teachings; and it is not a particular school or sect within Buddhism. Rather, it is a collection of texts and literature. These texts are a canonical source for certain Buddhist schools, such as the Sarvastivada, Sautrantika, and Theravada. The collection or "basket" of these texts – the Abhidharma Pitaka, along with the Sutra Pitaka and the Vinaya Pitaka (the collection of manuals for the Buddhist monastic order), form what are called the Tripitaka. These are the "three baskets" or collections of texts comprising the early Buddhist literature of the Pali canon.[1] The Abhidharma texts are thus one of three

---

1 The Pali transliterations of these are Abhidhamma Pitaka, *(continued)*

traditional sources and collections of texts (at least, that is, for Buddhist schools for whom the Abhidharma are canonical). The Abhidharma texts are regarded as presenting a systematic treatment and analysis of the Buddha's teachings. Indeed, the Abhidharma represent a first attempt to lay down, think through, and systematize the Buddha's teachings.

Gethin describes a dual aspect to the Abhidharma: "first, a set of books regarded by most ancient schools as the 'word of the Buddha' and as such forming the contents of the third basket of scriptures, the Abhidharma Pitaka; secondly, the particular system of thought and method of exposition set out in those books and their commentaries."[1] The status of the Abhidharma as being the "word of the Buddha" has to do with the source of the Abhidharma texts: as Gethin relates, they are presumed to be the "product of the first generation of the Buddha's disciples."[2] It is this closeness to the Buddha's own thoughts, through the record of his first generation of disciples, which grants the Abhidharma texts the status of being the "word of the Buddha." The proximity in time and lineage to the Buddha himself is regarded – at least among those schools for whom the Abhidharma texts are canonical – as conferring authenticity to the Abhidharma literature, and thus to its systemization. Coming so closely on the heels of the Buddha's original teachings, and being a first attempt at thinking through and systematizing these teachings, it sets a stage and standard upon which further developments in Buddhism build, and against which they react. In this regard, the Abhidharma may be seen as providing terms for Buddhist philosophical discussion and thought, including the Mahayana philosophy to be discussed in the following chapters.[3]

The Sarvastivada, Sautrantika and Theravada are three key Buddhist schools that find a textual source in the Abhidharma literature.

Sutta Pitaka and Tipitaka. Vinaya Pitaka is transliterated the same from Pali as from Sanskrit.

1 Gethin (1998), p. 203.

2 Gethin (1998), p. 54.

3 Williams affirms just this: "The name for Buddhist philosophy as a whole, it seems to me, is 'Abhidharma', in the sense that Abhidharma sets the agenda, the presuppositions and the framework for Buddhist philosophical thought ..." Williams (2000), p. 140.

Sarvastivada is a parent school of the Sautrantika, and together with the Theravada, they are the schools of which we have some significant knowledge. In the case of Sarvastivada, this is largely by way of Chinese sources and translation.[1] There are two principal Abhidharma texts among the sources and manuals of these schools. These are the *Abhidharmakosa* or *Treasury of Abhidharma*, a summary of the teachings of Sarvastivada by Vasabandhu,[2] and the *Visuddhimagga* or *Path of Purification*, by the Theravada monk Buddhaghosa. Buddhaghosa's name means "voice of the Buddha." His *Path of Purification* is a comprehensive discourse and guide that tries to organize the Buddha's teachings and provide a systematic analysis and understanding of the path to enlightenment.

The Abhidharma represents a certain way of thinking about the reality that is the focus of the Buddha's teachings. It provides an analysis of reality as it is experienced into irreducible constituents. These constituent elements are called 'dharmas', and it is held that the basic teachings of the Buddha – the Dharma – are ultimately about the reality that is formed of these dharmas.[3] A taxonomy of the dharmas reads like a periodic table of elements. Different Abhidharma schools present varying taxonomies with different categories and numbers of dharmas. For instance, for the Sarvastivadans, the number of types of dharmas is seventy-five, and for some Theravada schools the number of dharma varieties is eighty-two.[4] The dharmas, like atoms, are held to be the building blocks of reality. But there are notable differences between dharmas and physical atoms and these will be discussed in the next section.

---

1 At one point there were said to be eighteen different schools with different interpretations of the texts. Despite the differences between them, as Siderits points out, "Most of those disputes lack any major philosophical significance." Siderits (2007), p. 116.

2 Most likely not the Vasabandhu of Yogacara Buddhism.

3 As noted earlier, there are no capital letters in Sanskrit. Nonetheless, the transliteration 'Dharma' is capitalized to signify the standing of the term, and also to distinguish more clearly from the dharmas.

4 Gethin (1998), p. 210.

Dharmas and Atoms

The Dharma is the basic doctrines and teachings of the Buddha. The Dharma is believed to describe the way things really are. The dharmas are constituents of the reality described by the Dharma, and so the Dharma may be said to be ultimately about the dharmas. The dharmas are mental and physical constituents of the "world of our experience."[1] This notion of the "world of our experience," as opposed to the world as it may exist independently of being experienced, warrants elaboration. This will be a focus of the next section, which concerns dharmas as ultimate reality. This section will begin the discussion of the nature of dharmas and will focus on similarities and differences between dharmas and physical atoms.

Gethin compares dharmas with physical atoms:

> Ultimately dharmas are all that there is. In this respect dharmas are very like atoms ... Thus just as a table might be analysed by a chemist as consisting of innumerable atoms, so a person is analysed by Abhidharma as consisting of innumerable dharmas ... just as the wood that makes up a table can be analysed into atoms of various elements, a person's mind and body can be analysed into dharmas of various classes ... dharmas are not enduring substances, they are evanescent events, here one moment and gone the next – like dewdrops at sunrise or a bubble on water, like a mirage or conjuring trick.[2]

Dharmas, says Gethin, are like atoms for both are basic building blocks. As he notes, the composition of a table may be analysed by a chemist or physicist into a number of different types of atoms. In the Abhidharma, instead of the chemist's or physicist's analysis, the composition of a person's mind and body is analysed into a number of different types of

---

1 The phrase comes from Williams (1989), p. 15. The passage in which it is contained is discussed in the next section.
2 Gethin (1998), pp. 209-10.

dharmas. A mind is composed of mental dharmas, and a body of physical dharmas. We might respond that a person's body is also made up of atoms (and a person's mind, conceived in terms of an underlying brain, is similarly made up of atoms). This again raises the question of how dharmas are different from atoms.

First, and most simply, atoms are the building blocks of physical objects, like tables and chairs and human bodies. But atoms can be broken down into further constituents, such as quantum particles, and these constituents can perhaps be broken down even further (physical atoms are not *philosophical atoms*, as this term is used). Dharmas, though, are held to be irreducible *simples* (i.e., they are philosophical atoms in the proper sense).

Second, dharmas are intrinsically connected to experience in a way that physical atoms are not. For instance, while we may say a tree is composed of atoms, it is not quite right to say that a perception of a tree – or a mental image or imagining of a tree – is composed of atoms. This is not how we would describe the parts of a perception or mental image. The neuronal brain state that underlies the mental image of the tree is comprised of molecules, which are themselves composed of atoms. But again, we do not speak of the mental image, *qua* mental image, as being composed of atoms. This is not to say the mental image is non-physical. Rather, it is to say that the description of the mental image and its parts do not involve a description of molecules or atoms. The physicist's atoms are not the constituents of our experiences of the world as we are aware of these from a first-person point of view.

The Theravada Abhidharma divides dharmas into fifty-two categories of mental constituents and twenty-eight categories of physical constituents. The physical constituents include, for example, earth, water, air, fire; and the mental constituents include, for example, compassion, greed and non-greed, volition, concentration.[1] Dharmas that are mental constituents, such as compassion, are clearly unlike physical atoms (there is no atom for compassion). But dharmas that are physical constituents are

---

1 Williams (1989), p. 15.

also unlike atoms. These dharmas constitute experienceable qualities (to use Western philosophical terminology, we could say that physical dharmas involve secondary qualities). For instance, the dharmas of earth and water speak, respectively, to the aspects of solidity and liquidity or wetness that we experience with physical objects. The experience of holding a rock in your palms is different from that of cupping water, and this difference in quality (or qualia, to use another Western philosophical term) is accounted for in terms of a difference in dharmas. The former involves more earth dharmas for these are thought to confer the quality of solidity, and the latter more water dharmas. A difference in type, number and order of dharmas constitutes the difference in perceptible qualities of the rock versus the water.

Let us consider the example of the tree once again. A tree is composed of physical atoms (the atoms compose molecules which form chemical bonds which make up the material of the tree). But the experience of a tree involves perceptions, and these perceptions, in the appropriate sense, are not composed of atoms. Once again, this is not to deny that the brain event that underlies a perception of a tree is composed of atoms. However, the perception of the tree itself – the aggregate that is encountered in our mind's eye – is observed in terms of the specific perceptible qualities that combine to make up the perception, and these are held to be dharmas. Different dharmas come together to form the tree as it is perceived. For instance, the visual perception of a tree involves an experience of greenness (assuming the tree has green leaves), an experience of brownness (assuming the bark is brown), and these are experienced as being arrayed in a specific way. These different colour and shape components are said to involve different dharmas (in this example, the dharmas are somewhat like coloured pixels forming an image;[1] this analogy should not be taken too far though, in particular as visual perception is but one aspect of our experience of the world). A perception, such as

---

1 C.f. Gethin: "… rather like the way in which a colour photograph in a printed book is seen as an unbroken whole when it is in fact made up of countless tiny dots of just four colours, so consciousness is made up of separate dharmas." Gethin (1998), p. 211.

of a tree, involves dharmas of different sorts to account for the different perceptible qualities we encounter (solidity, texture, colour, shape,
smell, etc.). Experiences such as fears, desires, loves, hates, etc., are said
to be composed of mental dharmas of different types.

The difference between mental and physical dharmas does not mark
a fundamental ontological division in the world, but rather a broad division between kinds of experience (by and large between internal and
external experiences). Physical dharmas such as earth and fire, which
speak to the qualities of solidity and heat, make up external experiences.[1]
Mental dharmas such as compassion and greed make up internal experiences. The totality of these kinds of dharmas, arrayed into different
forms, constitutes the world in which our lives unfold. Dharmas do not
constitute the world as it may exist independently of our experience of it
(as we think physical atoms do). Dharmas pertain to categories and kinds
of human experience in a way that physical atoms do not. This intrinsic
connection to experience is the second disanalogy with physical atoms.

To put it another way, the Dharma, being the teachings and truths
of the Buddha, is supposed to describe the way things really are. But
the teachings and truths of the Buddha are aimed at the human condition and overcoming suffering in the human condition. They are not
scientific doctrines that aim to describe the world at large, in terms that
are independent of how it is experienced by humans. Physical atoms
constitute this world, and this is described by physicists. Dharmas constitute the world of human experience, both of the inner mind and the
outer world. It is within experience that suffering arises and the idea is
that a systematic account of this world of experience – of the specific
constituents of human experience – will allow for a close understanding
of the sources of suffering and of the human condition in general. The

---

1 Just as seeing a red apple involves physical dharmas, so should imagining a
red apple in my mind's eye; the sensations, after all, may be the same. But
the latter, it would seem, is not an external experience. This means that the
broad correspondence between mental and physical dharmas and, respectively, internal and external experiences is not without exception. Mind
sensations and perceptions seem to be internal experiences that involve
physical dharmas.

Buddha's doctrines and teachings – his Dharma – is based on a careful observation of the human condition. The dharmas are held to be the minute constituents of what he observed. They are, in other words, the constituents of the aggregates.[1] The notion of the totality of dharmas constituting the world of our experiences will be further discussed the next section.

Continuing on to the third disanalogy, Gethin states in the above passage that dharmas are not enduring entities but rather are "evanescent." Mark Siderits uses the word 'occurrences'; he states: "… an earth atom dharma is not a tiny solid particle. It is just a particular occurrence of solidity. Likewise a fire atom is not a hot thing, it is just a particular occurrence of heat."[2] What is meant in saying dharmas are evanescent, or occurrences, is that dharmas are events and not enduring objects. That is, dharmas are not microscopic things. They are transient events. This is a third point of disanalogy with physical atoms.[3] However, dharmas are unlike other events. For instance, they are not like sunsets or changes in weather. These events are quite complex and involve parts changing over time. Dharmas are irreducible simples, not complex events, and thus cannot have changing parts. This means that the kind of change dharmas undergo cannot involve having changing parts. Instead, the kind of change dharmas undergo is the movement from one dharma to another. This is the arising and passing of dharmas. And this, of course,

---

1 Insofar as the first aggregate, bodily processes, is read to refer to the physical processes themselves, then the dharmas that compose these would be more like physical atoms (and this would introduce an ontological division between these dharmas and the dharmas that constitute other aggregates). But insofar as the first aggregate is read to refer to our experiences of physical processes – i.e., the perceptible qualities of our bodily states and processes – then the dharmas that compose these would be like the dharmas that compose the other aggregates and unlike physical atoms. This is a further reason for reading the first aggregate in a manner similar to the other aggregates (i.e., as referring to our awareness of bodily states rather than to the physical states themselves).

2 Siderits (2007), p. 113.

3 This may not be a disanalogy with subatomic particles which can be construed as waves or units of change.

is to say dharmas are subject to Impermanence as described in Chapter Nine.

The first disanalogy with physical atoms, noted above, was that dharmas could not have parts; they were irreducible simples. The third disanalogy is that dharmas are events, not objects. These two points together raise a conceptual challenge, for a simple event is more difficult to conceive than a simple object. A simple object is one that cannot be broken down any further; it is fundamental in this sense. It is impartite. But conceiving of a simple event is more problematic. Any event, no matter how brief, must transpire over a period of time; it must take time to occur. Hence, any event, it would seem, must be able to be further subdivided into smaller temporal parts. Any event must have a duration, and any positive duration can be further parsed. A duration must have a beginning, middle, and end, and this should be a way to further distinguish and divide an event. Simple events raise a greater challenge to our abilities to conceive than do simple objects. This is a comment on the apparent ontology of events as opposed to objects. This issue will be discussed in the last section, which concerns the duration of dharmas.

Dharmas as Ultimate Reality

According to the Abhidharma, the world we experience is composed ultimately of dharmas and nothing else; they are the building blocks of this world. This is to say that dharmas have *svabhava*. This term is variously translated as self-being, own-being, substance, and essence. 'Own-being' is a closely literal translation and we will stick mainly with this translation. Dharmas have own-being because they are irreducible simples of which everything else in the world we experience is constructed. That is, dharmas have own-being because they are basic constituents; they do not depend on composing parts, and in this sense, dharmas exist independently.

In contrast, everything constructed of dharmas does not have own-being and exists only dependently. Williams elaborates:

The concept of self-existence or essence (svabhava) was a development of Abhidharma scholars, where it seems to indicate the defining characteristic of a dharma ... In the Abhidharma only dharmas, ultimate existences, have essences. Conventional existents – tables, chairs, and persons – do not. This is because they are simply mental constructs out of dharmas – they therefore lack their own specific and unique existence.[1]

We might respond to this by saying that dharmas too are dependent: they are dependent on physical atoms and particles. For instance, there would be no perceptible quality of yellow without photons reflecting off of surfaces at specific wavelengths. This means that there would be no dharma of yellow, or yellowness, without these reflecting photons. Or, there would be no dharma of fire, or heat, if there were not molecules moving within spaces. Using Western philosophical terminology, this would be to say that secondary qualities, such as yellowness and heat, are dependent upon primary qualities, which include fundamental particles and their properties. Likewise, we might say that there would be no dharma of compassion if there were not specific neurophysiological goings-on in the brain. This line of response contends that dharmas are dependent upon physical atoms (or to use another Western philosophical term, dharmas are supervenient upon physical atoms and their properties). This dependence on atoms would suggest that dharmas do not exist with own-being, or as ultimate existences. Clearly, the Abhidharma would resist this. It is worth elaborating on why this would be.

The Abhidharma analysis that yields dharmas rigorously applies the Buddha's empiricist method. The idea is that close observation uncovers dharmas, not atoms. When we encounter the world around us, our experience is of colours, shapes, smells, tastes, textures, etc. These are all perceptible qualities that, according to the Abhidharma, involve specific dharmas. Likewise, when I look inwardly into the contents of my mind – although this is a metaphorical looking it is nonetheless

---

1 Williams (1989), p. 60.

an experiencing of my mind – I encounter not atoms but feelings and desires, memories and thoughts, and other mental events. Even if I peer into an electron microscope and see an atom or its effects close up, I still only encounter various perceptible qualities (shapes, sizes, colours, etc.), and these perceptible qualities, according to the Abhidharma, are composed of dharmas. The belief that there must be something behind the dharmas – such as physical atoms – that account for the perceptible qualities of dharmas is based on inference, not direct observation. What is directly observed or experienced are only perceptible qualities, that is, dharmas. Our experiences of the world – such as of a tree – are complex. Many different perceptible qualities come together to form the experience. Dharmas are the finest or smallest units of what we experience. They are the simples of which complex experiences are formed. And the different categories of dharmas are the different kinds of ingredients that join together in myriad ways to form our manifold experiences.

It is worth drawing a brief comparison with the history of British Empiricism (once again), for the thinking is, to an extent, similar.[1] According to the empiricist George Berkeley, there is no justifiable distinction to be made between a perceptible quality (such as yellow) and an external reality behind the perceptible quality (the thing that is yellow). Berkeley, being an empiricist, asserted that all we experience are perceptible qualities and not an external world behind the perceptible qualities. He concluded, on the basis of this empiricism, that there was no external world independent of perceptible qualities. This is akin to saying only dharmas exist, and no physical atoms apart from dharmas, because all that direct observation justifies are dharmas. However, Berkeley inferred that immaterial minds also exist, because perceptible qualities require minds to perceive them. And so he concluded that, while an external mind-independent world cannot be justified, immaterial minds can. This position, according to which only minds and their contents exist, is called 'metaphysical idealism'. But this conclusion is not justified by observation: no minds independent of perceptible qualities are

---

1 In Chapter Four, the methodologies of the Buddha and David Hume were discussed and compared.

observed. Only the perceptible qualities are observed. Berkeley inferred the existence of minds, thinking that they are necessary for there to be perceived qualities, but does not directly observe them. This point was made by David Hume (who applied the empiricist method more fully and consistently than Berkeley, and whose empiricism did not lead him to metaphysical idealism). The view that only perceptible qualities exist (i.e., that all objects – mental and physical – are no more than collections of perceptions) has commonly been attributed to Hume.[1] For instance, Roderick Chisholm contends that for Hume a peach would be no more than its perceptible qualities: fuzziness, roundness, firmness, etc.; this is conceptually on par with speaking only of dharmas.[2]

At any rate, we can see why a consistently employed empiricism could lead to the view that all that ultimately exists are dharmas. And we can see why these dharmas are asserted to exist independently, or with own-being, since there is nothing else observed upon which they depend. And everything which is constructed of dharmas is, as a consequence, not ultimately real. Instead, it is said to be only conventionally real, or dependently real. Thus, tables and chairs are only conventionally real. Likewise with persons or selves: the composite self, composed of the ever-changing aggregates, is only conventionally real.

Consider this passage from Williams, introducing this distinction between ultimate and conventional, or between what is true and real and what only appears to be so:

> All Buddhist traditions accepted an analysis of the human being into the five psycho-physical constituents. As we have seen, there

---

1 This view of Hume was held by Thomas Reid. Wade L. Robinson states: "Thomas Reid took Hume to be at the tail end of a chain of diminishing ontological commitments. Locke claimed that all knowledge has its sources in ideas and yet committed himself to the existence of material and immaterial objects as well as God. Berkeley pointed out the inconsistency of being empiricist in such a way and yet holding that material objects exist. Hume is read as going the further step of deleting immaterial objects and God as well.... Reid's reading of Hume was a common one in his day and has remained common." Robinson (1976), p. 39.

2 Chisholm (1969), p. 8.

is no independent being, he or she is really made up out of an ever-changing series of physical matter, sensations, conceptions, volitions and so on, and consciousness. Implicit in this very old analysis, therefore, is a distinction between what appears to be true and what is really the case. Eventually, in the Abhidharma traditions, this issues in a distinction between conventional and ultimate truth (or reality). The conventional reality is the world in which we live. Ultimate realities are the elements which really compose the world of our experience ...[1]

For Williams, the distinction between ultimate and conventional truth (or reality) is a distinction between reality and appearance. Williams further notes, and carefully so, that the dharmas, or "ultimate realities," constitute the "world of our experience." He also notes that what is conventionally true does not compose the "world of our experience"; rather, "conventional reality is the world in which we live." The "world of our experience" is thus distinguished from the "world in which we live." Also, given that what is conventionally real is only apparently real, it follows that the "world in which we live" is an appearance. These points will be elaborated.

It was earlier pointed out that the Buddha was not a metaphysician or scientist out to describe the universe at large. He was, rather, a careful observer of himself and the human condition. Through careful observation he was led to judgements about what is true and what is untrue, or between what is true and what only appears to be true, in human experience. The aggregates are what he observed, and they are supposed to encompass all our experiences. They include external experiences such as sensations and perceptions of the external world (in the Abhidharma systems, these are composed of physical dharmas), and internal experiences such as desires, hopes, feelings, willings, and much more (and these are held to be composed of mental dharmas). The distinction between ultimate truth and conventional truth, or between what is real versus

---

1 Williams (1989), pp. 14-15.

what only appears to be real, may be thought to be a distinction between the way the physical world really is and the way it is experienced. But this is not the way it is applied in the Abhidharma. Rather, the distinction applies to the "world of our experience," for experience itself is real and, if we pay close attention, is something in which we can discern truths from apparent truths. The world of our experience is ultimately composed of dharmas according to the Abhidharma.

The Buddha observed and judged that there is no permanent self among the aggregates. This is a truth about the world of our experiences. There only appears to be a permanent self – not in the sense that we can observe or see one, but because we, or at least the unenlightened among us, are attached to one and may firmly believe in one. This is an aspect of the world in which we live, and is only apparently or conventionally real. Just as appearances can mislead the incautious scientist about the world he observes, they can mislead the incautious observer about himself. Without careful observation, the conventional may be taken for ultimate, and what only appears real, such as the self, may be taken for real.

The Abhidharma's concern with the "world of our experience" is also the Buddha's concern. Consider, for instance, the doctrine of Impermanence. The Buddha's empiricist methodology would not support a metaphysically substantive claim such as that there is no permanence anywhere in the universe. As described in Chapter Nine, such a claim not only goes beyond what the Buddha could have observed, but would have been contrary to much of what he actually would have observed (a rock, for instance, would appear to not undergo change for long stretches, let alone appear to undergo constant change). It was not in his expertise, or interest, to make judgements about the nature of the physical universe independent of human experience. The Buddha was not a physicist, or a speculative metaphysician, and he was not trying to be or interested in being one. He was, though, a careful observer of his own condition and of the human condition in general. And it was within his expertise as a careful observer of himself to judge that there is no permanence in experience, or among the contents of his mind's awareness.

It may be thought that, as long as experiences are veridical, to describe our experiences is also to describe the mind-independent world or the world as it exists independently of being experienced. But this is to miss the focus and agenda of the Dharma. The Dharma – in particular, the Noble Truths and the basic doctrines including No Self, Impermanence and Dependent Origination – are directed at overcoming the experience of suffering. The focus of the Dharma is on describing the nature of human experience and what is necessary for overcoming suffering in that experience. And as human experience is the focus of the Dharma, it is also the focus of the dharmas: they are the constituents of human experience, and as a totality, constitute the world of human experience. The "world of our experience" includes experiences of tables and chairs, trees and buildings, as well as desires and fears, thoughts and memories, and much else. This totality of experiences is the world in which we live (our desires are real to us just as trees are real to us, and both are aspects of our experiences and lives). The Buddha considered his experiences closely and grouped them into aggregates. The Abhidharma analysis can be seen as an extension of the Buddha's empirical analysis, for each aggregate can be observed to be complex. The aggregates can be seen to have parts when looked at closely and these parts can be seen to fall under different types. These ultimate parts are the dharmas, and in the Abhidharma view, they are what are ultimately real in the "world of our experience."

Dharmas and Mindfulness

There is an important connection between the observation of dharmas and mindfulness. Gethin points this out:

> Essentially Abhidharma is a device for promoting mindfulness and understanding. The study of Abhidharma encourages the practitioner to pay attention to the kinds of mental states that are occurring whatever he or she is doing. It also draws the practitioner's attention

to the way in which the spiritual process is understood to unfold. To this extent it can be seen as simply the elaboration of the analysis of the five aggregates and the twelvefold chain of dependent arising.[1]

The observation of dharmas involves looking very closely at experiences – internal and external – for in observing dharmas we are observing the smallest units or constituents of our experiences. An observation of dharmas allows for a more careful view of causal interconnections because it involves observing the causal inter-workings of the component parts of experiences, rather than just causal connections between whole experiences, or complex experiences. That is, part of paying very close attention to the causes of experiences is paying attention to the constituents of experiences – the smallest units – and how these come together to form the experiences we undergo. With the systematizing of dharmas, dharmas that are causes can be understood to be causes of certain types. This means that types of causes can be linked to types of effects, and the causes that lead to suffering can be identified by their type. Noticing the relations between types of events is necessary for making predictions that certain kinds of effects will follow from certain kinds of causes. A mindful exercise of Dependent Origination requires not just carefully noticing events and their causes but types of events, and the causal relationships between types of events. In this way the Abhidharma analyses which group dharmas into types and classes helps to put into practice Dependent Origination, and to overcome suffering by identifying which causes to eliminate.

An observation of dharmas is part of a refined and discerning mindfulness. This is because in being mindful of dharmas, an adept is observant of the smallest and briefest units of experience; attentive to the quick succession between arising and passing, and of the encroachment of attachment to self within this quick succession; and aware of causal relations between experiences – internal and external – at a fine-grained

---

1 Gethin (1998), p. 217.

level of inspection. Mindfulness of dharmas should seem to be a very close and keen mindfulness. The proper taxonomy of the dharmas is open to question, and is viewed a little differently by different schools associated with the Abhidharma. Nonetheless, the principle is still supposed to stand that a mindful awareness of experiences – of the arising and passing of aggregates from the mind's attention – will be all the more attentive for paying mind to the dharmas, the constituents of the aggregates, for these are the minutiae of experiences.

For dharmas to play this role in the exercise of mindfulness, they must be observable. This condition of being observable places conditions on the duration of dharmas and this will be considered next.

What Is the Duration of a Dharma?

Dharmas are subject to the doctrine of Impermanence, which is to say that they arise and pass from the mind's attention. These dharmas may compose external experiences (such as sensations and perceptions of the external world) or internal experiences (such as desires and fears). Either way, the succession of aggregates in the mind's attention, and thus the succession of the dharmas which constitute these aggregates, is often very quick, dashing from one to the other, and often seamless. This movement of aggregates and the dharmas that compose them is portrayed with the analogy of monkeys swinging along from branch to branch. The analogy conveys that there is a continual succession of dharmas, and that the mind is really only focussed upon one aggregate of dharmas at a time (although the very quick succession may make it seem like more).[1]

---

1 Gethin elaborates: "The arising and passing of each moment of consciousness is understood to occur extremely rapidly ... consciousness is experienced as a continuous flow, but is in fact made up of the rapidly occurring sequence of consciousness moments, each with a particular object. We may think that we are thinking of two or three things at once, but according to the Abhidharmikas we are just very rapidly turning from one thing to another and back again." Gethin (1998), pp. 211-12.

Dharmas are brief, fleeting events, not small enduring things. As noted earlier, this raises a conceptual difficulty: it seems that dharmas, while they may be very brief or evanescent, must have some positive duration; and any duration can be conceived of as having temporal parts – a beginning, middle, and end. While we may not be able to perceive events with very brief durations (such as a nanosecond), any finite duration can, in principle, be further subdivided. No duration is impartite. And this suggests that dharmas with durations cannot be simples.

To avoid this result we may be pressed to admit that dharmas have no duration. But this cannot be. If a dharma has no duration, it cannot be an event (for an event that lasts for no time is no event at all). And just as zero plus zero is zero, an aggregate of dharmas that have no duration would also have no duration, and thus dharmas could not come together to form an aggregate. One might reply that this sort of aggregation does make sense. After all, a line with non-zero length is, by analogy, thought of as being composed of zero-length points. But of course, geometrical points are theoretical constructs, not objects we can perceive. Likewise zero-duration dharmas would be imperceptible theoretical objects, contrary to the clear Buddhist empiricism about them. So we ask: do dharmas have a duration, and if so, what is it? As we will see, there is no clear answer. This section will pursue this enquiry by considering and assessing four possible, exhaustive answers. After this, the views of specific Abhidharma schools will be briefly considered and situated among these possible answers.

The four exhaustive answers are: (i) dharmas have no duration; (ii) they have a duration but it is too brief to be noticed; (iii) dharmas have a duration, and this can be noticed, but no parts to the dharma can be further noticed (i.e., this duration is too brief for us to experience anything more than the dharma's occurrence); and (iv) dharmas have a duration which lasts long enough for us to notice parts.

The first answer is that dharmas are events with no duration. We already noted why this cannot be correct. If there is no duration, then there is no event. There cannot be any arising or passing if there is literally no time for something to arise, to pass, or to persist between arising and passing. Dharmas without duration could not be aggregated into anything that can be observed or experienced (for as noted above, zero plus zero is still zero). Since dharmas are supposed to constitute our experiences, and since they are supposed to be observable in an exercise of mindfulness, they must have some positive duration.

The second answer is that dharmas have a positive duration, but this duration is so brief that it escapes human perception. Such dharmas could be aggregated together to form events of noticeable durations (just as a table is composed of particles that are too small to be seen, but when aggregated, the table can be seen). But if a dharma is too brief to be noticed, like an elementary particle is too small to be seen, then such a dharma cannot be noticed in the exercise of mindfulness. These are dharmas that we would not observe to individually arise, or pass, and we would not observe causal connections between them. But the observation of dharmas is an important part of the exercise of mindfulness. Williams makes this point:

A monk developing the insight meditation, wishing to see things the way they really are, develops the ability constantly to analyse his experiences into their constituents. He is said to dwell peacefully, observing the rising and falling of dharmas, thereby dissolving the objects of his attachment and cutting at the root of desire. Thus by learning to see things the way they really are he brings his ignorance to an end.[1]

The observation of dharmas is supposed to be an important part of mindfulness and meditation, and this conveys that dharmas should be able to be observed (and not just observed when they are aggregated together to form complex experiences). In addition, we may note that if dharmas escape observation, then they cannot even be judged to exist based on observation (and this is contrary to the Buddha's empiricist methodology). So far it seems that dharmas must have a duration and this duration must not be so brief or quick so as to escape notice.

---

1 Williams (1989), p. 15.

On the third answer, the duration of a dharma is neither too brief for the dharma to go unnoticed nor long enough for temporal parts to be noticed. This is a duration in which dharmas are observed as simple events and not as complex events. Since these dharmas are observable, they can be the objects of a mindful awareness. These dharmas can then be aggregated to form complex events or experiences of a longer duration. As noted above, any duration, no matter how brief, can be further subdivided. However, at some point, when the duration of an event is too brief, the event cannot be humanly registered. The duration of a dharma on this third answer is the briefest observable duration (we might say it is an experiential simple). This view also faces difficulty, but this is more complicated and will be picked up a little further below.

The fourth answer is that dharmas have finite durations that can be noticed, and these durations are long enough to notice parts. However, under this possibility, dharmas are complex events, not simple events. Thus, this fourth answer is not admissible.

These four answers present exhaustive possibilities. Either a dharma has (i) no duration; or (ii) a duration that is so brief that it can't be noticed; or (iii) a duration that can be noticed but no parts to the dharma can be noticed; or (iv) a duration that can be noticed but is long enough to notice parts to the dharma as well. Let's sum up the assessments so far. The first answer admits no duration, but this means that there is no event, and no opportunity for a mindful awareness of the dharma. The fourth answer treats dharmas as complex events, rather than as simple events. Complex events would be composed of further constituents, and so these are not dharmas. The second answer holds that dharmas have positive durations, but these are too brief to be humanly perceived (these dharmas would only be noticeable in aggregated form, as complex experiences and not as the irreducible simples that they are). Such dharmas cannot be the objects of a mindful awareness and the observation of them cannot be a part of overcoming suffering. Also, the existence of dharmas on this view cannot be justified by observation (and as noted, this is at odds with the Buddha's empiricist methodology). This leaves answer three. The third answer asserts that dharmas have a duration that is long enough to be observed, but not long enough to notice parts. Like Goldilocks after trying other not-quite-right bowls of porridge, this one seems just right. The duration of a dharma on this answer is the briefest humanly noticeable duration. Like a flash, we might say it lasts for a moment's notice.

However, there are difficulties with the notion of a briefest noticeable duration. The duration of a dharma under this third answer must be long enough to be noticed, but not long enough to notice parts to the dharma. But these limits are open to variation. Different creatures, with different sense organs and different cognitive capacities, may be able to notice events of very brief durations that humans cannot, while others may not notice events that humans can. Such differences also exist amongst human beings, of course, due to age, ability, training, or just circumstances of alertness at any given time. That is, at some times, some of us may be able to notice events of a very brief duration while at other times, we may not. The duration of a dharma on this view is circumscribed between upper and lower limits that are variable and physiologically and circumstantially dependent. If we were to opt for a lowest common denominator – a duration that is at least noticeable by all humans regardless of how alert they are – then this duration would be long enough for many alert humans to notice parts to the dharma and so for them it would be complex and not simple (i.e., it would fall under answer three for some people and answer four for most others). Alternatively, if we were to opt for the briefest duration that is humanly noticeable, then it would be too brief for many humans to notice at all (i.e., it would fall under answer three for the most alert of individuals, and answer two for the rest of us). The point that should be coming across is that it is exceedingly difficult, and seemingly impossible, to specify the duration of a dharma under the conditions of answer three that would apply to all individuals at all times.

Perhaps then we should just say that dharmas have no fixed duration while still being simples. That is, the duration of a dharma is just what a given person, at a given time, is mindfully able to be aware of as a simple event. This would mean that durations of dharmas could vary across times, situations, and people in which case there is no common answer to the duration of a dharma. A difficulty with this is that dharmas are supposed to be the *independent* constituents of our experiences. They are supposed to have *svabhava*. But on this answer, the duration of a dharma is dependent on, and can vary with, physiology, age, and other circumstances affecting attentiveness at any given time. Dharmas are events, and so having a duration is an *intrinsic* aspect of what a dharma is (just as having size is an intrinsic aspect of being a physical object; note that under answer one dharmas have no duration, but as described, they cannot then be events). However, on this third answer, the duration of a dharma is dependent on a variety of factors that can affect attentiveness and mindfulness. This means that dharmas are rendered as dependent rather than independent events. This is not in keeping with the independent existence or own-being that dharmas are supposed to have. Perhaps this answer is the most appealing, but it is certainly not without its difficulties.

At any rate, no clearly correct answer on the duration of a dharma is in the offing. It is notable that Buddhist schools associated with the Abhidharma canon did not reach a clear consensus on the duration of a dharma. To finish off this chapter we will briefly consider the positions of two of these schools on the duration of dharmas. Gethin, drawing on textual sources for both the Sarvastivada and the Sautrantika, states:

> There is no Sarvastivadin consensus on the length of a moment but figures given in the texts work out at between 0.13 and 13 milliseconds. Yet, object the Sautrantikas, if something endures unchanged for even a moment, then the fundamental Buddhist principle of impermanence is compromised. If things are truly impermanent, then they must be changing continuously and cannot remain static for any period of time, however short. This kind of thinking led to the conception of moments as point instants of time which, just as geometric points have no extension in space, have no duration in time.[1]

---

1 Gethin (1998), pp. 221-22.

The above passage states that, for the Sarvastivadins, the duration of a dharma is between 0.13 and 13 milliseconds. The shorter duration is too brief to be humanly recognized, and so it fits under answer two considered above. The upper figure is less clear. On the one hand, a normal motion picture film involves 24 frames per second, that is, about 42 milliseconds for each frame; but we do not perceive individual frames. A motion picture involving 12 frames a second (each frame lasting 83 milliseconds) has barely noticeable individual frames. On the other hand, an image on a cathode-ray tube (the older type of computer and TV screen), which is adjusted to have dark intervals of 16 milliseconds between screen renewals, has a noticeable flicker. A dharma duration of 16 milliseconds may thus fall under answers two or three (and perhaps even four for the most alert of individuals). Presumably the same holds for an event lasting 13 milliseconds (as the durations are quite proximate): in some cases it may arise and pass without being noticed; in other cases, it may be noticed but no parts to the event are noticed; and perhaps in other cases, under very alert conditions, it may be noticed and parts also noticed (such as a beginning distinct from an end). Thus, a dharma duration of 13 milliseconds seems as if it may fall under answers two, three and perhaps even four depending on conditions of alertness and other circumstances while a duration of 0.13 milliseconds would fall under answer two. In short, the point can be reasonably made that the Sarvastivadan band of 0.13 to 13 milliseconds runs the range of answers two to four, and provides us with no clear understanding of the duration of a dharma.

In contrast, the Sautrantika position described by Gethin clearly falls under answer one above. As explained, the difficulty with this option is that if dharmas are mere "point instants" with no "duration in time," then they cannot be observed. It does not even allow for observable aggregates to be formed from dharmas (for again, zero plus zero is still zero). The reason presented in the above passage for the Sautrantika position is that any duration seems to violate the doctrine of Impermanence. This view is worth elaborating. Dharmas are simples. They cannot have parts. This means that dharmas cannot undergo any change that involves a change in parts (dharmas, of course, may change by succeeding each other, by arising and passing, but this is a change from one dharma to another and not a change within a dharma). It follows from this that if dharmas have a duration, this must be duration of time during which there is no change (for there are no parts to change). This duration of time (between the arising and passing of a dharma) would be a duration in which there is permanence. And thus, in the Sautrantika view, a dharma with a duration is thought to violate the doctrine of Impermanence. In Chapter Nine, it was described that there must be a duration of time between the arising and passing of the aggregates for otherwise the aggregates would not be noticeable. They could not be objects of mindful attention if they did not persist for even a very brief time. Indeed, if there was no duration between the arising and passing of an aggregate, there would be no aggregate (for any event requires some duration during which it occurs). This implies that dharmas, and the aggregates they compose, must persist for some positive duration. This is certainly what we observe when we pay attention to the contents of our minds: mental states – be these desires or fears, perceptions or memories – enter into our awareness, persist for a time, and then pass. Sometimes they persist very briefly and sometimes longer. The empirical evidence of observation conveys that aggregates have some finite duration (even though this duration is unfixed). Since the dharmas are supposed to come together to form the aggregates, and to be observable in themselves, dharmas must have some finite duration as well.

Coming to an understanding of what this duration is runs into considerable difficulties, as we have seen. This may be why there is no clear consensus on this issue. One approach to dealing with these difficulties is simply to say that there are no dharmas, for then there is no problem in accounting for the duration of dharmas. The idea here is that dharmas should not be ontologized as existing independently or ultimately. This sort of view is advocated in the original literature of Mahayana Buddhism – the *Perfection of Wisdom* sutras – wherein it is asserted that dharmas are "empty." Specifically, the dharmas are held to be empty of *svabhava* or own-being and this is contrary to what the Abhidharma affirm of the dharmas. This will be discussed in the next chapter.

XIII

The Concept of Emptiness in Mahayana Buddhism

Introduction to Mahayana Buddhism

MAHAYANA BUDDHISM IS A movement that begins centuries after the Buddha's death, as early as the first century BCE in India. Its origination involves the appearance of specifically Mahayana sutras or scriptures. In addition to the *tripitaka* (the 'three baskets' of early Buddhist literature that include the sutras – *Sutra Pitaka*, the monastic rules – *Vinaya Pitaka*, and the 'higher' *Dharma* – *Abhidharma Pitaka*, discussed in the previous chapter), texts began to appear that were not part of the early textual tradition. These texts were held, within Mahayana Buddhism, to be the true meaning and word of the Buddha, which was revealed only to more advanced disciples. These sutras thus claim legitimacy and importance, and due to their being revealed to only more advanced disciples, they are also held to be more difficult and privileged.[1] These sutras include the

---

1 The idea that the Buddha spoke differently, or taught differently, based on the level of spiritual understanding of the audience is itself an (*continued*)

219

Astasahasrika sutra, or the 8000 line sutra, which is thought to be the earliest of this literature, the *Heart* and *Diamond* sutras which are considerably shorter and more widely read and renowned, as well as several others.[1] Particularly significant in the East Asian Buddhist tradition is the *Lotus* sutra. It is held that these scriptures describe a superior awakening based on the example of the Buddha and his enlightenment.

The Four Noble Truths constitute the Buddha's first preaching upon enlightenment, and they assert a diagnosis of suffering and a prescription for its eradication. The Noble Truths state that freedom from suffering can be achieved by following the Noble Eightfold Path. It is presumed here that one can reach enlightenment as a goal pursued for oneself. This is not to say that enlightenment can be successfully achieved while selfishly pursued (for selfishness conflicts with steps on the Noble Eightfold Path). Rather, the point is that one may pursue the end of suffering as an individual goal. The Buddha may have spent the greater part of his life helping others overcome suffering, but the Noble Eightfold Path does not state that a Buddhist adherent must do the same. A commitment to helping others, let alone a commitment to helping others to an extent similar to the Buddha's, is not a stated requirement.

It is not that the Noble Eightfold Path or the Noble Truths are incorrect in the Mahayana view. However, the Mahayana path does require more, if not to reach enlightenment, then to reach the sort of enlightenment of the Buddha. To reach *this* enlightenment, it is claimed, not only must the Buddha's teachings be followed, but his compassionate example as well. Early Mahayana teachings and scriptures look beyond the explicit terms of the Noble Truths and Noble Eightfold Path to the life of the Buddha, and note that while the Buddha attained enlightenment as an individual, he was committed to ending the suffering of everyone. The Buddha's example, it was thought, conveys a message not

important element of Mahayana Buddhism called 'Skillful Means'. This will be described in the next chapter.

1 C.f., Edward Conze: "the Diamond Sutra and Heart Sutra are in a class by themselves and deservedly renowned throughout the world of Northern Buddhism." Conze (1973), p. 9.

fully captured in the early writings and scriptures. The Buddha's example conveys a commitment to helping others overcome suffering, and this compassionate commitment is an essential aspect of the Mahayana path to enlightenment.

A distinction is made between degrees of enlightenment. Someone who pursues individual freedom from suffering, rather than helping others and trying to achieve a collective freedom from suffering, is said to be only able to reach a lesser enlightenment. Someone who achieves this personal enlightenment is called an Arhat. But those who follow the Noble Truths, the Noble Eightfold Path, *and* the compassionate example of the Buddha by selflessly helping others to overcome suffering are said to be able to achieve an enlightenment similar to the Buddha's own. A being who commits to a life of helping others, to the extent of putting the alleviation of their suffering above his or her own, is on a path towards becoming a Bodhisattva. The term 'Bodhisattva' literally means 'enlightened being'. The path of the Bodhisattva aims for the benefit of all, and not just the individual, and this is considered within Mahayana Buddhism to be a nobler ideal, one that is true to the path of the Buddha himself. The Bodhisattva is held in higher esteem than the Arhat, and to have achieved a greater enlightenment.

Mahayana Buddhism spread as Mahayana monks and practitioners travelled. These travels led primarily northwards and eastwards. Mahayana Buddhism is the dominant form of Buddhism presently found north of India – in Nepal and Tibet, and in East Asia – China, Korea, and Japan. The varieties or forms of Buddhism associated with the Theravada tradition spread mainly in a southerly and easterly direction from India, and are the dominant forms of Buddhism found today in Sri Lanka, Burma, Thailand, and Laos (both Theravada and Mahayana are commonly practiced in Cambodia and Vietnam). 'Theravada' literally means the 'teachings of the Elders [*Thera*]', and finds its sources in the older texts of the Pali canon. Speaking quite generally, Mahayana Buddhism admits a greater possibility for lay people to achieve enlightenment than does Theravada Buddhism and non-Mahayana traditions (wherein the possibility of enlightenment is largely limited to those who have pursued a monastic life or who have "gone forth" from society). Also, there is often a close relationship between laity and monks in communities practicing Mahayana Buddhism. This should be expected given the emphasis and expectation of Mahayana monks and adepts to be compassionate and help others overcome suffering.

The Mahayana commitment to helping others is expressed in the very name 'Mahayana', which means great or greater vehicle. 'Yana' means vehicle or vessel, and 'Maha' indicates greatness.[1] Mahayana Buddhism is so called for its concern that all should be delivered from suffering (in a great vehicle) rather than a concern for individual freedom from suffering. This latter ideal is associated with what is called 'Hinayana' (lesser vehicle), and traditional schools of Buddhism that advocated Arhatship were grouped under this title. This would include schools associated with the Abhidharma canon such as Sarvastivada, Sautrantika and Theravada. The title 'Hinayana' has a pejorative connotation (because it suggests a less compassionate and perhaps selfish interest in enlightenment), and non-Mahayana schools did not use this term to describe themselves. Still, the contrast between the terms 'Hinayana' and 'Mahayana' does illustrate how Mahayana Buddhism saw itself: as a "greater vehicle," emphasizing compassionate service on the path to enlightenment.

Besides compassion, the other principal differentiating feature of Mahayana Buddhism is the emphasis placed on the "perfection of wisdom." The key to a "perfect wisdom" in Mahayana Buddhism involves realizing what is called 'emptiness' (sunyata). The Bodhisattva, it is said, sees the world as empty. He or she realizes that all things, including objects, selves, aggregates and dharmas, are empty. Even the very truth of emptiness is asserted to be empty. This chapter focuses on the concept of emptiness; the next chapter focuses on the figure of the Bodhisattva, the role of compassion, and the idea and employment of what are called 'Skillful Means' in Mahayana Buddhism. In so doing, these two chapters

---

1 Thus, for instance, the term mahatma (maha and atma), means great soul (an honourific title associated with Mohandas K. Gandhi).

aim to give, not a full presentation of Mahayana Buddhism, which would involve delving into its several influential schools, figures, and regional developments, but a thematic presentation of the tradition through a discussion and examination of central concepts and aspects.[1]

The Perfection of Wisdom and Emptiness

The *Prajnaparamita* or *Perfection of Wisdom* sutras are key texts of the Mahayana tradition. As noted above, representative sutras from this collection include the *8000 Line* sutra, the *Heart* sutra and the *Diamond* sutra. 'Prajnaparamita' refers to a wisdom (*prajna*) that has gone beyond and is from the other side, as in from the other side of a river. The connotation is a wisdom that is an enlightened understanding. This wisdom is carried from the experience of enlightenment back to Samsara, and used to help those caught up in the cycle of Samsara and suffering. This perfect wisdom and great compassion are the distinguishing features of the Bodhisattva.

According to the Abhidharma, there is no self that is independent of the ever-changing aggregates. The aggregates are composed of dharmas, and according to the Abhidharma, only the dharmas are ultimately real.[2] The *Perfection of Wisdom* sutras reject this. They assert that all is empty and without substance, including the aggregates and dharmas.[3] The *Heart*

---

1 This was also the approach taken in the discussion of the Abhidharma in Chapter Twelve. There are many good resources for the reader to follow up on schools and regional developments in Mahayana, such as Madhyamaka, Yogacara, Tibetan, Hua Yen, Chan or Zen Buddhism; the Bibliography provides some information on these.

2 C.f., Williams: "But while there is no Self at all, and all things are empty of Self, for the Abhidharma there must exist some things which have primary existence ... The absence of Self cannot mean that there are actually no primary existents at all." Williams (2000), pp. 134-35.

3 Williams describes this feature of these texts: "What is immediately apparent to anyone who glances at a Perfection of Wisdom text is the endless list of things that are said to be 'empty, like a magical illusion'. This is indeed the principal philosophical teaching of the Prajnaparamita literature." Williams (2000), pp. 134-35.

sutra portrays the Bodhisattva Avalokiteshvara (or Avalokita, as in the passage just below), who is regarded as the Bodhisattva of compassion. In this sutra, Avalokiteshvara describes the perfect wisdom of enlightenment. His audience includes Sariputra, who is a disciple of the Buddha, and is portrayed as a representative of Abhidharma thought. The sutra tells us: "Avalokita, the holy Lord and Bodhisattva, was moving in the deep course of the wisdom which has gone beyond. He looked down from on high, he beheld but five heaps, and he saw that in their own-being they were empty."[1] In this passage, Avalokiteshvara sees himself and sees only "five heaps," which are the five aggregates, which he then sees are "empty" and without "own being." This passage conveys, not only that there is no self apart from the aggregates, but that there is no substance to the aggregates; they, as with the self, are "empty." To be empty is to lack own-being (svabhava).

The Argument from the Aggregates, discussed in Chapters Four and Eight, is an argument for the doctrine of No Self. The method of argumentation employed in the Argument from the Aggregates is empiricist: no permanent self independent of the ever-changing aggregates is observed. Instead, all that is observed are the ever-changing aggregates. The argument concludes that a permanent self independent of the aggregates is not justified. However, the existence of the aggregates and the dharmas that compose them does seem justified for these are observed. Furthermore, on the basis of this observation, the dharmas may be said to have own-being. This is because everything else is observed to be composed of dharmas, but the dharmas are not observed to be composed of anything else; they are the endpoints of analysis, the smallest units observed. This is the view of the Abhidharma. However, Avalokiteshvara takes issue with this. He asserts that the five aggregates are empty of own-being. Likewise, the dharmas – the constituents of the aggregates in the Abhidharma systems – are empty as well. This is not to assert that the dharmas are impermanent or passing substances (which the Abhidharma fully endorses), but that they are not independently real

---

1 From the *Heart Sutra* in *Buddhist Texts Through the Ages*, p. 152.

substances or existents at all, impermanent or not. The self is empty of own-being; the aggregates are empty of own-being; and the dharmas are empty of own-being. And since the world of experience is ultimately composed of dharmas in the view of the Abhidharma, the implication is that nothing in this world has own-being. Everything is empty.

Consider again Nagasena's analogy of the self with a chariot. Nagasena tells King Milinda that his name is 'Nagasena', but then adds that this is a mere label and does not stand for an ego or self. He explains that he is no more than a composition of impersonal parts, similar to how a chariot is a composition of parts, without an essence or core. The analogy is used to convey that Nagasena is empty of a substantive self. But in doing so, it seems to imply that the aggregates – the composing parts – are real. After all, while the chariot may not be an independently existing entity for reason of being composed of parts, it would seem that the parts of the chariot exist with own-being (presuming these parts don't themselves have parts, in which case it would be the ultimately impartite composing parts which would seem to have own-being). They should be what ultimately exists for it is these parts which come together to form the chariot (and without which there would be no chariot). By analogy, while the self may be empty of own-being, it would seem that the ultimate parts of the self – the dharmas – must have own-being (*svabhava*). This is the implication that the Abhidharma draws. However, this implication is not drawn in the *Perfection of Wisdom* literature. Again, the self is empty, and so are the aggregates, and so are the dharmas of which they are composed. All is empty, says Avalokiteshvara to Sariputra in the *Heart* sutra: "Here, O Sariputra, all dharmas are marked with emptiness; they are not produced or stopped, not defiled or immaculate, not deficient or complete."[1]

All truths and teachings are said to be empty as well, and this includes those teachings pertaining to the very notion of emptiness itself. Gethin describes this point:

---

[1] From the *Heart Sutra* in *Buddhist Texts through the Ages*, p. 152.

The teaching of emptiness should not be read, as it sometimes appears to be, as an attempt to subvert the Abhidharma theory of dharmas as a whole. After all it applies to the constructs of all Buddhist theory, including the Mahayana and, crucially, itself: there are no bodhisattvas and no stages of the bodhisattva path. Two points are of importance here. First, we are concerned here with the perfection of wisdom, how the world is seen by the awakened mind. Secondly the perfection of wisdom texts presents what they have to say about wisdom not as an innovation but as a restatement of the original teaching of the Buddha.[1]

Emptiness extends to truths and concepts. For a concept to be empty means it makes no ultimately real distinction. This is contrary to the way we ordinarily comprehend concepts, which is to think of them as making real distinctions. Likewise, we ordinarily view objects as having own-being. For instance, I look at a pen and paper on my desk and see them as distinct and independent objects. I can look at each and see it without seeing or thinking of a connection between them or with anything else. Likewise, the concept 'pen' and the concept 'paper' mark real distinctions in my thoughts. Each of these objects is causally dependent (i.e., they wouldn't be on my desk were it not for a series of anterior causes which led to them being here). Nonetheless, they are experienced by me as being independent objects and without thought given to their causes. In short, I see the pen and paper as having own-being, and thus as non-empty. This applies not only to the pen and paper, but to other objects I encounter, including the contents of my mind. For instance, I look within and encounter different thoughts and feelings, memories and images. While these are not without their interrelations, I can still observe each in my mind's eye as being an independent mental state. Since we ordinarily see things, both internally in our minds and externally in the world, as having own-being, emptiness is contrary to our ordinary approach to seeing things. And since we ordinarily take

---

1 Gethin (1998), p. 236.

concepts to make real distinctions between objects or events, emptiness is contrary to our ordinary approach to employing concepts. Seeing and conceiving in the way we ordinarily do, it is held, is the unenlightened perspective.

The enlightened viewpoint is supposed to not objectify or attach to objects of any sort, including objects in our minds such as thoughts and feelings. There simply are no independent objects of awareness. Avalokiteshvara further states in the *Heart* sutra: "Here, O Sariputra, form is emptiness, and the very emptiness is form; emptiness does not differ from form, form does not differ from emptiness; whatever is form, that is emptiness, whatever is emptiness, that is form. The same is true of feelings, perceptions, impulses, and consciousness."[1] This is not to say that the enlightened mind experiences no thoughts or feelings, but that the awareness of these does not involve viewing them as independent objects or events in the mind. Our use of different words to refer to different thoughts and feelings suggests to us that they are independent mental events. However, the enlightened viewpoint sees them, along with everything else, as empty.

Notice that this is not merely to advocate for a belief in emptiness, for someone may believe all objects are empty of own-being but still experience their surroundings and the contents of their minds as populated by distinctly existing objects and events. Instead, the enlightened viewpoint involves *seeing and experiencing* the world as being empty of own-being. Again, this is not to say distinctions and objects are no longer observed. The experience of emptiness, we can say, is not an experience of an

---

1 Also from the *Heart Sutra*: "Therefore, O Sariputra, where there is emptiness there is neither form, nor feeling, nor perception, nor impulse, nor consciousness; no eye, or ear, or nose, or tongue, or body or mind; no forms, nor sound, nor smell, nor taste, nor touchable, nor object of mind; no sight-organ-element, and so forth, until we come to: no-mind-consciousness-element; there is no ignorance, nor extinction of ignorance, and so forth, until we come to: there is no decay and death, no extinction of decay and death; there is no suffering, nor origination, nor stopping, nor path; there is no cognition, no attainment, and no non-attainment." From the *Heart Sutra* in *Buddhist Texts through the Ages*, p. 152. See also the *Heart Sutra* in *Buddhist Scriptures*, pp. 162-63.

overwhelming grey muddle with no observed distinctions in the world.[1] But it does mean that distinctions and objects are not observed or experienced as being fundamentally real, and herein is supposed to lie the "perfect wisdom."

The enlightened or awakened mind is supposed to see all things as empty, including emptiness itself. Experiencing emptiness entails not seeing things as having own-being, and not thinking of concepts as making real distinctions, for it is things and distinctions that are said to be empty. The distinction between empty and non-empty is not, in the Mahayana view, an ultimately real distinction because the very notion of an ultimately real distinction is contrary to emptiness. The claim of emptiness does not exclude itself when it holds all concepts to be empty. The emptiness of emptiness is due to a dependence on things being empty, that is, on things being conventionally dependent. To elaborate, things and selves are said to be empty of own-being; they are conventionally arrived at, not ultimately real, and to see emptiness is to see them as such. To see emptiness in the world is to see the conventional dependence of things and concepts. This means that if there were no empty things, or no empty concepts that mark distinctions between empty things, then there would be no emptiness; there would be nothing to be empty. Emptiness is thus differentiated from nothingness: if there are no empty things; if there are no conventionally derived objects or distinctions, then while there may be nothingness, there is no emptiness. Emptiness is a claim about conventional existence, and its truth is dependent on this conventional existence. And this is again to say emptiness is itself empty. There are no ultimate truths or independent existences, according to the claim of emptiness, but only that which is conventionally true and dependently arisen. Garfield, in speaking of Nagarjuna, the great Mahayana philosopher of the *Madhyamaka* school, explains this as follows:

---

1 The American philosopher William James claimed that conceptual distinctions are the basis of all thought and coherent experience: that when a baby has experiences but still lacks ways of making distinctions, the baby's world is merely a "blooming, buzzing confusion."

To see the table as empty, for Nagarjuna, ... is to see the table as conventional, as dependent. But the table that we so see when we see its emptiness is the very same table, seen not as the substantial thing we instinctively posit, but rather as it is. Emptiness is hence not different from conventional reality – it is the fact that conventional reality is conventional. Therefore it must be dependently arisen, since it depends upon the existence of empty phenomena. Hence emptiness is itself empty.[1]

The status of emptiness in Mahayana Buddhism is not like that of dharmas in the Abhidharma. Emptiness does not have own-being. The Bodhisattva who sees all things as empty does not see himself, or his view of the world, as ultimately true or real, for this would not be to view all things as empty. The perspective of emptiness – the enlightened perspective that comes "from beyond" – thus involves humility.

The distinction between Samsara and Nirvana, or between unenlightened existence and enlightened existence, is also recognized to be empty. There is no real distinction between Samsara and Nirvana. This point, and the emptiness of distinctions in general and of emptiness itself, is made with expansive consideration by Nagarjuna in his *Mulamadhyamakakarika* (*Fundamental Verses on the Middle Way*). In Chan or Zen Buddhism, this point is expressed in saying that we all already have Buddha Nature or enlightened nature (for if all distinctions are empty, so is the distinction between not being enlightened and being enlightened). There is no fundamental distinction between not being a Bodhisattva and being one. Thus, the task of becoming enlightened is not one of becoming something different from what we are, but of realizing what we are already. And this involves realizing the emptiness of the distinctions we apply and that distance us from realizing what we are already. There is an epistemic challenge here that involves coming to not know what we think we know, and take for granted, in our ordinary experiences of ourselves and the world, in which we readily apply

---

1 Garfield (1994), p. 232. Also see Garfield (2002).

concepts and presume the distinctions we arrive at to be non-empty and real.

The doctrines of Impermanence, Dependent Origination and No Self are based upon an observation of the aggregates. The aggregates are observed to arise and pass; causal connections between the aggregates are observed; and no permanent self independent of the aggregates is observed. The empirical method is used to justify these doctrines but, as noted, this same method seems to justify the existence of the aggregates and dharmas (for while no self is observed, the aggregates and dharmas are observed). The method of observation, it seems, justifies the non-emptiness of the dharmas and aggregates. The claim of emptiness denies this, but that does not mean that emptiness is at odds with these basic doctrines, or with the method of observation employed in their support. This warrants elaboration.

The *Perfection of Wisdom* sutras do not reject the observational or experiential method, which is the key methodology of the Buddha. Indeed, the realization of emptiness itself relies on this method. The would-be Bodhisattva is supposed to be able to see, and experience, the emptiness of all things for him or herself. The truth of emptiness is supposed to be observed, just as the truth of the basic doctrines is supposed to be observed. Instead, what the *Perfection of Wisdom* literature takes issue with is the reifying, or ontologizing, of entities and distinctions on the basis of observation. The basic doctrines of No Self, Impermanence and Dependent Origination are among the first teachings of the Buddha upon gaining enlightenment. As Gethin relates in the passage quoted earlier, "the perfection of wisdom texts present what they have to say about wisdom not as an innovation but as a restatement of the original teaching of the Buddha."[1] The *Perfection of Wisdom* sutras do not challenge these basic doctrines. They try to restore them. They challenge the Abhidharma interpretation of these doctrines which involves an analysis of the aggregates into ultimately existing dharmas. The observations of the aggregates do support the basic doctrines. But the *Perfection of Wisdom*

---

1 Gethin (1998), p. 236.

sutras assert that these observations do not additionally require seeing the aggregates as existing independently or with own-being. Seeing own-being involves bringing certain ontological commitments to what is seen, and, according to the Mahayana, reflects an unenlightened and unmindful way of seeing. It involves presuming conceptual distinctions to be fundamental, as opposed to being conventionally arrived and useful. This way of seeing, that sees things, self and others as having independent existences, is what the realization of emptiness is supposed to overcome. The enlightened perspective still observes dharmas and aggregates to arise and pass, to be without self, and to be causally interconnected. But more than this, it observes the dharmas and aggregates to be empty of own-being (*svabhava*).

Note that the observations which justify the basic doctrines of Impermanence and No Self are observations that the unenlightened can undertake. These observations do not require an enlightened perspective, or a viewpoint "from beyond." Indeed, conducting a mindful observation of the aggregates, and seeing their impermanence and that there is no self to be found among them, is a step along the Noble Eightfold Path *towards* enlightenment. We are supposed to be able to see for ourselves, from our unenlightened perspectives, that there is no permanence among the aggregates. In the Abhidharma view, these observations do more than justify these doctrines: they justify the ultimate existence of dharmas, for these are the starting points, the minutest particulars, of our observations. However, in the Mahayana view, this ontologizing of the dharmas steps beyond what is strictly there to be observed. While dharmas are observed, the own-being or ultimate existence of dharmas is not truly observed; it is something assumed in what is observed, and so it may *seem* directly observed. Seeing own-being is not to see things as they are, that is, as dependently arisen. It is not a necessary way of seeing; it is a conventionally affected way of seeing. And while this point may be accepted, seeing emptiness involves more than this recognition: it involves directly seeing this conventional dependence in all things, and this is not easily achieved.

Emptiness and Dependent Origination

The doctrine of Dependent Origination is a doctrine about causal interconnection. The aggregates are caused to arise and caused to pass, without any truly uncaused causes. However, causal dependence does not, by itself, imply that causes and effects cannot also be viewed as being independent. Dependence in one sense does not deny independence in another. To elaborate, there is a clear dependence between causes and effects: an effect would not exist without its cause, and a cause would not be a cause if it did not have an effect. But there is also independence: a cause is presumed to be a distinct event from its effect and vice-versa, assuming effects are not self-caused. Thus, something can be both caused and considered independent at the same time. To illustrate, I may describe my existence in causally dependent terms: my existence is dependent on my parents having existed, on a continued supply of water, food, air, and much besides. Nonetheless, for all these causes and dependencies, I can still view myself, and be attached to myself, as an independent person.

And so, despite acknowledging that objects and selves are dependent upon causes, we can still readily see them as having independent standing, that is, as being non-empty. These causes and dependencies may not figure into how we see something; for instance, we may think that these causes exist just in the past, and do not bear on a thing's current standing or nature. In contrast to this, emptiness requires that the causal interdependence of the doctrine of Dependent Origination be interpreted more strongly. The nature of this dependence isn't such that something can be caused and thereafter be an independent object (as in the example of me being caused by my parents but thereafter being an independent person). Rather, in the perspective of emptiness, everything is always viewed as interdependent and not as a thing unto itself.

Consider another illustration: a spider's web. A spider's web seems like it should be a good analogy for causal interdependence as a web is a network of interconnected strands. Nevertheless, when we observe the web we can focus our attention on individual nodes, or individual strands (or focus on groups of nodes and strands for that matter). The nodes and strands are causally dependent: each node of the web is a product of crisscrossing strands, and each strand is how it is because of its relation to the other strands and the nodes. However, this dependence need not be something we are aware of as we attend to the nodes or strands. Instead, as we focus our awareness on one, we can come to see it as an object unto itself, independent of its surroundings (i.e., the other nodes and strands). In attending to something we can easily find ourselves objectifying it, that is, seeing it as an independent object. When we do this we don't see Dependent Origination, at least not according to the Mahayana view of Dependent Origination, which involves seeing interdependence. This is what emptiness requires. We may believe that everything exists dependently, but the realization of emptiness involves experiencing and seeing this in all that we experience and see, without exception. This is none too easily done given our ordinary way of seeing ourselves and the world.

When I look around my office, for instance, I see papers, pens, cups, books, lights, and many more things. I know that each item is causally dependent, and would not be in this room were it not for a history of causes that led to its being here. Still, in attending to these items I see them as independent objects. I see the things for which I have specific names. I see what I can conceptually distinguish. I see what I can objectify. I generally don't see the interdependencies. It is not part of my ordinary experience of my surroundings, or of the world in general. Even our concepts of dependence and relation prioritize objects for dependencies and relations, we tend to think, only exist between objects; objects are logically prior, for it would seem that they must exist for there to be dependencies and relations between them. To see an object as existing independently is to see it as non-empty. Though once again, emptiness does not entail not noticing objects or distinctions at all. It does not mean not being able to focus on things, such as nodes or strands in a web. Instead, it means seeing these objects and distinctions without also according them an independent standing or reality. All things are to be seen as dependently originated.

Despite the apparent synonymy of 'emptiness' and 'nothingness', they are not the same. Experiencing emptiness is portrayed as experiencing interdependence. This is Interdependent Arising, or as the doctrine is called in this book, Dependent Origination. As indicated above, this doctrine can be interpreted in a weak and strong sense. In a weak sense, it conveys that all things are caused, and are thus dependent upon their cause. However, aside from this dependence – which may have been at some point in the past – a thing can exist independently. This is the approach to the doctrine in the Abhidharma. The dharmas are caused to arise and pass – Dependent Origination does apply to dharmas in this respect – but nonetheless, dharmas are considered to be independent existents. Consider a cup on my table. The Abhidharma takes my experience of the cup and considers it closely. My perception of the cup is complex; it has distinct parts. This is taken to mean that the perception is dependent upon these composing parts (for if the parts were different, or came together differently, my experience of the cup would be different as well). However, the composing parts, if they don't have parts themselves, are not dependent in this way. These ultimate parts are dharmas. The dharmas are said to be independent existents, not because they are uncaused events, but because they are not dependent upon composing parts themselves (and likewise, they are presumed to not be dependent on convention as well). They are independent particulars that come together to form the world of our experience. To be clear, the dharmas are not regarded as an exception to Dependent Origination. To the contrary, the Abhidharma promotes a view that is alleged to be in line with, and also explain, the basic doctrines. The aggregates and the dharmas that compose them are caused to arise and pass. They are portrayed as monkeys swinging along branches and this movement in and out of our attention is not without cause. But having causes is not taken to imply a lack of *svabhava* or own-being. However, according to the Mahayana view of emptiness, interpreting Dependent Origination so as to allow for the independence of dharmas is interpreting it weakly, and also wrongly.

According to the *Perfection of Wisdom* sutras, this was not the original understanding of Dependent Origination of the Buddha. The original

understanding, it is alleged, is of emptiness. This understanding is supposed to reflect the enlightened point of view, and was shared only
with the Buddha's advanced disciples who were ready to appreciate it.
Correctly interpreting Dependent Origination is not merely an academic
concern. It is thought to be integral for fully overcoming attachment
and suffering. In Chapter Ten it was noted that the Buddha rebuked
his disciple Ananda when he asserted that Dependent Origination was
simple (after all, causal dependence, at first sight, does not seem to be a
problematic notion). The Buddha responded that it was subtle and profound. In the Mahayana view, this is because it is about emptiness. The
enlightened perspective of emptiness involves not seeing the world as
comprised of independent objects, be these dharmas or anything else.
But this does not entail it is an experience of nothing or nothingness.
It involves seeing and experiencing the interdependent nature of reality, with no exceptions, as Mahayana Buddhism attests that Dependent
Origination was originally intended.

Emptiness and Non-Duality

All distinctions are empty, according to the claim of emptiness. None
is ultimately real. This includes not just distinctions between objects.
It also includes the distinction between subject and object. Thus, the
distinction between my observation of an object and the object observed
is, from the perspective of emptiness, not an ultimately real distinction.
This is a non-dualistic perspective, and it is worth making clear just
how extraordinary this is. For instance, we tend to think that there is a
real distinction between my perception of a can of Grape Crush and the
can itself; and between my internal observation of my desire for Grape
Crush and the desire itself. We presume that there is a real distinction
between our subjective appreciation of an object and the object itself,
whether this is an external object or an internal object in our mind's eye.
Our experiences and observations, both internal and external, are generally dualistic. We distinguish between self and world. We distinguish

between experience and the world we experience. From the viewpoint of emptiness, however, all such distinctions are empty. Once again, this is not to say that these and other distinctions cannot be observed from the viewpoint of emptiness. Rather, it is to say that they are observed with the appreciation of being empty, insubstantial and only conventionally real. The Bodhisattva is supposed to be able to observe the aggregates and dharmas, see them arise and pass, and see that there is no permanent self among them. He is supposed to be able to do this without experiencing the aggregates and composing dharmas as being independently real entities; and furthermore, without experiencing the distinction between himself as observer and the aggregates observed as an ultimately real distinction. Rather, he is to see this distinction between subject and object, as with all other distinctions, as being conventionally dependent.

From the viewpoint of emptiness, the world and the experience of it are not independent of each other. From our ordinary, unenlightened perspective, the contrary seems true. While our experiences are causally dependent on the world, the world itself is taken to exist independently of our experiences of it. The objective world and our subjective experience of it are distinct, we think. But again, from the perspective of emptiness, there is no such independence. The object does not exist independently of the experiencing subject and vice-versa. It follows that the question of veridicality – of whether the experience of emptiness is true to the world, or correctly corresponds to the way the world really is – is inadmissible. This question presumes a real distinction between experience and reality that emptiness finds empty.

Emptiness does not represent the world as a dualistic experience represents the world. The two ways of experiencing are not commensurate in their ability to depict a reality existing outside of the experience, for this is only possible with a dualistic experience. With the perspective of emptiness there is no real distinction between experience and world, and this means that, for the one experiencing emptiness, the experience of emptiness is *ipso facto* the world. There just is no independent world outside of experience in the viewpoint of emptiness. This is not solipsism, however, for solipsism presumes that the self is real and non-empty.[1] The experience of emptiness is thus quite unlike ordinary and allegedly unenlightened experiences. Note that this does not mean that the experience of emptiness physically changes the world. In the view of unenlightened observers, the world is as it ever was. Clearly though, the world is different for the enlightened observer who comes to see it as empty.

Attachment to self, the source of suffering in the Buddhist sense, is dualistic. This is evident with cravings which involve a subject's attachment to objects of craving (be these external objects or states of mind). Also, attachment to self presumes a real distinction or separation between that which is self and that which is not self. This is a discerning attachment that gives distinction and privilege to its own states. Alternatively said, attachment to the aggregates involves attaching a core sense of self to the aggregates such that they are distinguished as one's own and held fast and dear. In the perspective of emptiness though, the objects of cravings, and the boundary between self and not-self, are recognized as being insubstantial and not ultimately real. The experience of emptiness does not admit the conditions that are necessary for craving and attachment to self. As a result, the experience of emptiness is without suffering in the Buddhist sense.

It might seem that the experience of emptiness is similar to that of Atman and Brahman, respectively the True Self and Ultimate Reality of the Upanishads. Both involve non-dualism and both are identified with the end of suffering and enlightenment. Also, the interconnectedness or interdependence of all reality that is supposed to be realized with emptiness might seem similar to the oneness of all reality that is supposed to be realized with Brahman. Both emptiness and Brahman deny ultimate reality to distinctions between objects. Emptiness may thus seem to be monism by another name. While there are similarities, there are also crucial differences. Emptiness, as with No Self, is negatively conveyed. It is a repudiation of independent existence. Brahman and Atman are,

---

1 And neither is this metaphysical idealism, which presumes mind, or mental phenomena, are real and non-empty.

comparatively speaking, positively portrayed. Brahman is the Ultimate Reality, and Atman the True Self. This is a difference between negative versus positive descriptions of reality. However, this difference is not simply descriptive or semantic. It involves a difference in approach and objective.

To elaborate, both Upanishadic monism and Mahayana emptiness deny ultimate reality to distinctions between objects. But monism asserts that there is one true reality (or one true object we might say): Brahman. Emptiness abjures such talk and the metaphysics that comes with it. The *Perfection of Wisdom* sutras do not assert that emptiness is an ultimate reality. To the contrary, they assert that emptiness is itself empty. Emptiness is empty because the conventional dependence which underlies the reality of objects and distinctions also underlies the truth of the claim of emptiness. That is, emptiness is a claim about the conventional existence of all that is deemed true or real, and thus it applies to itself. Brahman, in contrast, does not exist dependently or conventionally; indeed, monism does not seem to even allow for relations of dependence (for if there is ultimately only one thing, then there are ultimately no relations between things). There is an affirmation of a metaphysics with Brahman and monism that is notably absent with emptiness. The contrast is stark: emptiness is a repudiation of independent reality whereas Brahman is an affirmation of an independent reality.

This repudiation of independent reality suggests a reduced potential for craving and attachment. This perhaps is the most significant difference. Brahman and Atman, at least from the Mahayana perspective of emptiness, retain a basis for attachment and thus suffering whereas emptiness conveys that there is no real basis for attachment. There is no ultimate reality to attach to according to the viewpoint of emptiness for even emptiness itself is deemed empty. Since attachment is at the root of suffering, an approach that eschews any real basis for attachment arguably facilitates the overcoming of suffering.

Still, significant claims are made about emptiness in Mahayana Buddhism and these are taken to be true. For example, the claim that no objects exist independently is held to be true and the contrary false.

While such assertions are made, and considered useful, they are not regarded as being ultimately true. Not from the perspective of emptiness, that is. They are only conventionally true, as with all claims to truth. From the perspective of emptiness, the distinction between true and false, or between ultimately real and conventionally real, is itself empty.[1] Statements about emptiness are but empty statements.

This warrants further explanation. Emptiness is spoken of *as if* it were an ultimate truth. The claim that all is empty is asserted with finality. The notion of two truths – between conventional and ultimate – is one that we have encountered previously. It is applied here as well, but differently. In the Abhidharma, the dharmas were considered to be ultimately real, and all that is composed of dharmas to be only conventionally and dependently real. With emptiness, however, the distinction between ultimate and conventional is not registered as an ultimately real distinction. To elaborate, conventional truth involves speaking of selves and objects. They are spoken of as if they were real, but recognized to be only conventionally real. Ultimate truth involves the recognition that selves and objects are empty and not ultimately real. This distinction between conventional truth and ultimate truth allows us to continue speaking of selves and things as distinct existents while recognizing that these are conventional ways of speaking and not ultimate truths. However, this distinction between conventional and ultimate is itself one of usefulness, that is, of conventional use. It does not mark a fundamental divide. This is to say that an ultimate truth has its ultimate standing only conventionally. All claims about truth and existence, which must make distinctions, are conventionally dependent. Garfield describes this succinctly: "Emptiness is, in short, nothing more than the fact that conventionally dependent phenomena are conventional and

---

1 This point is also made by Nagarjuna. The reader looking for a more in-depth discussion of emptiness is encouraged to look to Nagarjuna. A good place to start, though, is with secondary writings such as Garfield (1994) and Westerhoff (2009), or with Garfield's translation with commentary of Nagarjuna's seminal *Mulamadhyamakakarika*, for Nagarjuna is a notoriously cryptic writer.

dependent. It is simply the only way in which anything can exist."[1] The usefulness of the distinction between conventional and ultimate resides in legitimizing a way of speaking of selves and things. However, the distinction cannot, at the end of the day, be an ultimately real or true distinction from the point of view of emptiness. It is only linguistically useful or conventional. Notice we cannot even conceive of what it means for the distinction between conventional and ultimate truth to not be a real distinction, or not be ultimately true, without employing the very distinction being repudiated. This raises the question of speaking effectively about emptiness and this will be "discussed" in the next section.

Emptiness and Enlightenment

The perspective of emptiness is held to be "from beyond." It is the "perfect wisdom" of the enlightened mind. There are problems in accurately communicating this perspective and its way of understanding and looking at the world to the unenlightened mind. Our ordinary use of words, including even such basic words as 'experience' and 'world', involves making distinctions that we presume are not empty and insubstantial. We use words, among other things, to refer. Referring – whether this involves referring to people, things, events, ideas or feelings – involves distinguishing. Referring involves picking out specific objects or qualities from amongst others and speaking about them in their own right. Generally speaking, when we refer we presume the non-emptiness of the referent. Someone who experiences emptiness need not lose the ability to refer and speak, but the relation to words clearly must change. Those who describe experiences of non-duality, or mystical experiences in general, often use terms such as 'ultimate' or 'true' or 'real'. This is certainly the case in the Upanishads. These terms are presumably chosen for seeming appropriate, and used sincerely. Yet they must also fall short

---

1 Garfield (2002), p. 51.

in the case of emptiness. Words distinguish, and this presents an obstacle, seemingly insurmountable, to accurately describing the experience of the emptiness of distinctions, rendering that experience indescribable, or mystical in the proper sense of the term. And if emptiness cannot be accurately described, then it cannot be accurately conceived either (at least not insofar as conceiving involves thinking with words).

As explained in Chapter Six, descriptions of Nirvana cannot accurately convey the nature of the first-hand experience of Nirvana to those who have not experienced it (unlike a description of a new flavour of ice cream which need not fail to convey the nature of the taste). However, this failure need not be complete. If a full and accurate description is not possible, an inaccurate one may still serve. A negative or indeterminate description, which does not pin down a specific content, may still yield some understanding. Also, it may convey elliptically, as with the Buddha's "inspired utterance" on Nirvana discussed in Chapter Six. We will briefly consider this again to see what it conveys about emptiness. The Buddha states:

> There is, monks, a domain where there is no earth, no water, no fire, no wind, no sphere of infinite space, no sphere of nothingness, no sphere of infinite consciousness, no sphere of neither awareness nor non-awareness; there is not this world, there is not another world, there is no sun or moon. I do not call this coming or going, nor standing nor dying, nor being reborn; it is without support, without occurrence, without object. Just this is the end of suffering.[1]

This describes Nirvana using negative terms, which is not uncommon, but also employs contradictory terms (e.g., Nirvana is neither a something nor a nothing, neither of awareness nor non-awareness, etc.). The contradictoriness of this passage conveys elliptically that Nirvana involves a role for non-dualism. That is, the inference can be drawn

---

1 From Gethin (1998), pp. 76-77. Also in Williams (2000), pp. 49-50.

from contradictory dualistic descriptions that understanding Nirvana dualistically is impossible, and thus that there is a role for non-dualism in the realization of Nirvana. This was discussed in Chapter Six. We may add here that this "inspired utterance" seems to also be an expression of emptiness through its systematic consideration and rejection of content to Nirvana. The "inspired utterance" conveys that Nirvana is empty of any and all content. Nirvana does not involve reaching some other world (which, according to the "inspired utterance," would have to be a world without earth, water, fire, or wind; with neither awareness nor non-awareness, neither coming nor going, etc.). Instead, it involves experiencing this world as empty. All the distinctions named in the "inspired utterance" – between earth and water, coming and going, awareness and non-awareness, etc. – are to be experienced as insubstantial and empty. Although distinctions and dualistic categories may still be discerned, they are to be discerned without being accorded a substantive and independent reality. And this conveys that emptiness involves experiencing interconnectedness and unity.

Emptiness, as with Nirvana, is generally described negatively, in terms of what it does not involve. Indeed, the word itself – 'emptiness' – is a one-word negative description. A positive description provides a focus and goal that may be more susceptible to attachment than a negative description that does not carry ontological implications. For instance, and as noted in the previous section, the descriptions of Brahman as a permanent ultimate reality and Atman as the True Self are positive and assert a metaphysics that may be more prone to craving and attachment. In contrast, the negative descriptions of emptiness and Nirvana suggest the absence of a real basis for craving and attachment. The claim that all is empty – self, aggregates, dharmas, and all forms – conveys to us that there is truly nothing to grasp, nothing to attach to, and no possibility of grasping or attaching. There are truly no others, no objects, no experiences, no thoughts, no principles, no truths and no falsehoods to which to attach; and no self with which to attach. The lengthy listing of things that are empty signifies the importance and extent of non-attachment in the pursuit of enlightenment.

Emptiness and compassion are the key marks of Mahayana Buddhism. As noted at the beginning of this chapter, the name Mahayana – the "greater vehicle" – conveys the centrality of compassion, for the objective of the individual adept is not individual enlightenment, but enlightenment and freedom from suffering for all. The role of compassion will be discussed in the next chapter, but the point that will be briefly considered in closing this chapter is the relation between compassion and emptiness. These are both pillars of Mahayana Buddhism, and there is a close connection. The emphasis on compassion is an emphasis away from self. One's concern with ending one's own suffering is not to be put before a concern for the suffering of others. In fact, the ideal is that one's self-concern be put away in order to focus on alleviating the suffering of others. Compassion is not only to be realized in one's efforts, but also in one's intentions and motives. One is to be moved by the suffering of others, to feel for others and to want to help others. This is a genuine compassion and, by removing barriers between oneself and others, it helps lead to the realization of No Self (this will be elaborated more fully in the next chapter). In this respect, compassion furthers the realization of emptiness. Realizing emptiness involves seeing interconnectedness or interdependence, and this involves seeing oneself not as unique or special or more deserving of the alleviation of suffering. Attachment to self is an obstacle to realizing emptiness and the exercise of a genuine compassion helps to remove this obstacle.

Moreover, the emphasis on compassion in Mahayana Buddhism tells us that realizing emptiness is not simply a cognitive shift but also an affective one, a change in feelings and emotions. It is not simply a matter of changing perspectives, such as may be done by trying on a new pair of glasses, but is more fully transforming. Recall that Gautama, upon leaving his father's palace, met two yogis who taught him meditational techniques. The first yogi, Alara Kalama, taught him to enter the "sphere of nothingness" and the second, Udakka Ramaputra, the "sphere of neither cognition nor non-cognition" (which, on the surface, seems to have been a non-dualistic state). These experiences gave him a brief reprieve from suffering – a "comfortable abiding" – but his troubles and anxieties arose afresh afterwards. It was not the remedy he sought. His attachments remained firmly rooted. The implication to draw here is that the challenge of enlightenment is not merely cerebral or cognitive, such as getting oneself into a certain state of mind through a meditation technique. The challenge is to more fully transform. The whole person is to be made over. Mahayana Buddhism conveys that for this compassion is integral, and that this was always part of the Buddha's original message. The mind needs to be trained, and the body disciplined, but also the heart must go out to others. The idea is that to realize emptiness, one must not only see interconnectedness, but also feel interconnectedness. This involves feeling for others as for oneself. Mahayana Buddhism emphasizes both emptiness and compassion, and sees these objectives as united.

XIV

Compassion and Skillfulness in Mahayana Buddhism

Introduction

THE EMPHASIS ON WISDOM in Mahayana Buddhism is an emphasis on the experience and understanding of emptiness of the enlightened mind. This is the "perfect wisdom" of one who has "gone beyond" and is expressed in the *Perfection of Wisdom* sutras. This is one of two main areas of emphasis in Mahayana Buddhism. The other is compassion. According to the ancient Tibetan philosopher Tsongkhapa, the compassion of the Bodhisattva is the defining characteristic of Mahayana Buddhism.[1] As discussed at the end of the previous chapter, the wisdom and compassion of the Bodhisattva are not unrelated as it is thought that having perfect wisdom and seeing the interdependence of all things

---

1 See Williams (1989), pp. 47-48.

involves understanding and feeling for the suffering of others. Seeing emptiness in all things and feeling empathy for all beings are coupled in the Bodhisattva. This chapter will philosophically examine the role of the Bodhisattva, the significance of compassion, and the employment of what are called 'Skillful Means' in Mahayana Buddhism. These are key aspects of Mahayana Buddhism. It is by way of a focus on central concepts and aspects that this chapter and the previous one, which focused on the concept of emptiness, aim for a thematic presentation and general assessment of Mahayana Buddhism.[1]

Mahayana Buddhism accepts the Noble Truths and the basic doctrines of No Self, Impermanence, and Dependent Origination. Although, as was discussed in the previous chapter, Mahayana Buddhism places an emphasis on emptiness in its understanding of these early doctrines, in contrast to the Abhidharma and its emphasis on the dharmas. But the most significant difference between Mahayana and non-Mahayana traditions is not doctrinal but a matter of practice and its motivation. Specifically, the path to enlightenment is to be followed with a concern for overcoming the suffering of all, rather than a concern with alleviating the suffering of oneself.[2] This is the compassionate motivation, and oath, of the Bodhisattva.

The Bodhisattva

In the Mahayana tradition, it is held that the great compassion and self-sacrifice of the Bodhisattva leads eventually to Parinirvana. Parinirvana is held to be the final Nirvana of an enlightened being, generally thought

---

1 As described in the previous chapter, this is not to give a complete presentation of Mahayana Buddhism; this would involve a significant discussion of its schools and regional developments. The Bibliography does provide some sources for a further reading of Mahayana Buddhism.

2 As Williams states: "... in the final analysis what makes a follower of Mahayana is not robes, rules, or philosophy. It is motivation, intention. The Mahayana as a whole is a particular vision of what the final motivation and goal of serious practitioners should be." Williams (1989), p. 102.

to be achieved upon the death of the body and dissolution of the aggregates. That is, it is held to be not only an end to suffering (Nirvana), but a final end: an end to the cycle of rebirth or Samsara. For this reason it is also described, in "modern Buddhist usage," as "Nirvana without remainder," for it is without the causes and attachments that would lead to further rebirth.[1] The Bodhisattva is said to be able to achieve Parinirvana as a result of endeavouring towards ending the suffering of all. Whereas the Arhat, who is perhaps unfairly portrayed in the Mahayana tradition as being concerned primarily with his own suffering, is alleged to be unable to achieve Parinirvana.

The notion of a final Nirvana, without the possibility of a return to suffering, raises questions about whether and how Parinirvana is to involve a continued, unsuffered existence outside of the cycle of death and rebirth. If there is no continued existence for the enlightened being, then the finality of final Nirvana would seem to signify only the finality of death (i.e., there is no possibility of a return to a suffered existence only because there is no existence beyond death). If there is continued existence, and it is a personal continuation outside of the cycle of Samsara, then this would be an example of Eternalism and violate the doctrine of No Self.[2] Thus, the only continued existence that is admissible is an impersonal continuance and this may proceed as follows: the world continues on after death, and since the enlightened being realizes he is not truly distinct from the world (as this is entailed by his realization of emptiness), the continued existence of the world is his continued existence as well; this is not oneness with the world (Brahman), but a realization of the lack of a real separation from the world. In addition, Parinirvana is sometimes held to be a "fuller" Nirvana, or a higher level of Nirvana,

---

1 Williams notes that "'nirvana without a remainder' is sometimes referred to in modern Buddhist usage (probably incorrectly) as parinirvana, restricting 'nirvana' to 'nirvana with a remainder'." Williams (2000), p. 49. Williams cites Gethin who states: "Modern Buddhist usage tends to restrict 'nirvana' to the awakening experience and reserve 'parinirvana' for the death experience." Gethin (1998), p. 76.

2 Difficulties raised within Buddhism with the notion of a personal continued existence beyond death were also elaborated in Chapter Eleven on Karma and Rebirth.

that is superior in quality.[1] The Buddha is reputed to have said that he was neither man nor god, but a Buddha – an enlightened one, and for some this enlightenment is thought to confer a supra-human status. The Bodhisattva, like the Buddha, is similarly regarded as a superior being for reason of having achieved a greater enlightenment (i.e., greater than that of the Arhat). This greater enlightenment is Parinirvana. However, this notion of different levels of Nirvana – superior versus inferior, fuller versus less full – is unclear. While it makes sense to say there are degrees or stages leading up to Nirvana, the idea that Nirvana itself admits of degrees or stages is more difficult to comprehend. An experience of Nirvana that still included some suffering, or still included some attachment to self, is not Nirvana (i.e., it is not an extinguishing of suffering, but only approaching the extinguishing of suffering). An end to suffering may be approached, but the end must be an end and not a matter of degree. Or so it would seem.[2]

What is clear concerning Parinirvana is that it is regarded as the preserve of the Bodhisattva, not the Arhat. The Bodhisattva is described as being concerned with the suffering of others, to the extent of spending his or her life alleviating the suffering of others. The Arhat is described, and again this may be an unfair characterization from the viewpoint of non-Mahayana traditions, as not being similarly committed to alleviating the suffering of others. This commitment to others is a mark of the great compassion of the Bodhisattva. It is also said of the Bodhisattva, and not the Arhat, that he forgoes a personal release from suffering in order to

---

1   Williams states that the Bodhisattva forgoes the Nirvana of the Arhat (and the Pratyekabuddha, one who achieves enlightenment on his own) but does not forgo the "full Nirvana of the Buddha" which is attained through the selfless Bodhisattva way: "Generally, the Mahayana Bodhisattva does not postpone or turn back from nirvana. Rather he or she rejects the nirvanas of the Arhat and Pratyekabuddhas, at least as final goals, and aims for the full nirvana of the Buddha." William (1989), p. 53.

2   If Parinirvana is to be understood as superior to Nirvana only because there is no possibility of a return to a life of suffering thereafter, then this is at least conceptually clearer. This is the notion of a final Nirvana; it is superior because it is a final end to suffering. As noted, this raises its own questions and this is discussed immediately above.

help others overcome suffering. This forgoing of personal enlightenment is supposed to convey that the would-be Bodhisattva does not place ending his own suffering above that of ending the suffering of others. This renunciation of a personal interest in enlightenment is thus also a mark of the great compassion of the Bodhisattva.

To be clear, there are presumed to be two self-sacrifices here: committing one's life to helping others overcome suffering and forgoing personal enlightenment in order to fully commit to helping others overcome suffering. The first clearly involves self-sacrifice. The second is less clear and it is worth exploring why. This exploration will take the form of trying to understand and answer this question: must the adept – the would-be Bodhisattva – forgo personal enlightenment in order to fully commit to helping others overcome suffering? Helping others is a given for the Bodhisattva. And note that this means the would-be Bodhisattva does not become a Bodhisattva before significantly committing to helping others (this is why the terms 'would-be Bodhisattva' and 'adept' are being used). A Bodhisattva is *made* through great compassion. The question here is whether it additionally makes sense to say the would-be Bodhisattva must renounce personal enlightenment in order to fully commit to helping others. This is a question about whether the adept or would-be Bodhisattva undertakes two significant self-sacrifices (helping others overcome suffering and forgoing personal enlightenment) or really just one (helping others overcome suffering).

The first answer to be considered is that the would-be Bodhisattva does not forgo personal enlightenment in order to fully commit to helping others overcome suffering. The second is that the would-be Bodhisattva does forgo personal enlightenment for this reason. There are difficulties with both these straightforward answers. After this a third possibility will be introduced (at the end of this section; it will then be elaborated in the next section): the would-be Bodhisattva *chooses* to forgo personal enlightenment in favour of helping others overcome suffering, but does not thereby *actually* forgo enlightenment. This third answer will be preferred for reasons that will be discussed. The reason for working methodically through these three answers is that it is a fruitful way of coming to a clearer understanding of the Bodhisattva, and the role of compassion and sacrifice in the pursuit of enlightenment.

The first answer asserts that the would-be Bodhisattva *does not* forgo personal enlightenment in favour of helping others overcome suffering. A reason for holding this is that this was ostensibly the case with the Buddha: he spent forty-five years helping others overcome suffering, but only after he was himself released from suffering. That is, his enlightenment, at age thirty-five, preceded his many years of compassionate service towards others. The second answer asserts that the adept *does* forgo personal enlightenment in favour of helping to end the suffering of others. A reason for holding this is that, according to the Mahayana view, personal enlightenment should not precede a commitment to help others. That is not the path of the Bodhisattva. The Bodhisattva's vow requires that the adept not place his own release before that of others. Indeed, the very name 'Mahayana' indicates this: the path towards enlightenment involves a "greater vehicle" and not personal enlightenment to be followed by the enlightenment of others (this would be a small vehicle followed by a large one, like a tugboat pulling a barge). On this answer, it is specifically the personal enlightenment of the Arhat that is sacrificed. Also, as described, compassion and self-sacrifice are defining features of the Bodhisattva. This consideration further favours answer two over one for the adept willingly forgoes a personal release from suffering in order to help others overcome suffering. On the first answer, personal enlightenment is not sacrificed: one's own enlightenment can precede turning to help alleviate the suffering of others, and this suggests a lesser compassion. Based simply on which answer displays the greater compassion and sacrifice, answer two seems to fare better than answer one.

However, there are difficulties with the second answer also. One difficulty, already mentioned, arises with comparison to the Buddha's life. Mahayana Buddhism draws upon what it considers to be an original understanding of the Buddha's message, and the Buddha's life is upheld as an example *par excellence* of selflessness and compassion for the would-be Bodhisattva. The Buddha, by general account, achieved enlightenment at the age of thirty-five, and then spent the next forty-five years of his life selflessly helping others overcome suffering. It is important to note here that the Buddha was already enlightened at the time he turned to help others overcome suffering, and so he did not forgo or postpone an initial experience of enlightenment in order to help others overcome suffering. Parinirvana may have had to wait until he was at his deathbed, after spending many years helping others, but Nirvana did not. Comparison with the example of the Buddha counts against the second answer because it conveys that the would-be Bodhisattva, who does forgo individual enlightenment in order to help others, excels in compassion over the Buddha. The Buddha's initial enlightenment would be relegated to that of an Arhat, and this just does not accord with the way the Buddha's life is revered within the Mahayana tradition. The Buddha's compassion and enlightenment are upheld as exemplary and not deficient in any regard. The example of the Buddha conveys that enlightenment need not be sacrificed in favour of spending a life helping others. Indeed, for the Buddha, enlightenment was a precursor to such a life.

The second answer is also conceptually problematic. Forgoing personal enlightenment out of a preference to help others overcome suffering implies that these can be exclusive. This does not accord with the Buddhist sense of suffering which holds that suffering involves craving and attachment to self. It does not make sense that overcoming craving and attachment to self should be put aside or forgone in favour of extending compassionate service to others. To the contrary, overcoming one's cravings and attachment to self is *part of* extending compassion to others. Far from being exclusive, these are mutually complementary ends: being less attached to self helps to extend compassion to others, and service to others is a way to overcome self-attachment. Each serves the other. While there may be something fitting about the spirit of selflessness in forgoing personal enlightenment, it does not make sense to actually forgo the ending of attachment to self in order to provide compassionate service.

The difficulties raised by these two answers lead to a muddle. The Buddha is supposed to be an example of compassion for a would-be Bodhisattva, and yet his life story conveys that he did not live a prominently compassionate life until after his alleged enlightenment. Once again, this suggests that the Buddha, at the time of his enlightenment, is deficient in compassion compared to the would-be Bodhisattva who chooses to forgo personal enlightenment in favour of helping others overcome suffering. There is a contradiction in saying the Buddha is an exemplar of compassion for the would-be Bodhisattva but also, at the time of his enlightenment, was deficient in compassion compared to the would-be Bodhisattva. If this contradiction is to be resolved while also upholding the exemplary compassion of the Buddha, then this compassion must have been in place at the time of his becoming a Buddha. His compassion must have been a part of his becoming enlightened (i.e., the Buddha did not suddenly become greatly compassionate after his enlightenment, even though to look just at his actions suggests this). Specifically, the apparent contradiction can be resolved by admitting these two points: (i) becoming a Bodhisattva requires a sincere and consuming commitment to help others overcome suffering (and note that while the commitment is to be carried out, enlightenment does not have to wait for it to be carried out; it can proceed with this commitment fully in place). And (ii), the Buddha did take on just this commitment in becoming enlightened (for instance, perhaps during his six day meditation leading up to his enlightenment experience). In this resolution, the Buddha's initial enlightenment was not that of an Arhat but of a Bodhisattva. This is because his compassionate commitment towards alleviating the suffering of others, even though it was yet to be carried out, was the sincere and compelling vow of a Bodhisattva.

This takes us to the third approach to answering our question about whether the would-be Bodhisattva does or does not forgo personal enlightenment. On this third answer, the would-be Bodhisattva chooses to forgo personal enlightenment, but he does not thereby actually forgo personal enlightenment. These are different. Choosing to forgo enlightenment does not entail one actually forgoes. In fact, it can help achieve enlightenment. Choosing to forgo a personal release from suffering in favour of helping others is to take on a whole-hearted commitment towards others. This unequivocal commitment towards others is valuable for overcoming attachment to self. An adept who willingly puts aside his own pursuit of enlightenment and freedom from suffering in order to help others commits himself fully to selflessness, and this is important for overcoming suffering in the Buddhist sense. While the Buddha did not live a life of service to others prior to becoming enlightened, it is reasonable to think he was committed to doing so in becoming enlightened (and that is why his life took this direction upon becoming enlightened). This third answer to the above question is similar to the first in that the would-be Bodhisattva need not actually forgo personal enlightenment; and to the second in that he does still choose to forgo. However, it does not face the difficulties of these other answers, and is consistent with the example of the Buddha. It will be discussed further in the next section.

The Bodhisattva Renounces

As described above, becoming enlightened and choosing to help others cannot be a real dichotomy, for becoming enlightened is not at odds with a life spent helping others; they are instead mutually complementary ends. However, even though it is not a real dichotomy, this does not mean there cannot be a real choice. On this third answer, the adept renounces personal enlightenment, but need not actually forgo. In fact, renouncing personal enlightenment in order to help others can be integral to attaining personal enlightenment. It can be important that the adept renounce for this can achieve a selflessness that otherwise may not be possible. There need be no actual forgoing; it is the sincere commitment to forgo that counts. Renouncing personal enlightenment in favour of helping others is described by Williams as "exhortatory": "There are certainly texts which speak of the Bodhisattva postponing or turning back from some enlightenment ... It may be that it embodies a form of exhortatory writing – the Bodhisattva adopts a position of complete renunciation. In renouncing even Buddhahood the Bodhisattva precisely attains Buddhahood."[1] This idea will be further elaborated.

---

1 Williams (1989), p. 53.

Since suffering in the Buddhist conception involves attachment to self, trying to achieve an end to individual suffering faces a significant obstacle: a self-interested motive. Acting out of self-interest need not always involve attachment to self. For instance, it can be in my self-interest to eat breakfast, but eating breakfast need not involve self-attachment. However, eating breakfast in order to satisfy one's cravings, as opposed to eating only to meet one's bodily need, does involve self-attachment. Overcoming attachment to self requires not being attached to the view that the beneficiary of an end to suffering is the same self who is pursuing an end to suffering. That is, it requires not being attached to permanence in one's view of self. But then how is attachment to permanence of self to be overcome? How is Nirvana to be achieved for one's future self but also pursued without self-attachment? This third answer says that it is by renouncing a personal interest in Nirvana. By sincerely forgoing his claim to Nirvana in order to help others, the adept puts aside his concern for his own present and future suffering and thereby can achieve a selflessness that is necessary for experiencing Nirvana.

This is not contradictory.[1] It does mean that achieving Nirvana for oneself requires that ultimately it not be pursued just for oneself. Committing fully to alleviating the suffering of others is, on this answer, a necessary step for overcoming attachment to self. Sincere compassion leads to freedom from suffering for oneself. If this compassion and commitment to helping others is not sincere – that is, if it is motivated by a self-regard for personal enlightenment – then it will not be successful. Enlightenment must not be pursued just for oneself to be achieved. This means that at some point in the quest for enlightenment, one's motives must be divested of self-concern; one must cease pursuing freedom from suffering just for oneself. Williams affirms: "... the result of this is that one attains Buddhahood all the more quickly. This is indeed the true way to Buddhahood."[2] This third answer is consistent

---

1 Psychologists sometimes speak of "paradoxical intentions" that are somewhat analogous to this. Examples: the more you try to go to sleep, the more sleep eludes you; self-consciously trying to fix your golf swing makes it worse; trying to be happy makes you unhappy.

2 Williams (2000), p. 139.

with the doctrine of No Self, and the understanding of suffering as attachment to self.

It is also consistent with the example of the Buddha. The Buddha, after enlightenment, spent forty-five years helping others overcome suffering (this is not to say he never helped others before, but after enlightenment it is portrayed as a consummate effort). On this third answer, the whole-hearted commitment to help others overcome suffering was in place in his becoming enlightened, even though it was not carried out until afterwards. If one must actually spend a life helping others before reaching enlightenment, then the Buddha would not have become enlightened at age thirty-five but rather only at age eighty, at his passing. As also noted, the renunciation and commitment to helping others must be sincere and full, and the evidence of this is in the Buddha's carrying through on the commitment for the remainder of his life. If one makes a commitment to help others for a year, or twenty, after which one will live for oneself, then attachment to self has not been fully overcome in one's commitment. This third answer is consistent with the course of events in the Buddha's life.

While renouncing the goal of personal enlightenment may be a necessary condition for enlightenment, it does not seem to be sufficient. Presumably, if an adept forgoes the individual pursuit of enlightenment in favour of helping others, but has not undertaken other steps towards enlightenment (such as following through on the Noble Eightfold Path), then this renunciation will not be sufficient for enlightenment. The individual may be greatly compassionate, but the disciplining measures of the Noble Eightfold Path must also be undertaken. However, if the adept appropriately practices and follows the Noble Eightfold Path, *and* sincerely forgoes the goal of personal enlightenment in favour of helping others, then this may be sufficient for fully overcoming craving and attachment to self, and hence for becoming enlightened.

This third answer implies that the Arhat, despite being described as enlightened, is really only at a stage on the way to becoming enlightened. A divestment of personal interest is still required for the Arhat to reach enlightenment. Gethin observes that the Mahayana sutras provide two divergent attitudes on the path of the Arhat and the goal of individual enlightenment. The first attitude is that this is a real goal, but is "inferior and should be renounced for the superior attainment of Buddhahood." This superior enlightenment is that of the Bodhisattva. The second, "classically articulated by the Lotus Sutra," sees this as not a true goal at all. On this latter view, the ideal of the Arhat is "merely a clever device employed by the Buddha in order to get beings to at least begin the practice of the path; eventually their practice must lead to the one and only vehicle that is Mahayana, the vehicle ending in perfect Buddhahood."[1] On the first attitude described by Gethin, Arhatship is an inferior but nonetheless real enlightenment.[2] On the second attitude, Arhatship is not a real attainment of enlightenment at all; it is rather a stage on the path to becoming enlightened. The answer and interpretation being discussed in this section holds this second attitude.

Pursuing the end of suffering for everyone and not just for oneself may be taken as too demanding and off-putting. In contrast, the promise of a personal enlightenment, pursued by an individual for his or her own benefit, provides enticement and incentive. The goal of personal enlightenment can draw initiates onto a path that must, in this Mahayana view, eventually become something more than a pursuit of a personal goal. While individual enlightenment remains attainable, it must not be pursued for the benefit of the individual to be attained. Gethin further states: "From this perspective the difference between Hinayana and Mahayana is effectively the difference between progressive stages of the same path."[3] Personal enlightenment provides incentive for following the Noble Eightfold Path but this can only take one so far; to attain

---

1 Gethin (1998), pp. 228–29. Note that discounting the Arhat is not uncommon in the Mahayana tradition, and again, this is viewed as a prejudice by non-Mahayana schools that uphold the enlightened status of the Arhat.

2 As described earlier, the notions of lesser and greater enlightenment, that are respectively inferior and superior in quality, is problematic and unclear (for an end to suffering does not seem to admit of degree).

3 Gethin (1998), pp. 228–29. Here Gethin also writes: "What is characteristic of the Mahayana vision of Buddhism is the view that the attainment of the disciple falls so far short of full Buddhahood that it cannot be considered as a worthy spiritual goal; contrary to the traditional formula which states the arhat 'has done what has to be done' he or she in fact has further work to do."

enlightenment one's motive and goal must change. The Bodhisattva way is required to complete the journey. The idea that Arhatship is not a real enlightenment, but only presented as such so that it might provide incentive for undertaking Buddhist practice, involves a notion called "Skill in Means" or "Skillful Means." The idea here is that the Buddha promoted the goal of Arhatship as a "skillful" device to motivate followers along the Noble Eightfold Path. If it were asserted up front that a personal interest in Nirvana must be renounced in favour of pursuing the end of suffering of all humanity, then the ordinary self-interested person would be hard-pressed for motivation.[1]

Presumably, one cannot reach the goal of ending everyone's suffering; but the sincere commitment towards this objective achieves a selflessness that may not be attainable through a self-interested pursuit of enlightenment. However, it may not be the only way to dislodge a self-interested motivation in the pursuit of enlightenment. Buddhist practice undertaken without being directed by any objective or interest – be this self-interested or selfless – is an alternative. The idea of maintaining Buddhist practice while being indifferent towards whether one realizes enlightenment by it, to the extent of it ceasing to be a goal at all, is raised in Chan Buddhism (called Zen Buddhism in Japanese). In Chan Buddhism there is an emphasis on practice as discipline – a rigorous practice – without giving mind to the reason, purpose or end to be gained from the practice. Indeed, it is part of the disciplining that one pay no mind to the end or reason of the practice, but pay mind just to the practice. This is perhaps an alternative approach to a non-self-interested Buddhist practice. It removes a self-interested motive, not by replacing it with a compassionate and selfless interest in pursuing the enlightenment of all, but by having no interest in the end to be achieved from Buddhist practice. Still, it is – through continued discipline – committing to Buddhist practice all the same.

---

1 The notion of Skillful Means is also given vivid expression in the 'Parable of the Burning House' from the *Lotus Sutra*. This will be discussed in the next chapter.

Compassion and Suffering

Someone with great compassion feels the suffering of others. We might call this the suffering of empathy. As long as such an empathetic person knows someone else is suffering, he will suffer for them. Their suffering causes him suffering. Thus, overcoming the suffering of empathy requires helping others overcome their suffering. At first, this seems to fit with the idea that the Bodhisattva must renounce personal enlightenment in order to help others, for he cannot be free from suffering himself until all are free.

While it may be true that feeling great compassion involves a kind of suffering, this "suffering of empathy" is not the focus of suffering in the Buddhist conception. This is not a suffering to be eliminated for it comes with compassion. Feeling compassion may cause one to feel grief or disquiet, to be unnerved and perhaps even to feel physical pain in response to the plight of other beings. But these feelings are examples of suffering under the first grouping in the First Noble Truth. Likewise, a compassionate being may have a strong desire to rid others of their suffering, and not be satisfied until fully successful. But the presence of an unsatisfied desire is an example of suffering under the second grouping in the First Noble Truth. Neither of these are the focus of suffering in the Buddhist conception unless they also involve attachment to self (which is the understanding of suffering given in the third grouping in the First Noble Truth). Thus, someone who feels great compassion for others, and suffers from emotional and physical symptoms because of this, need not suffer in the Buddhist sense. This is because their empathy need not involve craving or attachment to self. Indeed, such a compassionate person would be less prone to self-attachment. The suffering that comes with compassion is not to be eliminated. If anything, it is to be nurtured for it is the kind of suffering that helps overcome the suffering of self-attachment.

Since suffering in the Buddhist conception involves attachment to self, we might conclude that it is this suffering specifically that should be the focus of the would-be Bodhisattva's concern. That is, the would-be

Bodhisattva should focus on helping others overcome attachment to self. Alleviating ills and pains is still a worthy objective for these are, for the unenlightened, generally experienced with attachment to self and thus are still suffered in the Buddhist sense. Solely to treat ills and pains, though, does not alleviate the suffering that is Buddhism's main concern. The Buddha, after all, was not a curer of pain and sickness, but he is described as leading a path out of suffering all the same. His focus was not pain and sickness, but to help others overcome attachment to self in their pain and sickness (and elsewhere as well). Notwithstanding, for the would-be Bodhisattva, alleviating the suffering of others in any form can be a selfless endeavour, and thus help in overcoming attachment to self. Accordingly, Mahayana monks would often (and still do) focus on alleviating physical suffering and providing medical care and other material aid to laity. Still, the teachings of the Buddha are focused primarily on overcoming suffering in terms of craving and attachment to self. It is towards alleviating this suffering that the Noble Eightfold Path and the basic doctrines are directed. Again, this does not mean neglecting the pain and sickness of others, but it does mean that what should be ultimately important, for the would-be Bodhisattva, in extending compassion and remedy is helping others to overcome the attachment to self in feelings of pain and sickness and not only the feelings themselves. This is the focus of compassion of the Buddha and it is clearly different from the focus of compassion of the medical practitioner.

Genuine Compassion

The goal of overcoming attachment to self, and its emphasis on detachment, may seem to involve a withdrawal from affect or emotion. However, the emphasis on compassion in Mahayana Buddhism is an acknowledgement that at least some affect or emotion is necessary. Principally, this involves feeling compassion but also other feelings connected to this, such as grief and pain when others suffer, joy when they are alleviated, and in general, love for others. With the requirement of

compassion, the Buddhist adherent is charged not just with acting com-
passionately, but being and feeling compassionate (and as just noted, this
brings other feelings with it). This compassion and these feelings, as will
be discussed in this section, must be genuine.

Compassion counteracts the effects of states such as hatred, jealousy,
and greed. The idea is that by being consumed by compassionate feelings and thoughts, the adept will be less susceptible to hurtful or hateful
feelings and thoughts, and can turn around these aspects of his character.
Compassion does not covet or seek to take, but to give and be helpful,
and thus compassion is an antidote to greed and grasping as well. It is a
means to personality change via focus on the opposite of the states we
wish to overcome. As discussed, compassion divests of self. It focuses
outwardly, rather than inwardly, in its attentions. And it has an emotive
or affective component. It involves the feeling of caring, and not just
caring behaviour. This means that the compassionate, enlightened figure
is not fully dispassionate. As emotions are often mixed with attachment
to self, detachment from emotions can be an important part of following
the Buddhist path. This detachment, as discussed in Chapter Seven, is an
aspect of the vigilant practice of mindfulness (for mindfulness involves
detaching to some extent from occurrent states of mind in order to be
mindfully aware of them). The emphasis on compassion in Mahayana
Buddhism, however, conveys that this is not a sweeping detachment
from affect or emotion. The enlightened figure is presented as being of
genuine caring, and thus a person of feeling.

As described above, compassion, because it turns our minds outwards
to the plight of others, and not inwards to our own suffering, helps
overcome attachment to self. Compassion for others serves to lessen
attachment to one's self, and thereby lessen one's own suffering in the
Buddhist sense. However, there is a catch: if one is being compassionate in the interest of overcoming attachment to self, and ending one's
own suffering, then the objective of overcoming attachment to self is
thwarted. If the motive for being compassionate is personal gain – even
if this gain is the ending of one's own suffering – then the role of compassion in overcoming attachment to self cannot be fulfilled. Simply put,

the objective of No Self cannot be met if pursued from a self-centred motive. Thus, compassion must be pure of heart and genuine. This means that the reasons one gives to oneself for being compassionate cannot draw from one's sense of self-interest. It is interesting that we can justify the exercise of compassion in Buddhism on the grounds that it can help lead to the attainment of No Self, and thus to the end of suffering in the Buddhist sense. Yet the justification to oneself for one's compassion should not be the reason of ending one's own suffering. It must appear, to oneself, as genuinely altruistic to have this benefit.

To further elaborate, consider the Noble Eightfold Path. Steps on this path certainly place importance on the consideration of others. For example, Right Action and Right Livelihood concern proper interactions with others. Nonetheless, the Noble Eightfold Path is supposed to be something one can undertake for oneself, to eliminate one's own suffering. This is a reason and motive for undertaking the path, including those steps which prescribe moral conduct towards others. Yet, as discussed, a personal motivation cannot succeed in fully realizing No Self. At some point in following the path, this reason for following – ending one's own suffering – must be let go. It must come to be followed without the motive of personal benefit. The Mahayana emphasis on compassion accomplishes this; it is a compassion exercised for its own sake (that is, for the sake of others and not for oneself). Compassion is not presented as a means towards achieving Nirvana, as is the Noble Eightfold Path. This is important for it is precisely in not being directed at one's personal freedom from suffering that the exercise of a genuine compassion can more effectively lead to one's freedom from suffering.

The Noble Eightfold Path is a path, and thus a means, and it is justified by the end to which it is supposed to lead. This end is usually conceived to be personal enlightenment. For one who is unenlightened, and attached to self, it is quite natural to think of freedom from suffering as a personal objective. In marked contrast, the emphasis on compassion in Mahayana Buddhism is not presented as a path leading to personal enlightenment. Compassion is emphasized for no other reason than the fact that others suffer. The justification ends there. The suffering of others is reason enough for the Mahayana goal of carrying everyone to freedom from suffering.

The life of the Buddha presents an example of compassion for the sake of others. Helping others overcome suffering is not presented as a requirement of the Buddha's enlightenment, for it comes on the heels of his enlightenment. Compassion, while it can be integral to overcoming attachment and attaining enlightenment, is not presented as a significant aspect of the Buddha's life leading up to his enlightenment. This presentation may have much to do with the requirement that only a genuine compassion – and not an instrumental compassion that is viewed as a means towards personal enlightenment – can help lead to enlightenment.

Skillful Means, the Arhat and the Bodhisattva

The Buddha is reputed to have spoken differently to different audiences, weighing and delivering his words to suit the level of understanding and spiritual maturity of the listener. This insight and ability, attributed to the Buddha, is described as speaking and teaching with 'Skill in Means' or 'Skillful Means' (*upaya kaushalya*). Followers may be at different stages of spiritual development, or face different obstacles and challenges, and for these people different – and perhaps even contrary – teachings may be appropriate. The same teaching, or the same presentation of a teaching, may not work as effectively for all audiences. The ability to adapt teachings to the level of understanding or concerns of an audience is wherein the skill in Skillful Means lies. The care and effort involved in considering the nature of an audience's suffering, and how they may need to be guided in order to overcome their suffering, is said to display the compassion of the Buddha. The Buddha's ability to tailor teachings to individual needs was thought by some to be magical.[1] While the judgement of magical ability will be presumed to be incorrect, it

---

1 C.f. Kalupahana: "His [the Buddha's] contemporaries, who failed to understand the psychological significance of this method of discourse, saw him

nevertheless conveys the psychological insight the Buddha was thought to have possessed in providing customized teachings.

The idea that the Buddha taught with Skillful Means has its origins early in the history of Buddhism but it gains significance, and is a central principle, in Mahayana Buddhism. The notion of Skillful Means may be applied to all Buddhist teachings, including those presumed central and basic, and it emphasizes a practical approach and an attitude of non-attachment to these teachings. Non-Mahayana texts provide a key source for the notion of Skillful Means: a simile between the Buddha's teachings – the Dharma (or Dhamma in Pali) – and a raft. The simile conveys that just as a raft is used to cross a river, Buddhist teachings should be used to help overcome obstacles or reach a certain point. And just as it would not be wise to haul a raft along on one's back after using it to cross a river, it would likewise not be wise to hold on to teachings beyond their usefulness. The Buddha states, "... the Dhamma is similar to a raft, being for the purpose of crossing over, not for the purpose of grasping." He adds, "Bhikkhus, when you know the Dhamma to be similar to a raft, you should abandon even the teachings, how much more so things contrary to the teachings."[1] The Raft Simile is commonly quoted but it is not the only analogy to make this point. Another involves comparing teachings to a series of chariots, with each one used to carry a person to a certain point whereupon another chariot is taken up.[2]

The value of a raft is presented as being instrumental; its value is its usefulness. Likewise with a teaching. To let go of a teaching once it is no longer useful does not mean that a teaching once believed to be true

---

as a person possessed of the magical power of conversion. Yet there was no magic or mystery involved. All that the Buddha did was carefully observe the intellectual maturity and psychological state of each person and provide a discourse that would produce beneficial consequences for him." Kalupahana (1992), p. 66.

1 *Alagaddupama Sutta, Majjhima Nikaya,* I 22, p. 229. Also see the *Mahatanhasankhaya Sutta, Majjhima Nikaya* I 261, p. 353: "... the Dhamma has been taught as similar to a raft, being for the purpose of crossing over, not for the purpose of grasping."

2 *Rathaavinita Sutta* (Discourse on the Relay of Chariots), *Majjhima Nikaya* I 24, pp. 240-45.

must now come to be believed false. But it does require being able to put aside a teaching even while it may still be considered true. This involves a pragmatic approach to Buddhist teachings. To say that a teaching, once learned and used, can become an encumbrance and must be put to the side, just as a raft can become an encumbrance, means that upholding a teaching can be an impediment to further progress on the path to enlightenment. This may be because one can cling to the teaching; one can become attached to what one believes to be true just as one can to a feeling, physical object or person. Or it may be because holding fast to the teaching impedes receptivity to something else, another teaching perhaps, which is needed for going further or overcoming a different obstacle. The analogy also conveys that we will not need the same raft again for crossing another river (for if we did, then it may indeed make sense to carry the raft with us until it is needed again). Thus, the path to enlightenment is portrayed as a progression involving different stages, and progressive teachings are needed to move along this path and navigate its steps and obstacles.[1]

The Arhat is said to have achieved individual enlightenment. Though as discussed earlier, a different interpretation, "classically articulated" in the *Lotus* sutra,[2] holds that in fact the Arhat is not yet enlightened. On this view, the Arhat is still attached to self because he views enlightenment as a personal goal and accomplishment. On *this* Mahayana interpretation, the Arhat is only at a stage on the path towards the genuine enlightenment of the Bodhisattva, which requires a renunciation of a personal interest in enlightenment and a compassionate dedication towards others.[3] A reason the Arhat is still presented as an enlightened being, and Arhatship as a legitimate goal, is because this is a Skillful Means. This will be further elaborated.

---

1 C.f. Harvey: "Thus the overall path of Buddhism is seen as a training which gradually moves towards the profounder teachings, just as the ocean bottom shelves down gradually from the shore into the depths (Vin.II.238)." Harvey (1990), p. 46. Harvey draws this analogy from the *Vinaya Pitaka* which deals with monastic rules for monks and nuns.
2 Gethin (1998), p. 228.
3 See again Gethin (1998), p. 229.

The Noble Eightfold Path is presented as a path leading to individual enlightenment, and this objective provides reason and motivation for treading this difficult path. If a follower is told that a personal interest in enlightenment must be given up at some point then he or she may not begin on the path at all, or continue further if already on the path. Beginners and others on the path to enlightenment are, to make an obvious point, unenlightened and this is to say they are attached to self. This attachment means motivations and reasons for actions, such as Buddhist practice, will work best if they speak to the interests of a self. It would be hard to make sense of why enlightenment should be pursued if personal enlightenment must be renounced before it is reached. Why begin on a difficult road, it may be wondered, only to renounce reaching its destination?

While renouncing personal enlightenment may be necessary for reaching enlightenment, to be told this too soon may discourage staying the course and rob motivation. The emphasis on the great compassion of the Bodhisattva, and the ideal of the Bodhisattva generally, are regarded as higher teachings for the more spiritually advanced. Teachings concerning Arhatship do not require renouncing personal enlightenment and thus do not lead to Buddhahood on this Mahayana interpretation. Nevertheless, these teachings can provide motivation and ready one for the way of the Bodhisattva.[1] Hence, the goal of personal enlightenment is both useful for providing motivation for the aspirant and an obstacle because it retains attachment to self. Teachings that promote personal enlightenment – or Arhatship – may thus be described as a raft – a Skillful Means – that leads only so far and must at some point be put aside for the raft of renunciation so that the journey can be completed.

The notion of renouncing personal enlightenment seems to involve Skillful Means in another way as well. The would-be Bodhisattva is

---

1 Harvey presents this view: "The Arhat was seen as still having a subtle pride, and as lacking in compassion in his hope of escaping the round of rebirths, thus leaving unenlightened beings to fend for themselves. For those who were prepared to listen further, the Buddha then taught that the true Nirvana was attained at Buddhahood, and that all could attain this, even the Arhats, who currently thought that they had already reached the goal." Harvey (1990), pp. 92-93.

said to renounce personal freedom from suffering in favour of working towards freeing others from suffering. But as described earlier, this choice presumes a dichotomy that is false. Given that suffering in the Buddhist sense is suffering from attachment to self, it does not make sense that ending this should be sacrificed in order to help others. As discussed, these ends are complementary. For instance, focusing on alleviating the suffering of others and not one's own helps one to overcome self-attachment. But as also discussed, while the dichotomy is false, approaching it as a real choice can have a real effect. The choice to renounce a personal interest in enlightenment can help to overcome the last vestiges of attachment to self that the personal pursuit of enlightenment allegedly cannot. In this respect, the Mahayana teaching that portrays the renunciation of personal enlightenment in favour of helping others as involving a real choice and dichotomy seems to be a Skillful Means. The choice to renounce is supposed to be treated seriously, sincerely, and not for personal benefit. Seemingly paradoxically, the effect of this can be the very personal enlightenment that is renounced.

For renunciation to be an effective means, one should not challenge the sense of the choice between pursuing personal enlightenment or putting aside personal enlightenment in order to help others achieve enlightenment. One should not question why one cannot simply pursue both together (for if one does challenge, and does not renounce personal enlightenment as a consequence, then there will not be the benefit of renunciation in helping to overcome attachment to self). Renouncing the objective of personal enlightenment in favour of helping others requires that one be little concerned about one's own suffering, and more concerned with the suffering of others. It also requires that one's desire for personal enlightenment be put aside in favour of helping others. While one's interest in personal enlightenment can be put aside, whether or not one becomes enlightened cannot be wilfully put aside in this way. The significance of being persuaded in the choice of renunciation requires skillfulness in its teaching.

To sum up, renouncing personal enlightenment in favour of the path of the Bodhisattva seems to involve two instances of the employment of

Skillful Means. The first is that, at least under the Mahayana reading of the Arhat and Bodhisattva offered in the *Lotus* sutra, the Arhat does not achieve a lesser enlightenment compared to that of the Bodhisattva, but rather is only at a stage on the way to becoming enlightened. The renunciation of personal enlightenment is still required for the Arhat to fully overcome attachment to self. The Skillful Means involves presenting Arhatship as a real, even if lesser, enlightenment for this provides initial motivation for following the Noble Eightfold Path. The second is that the choice between personal freedom from suffering and helping others overcome suffering is not exclusive. Presenting this as an exclusive choice is skillful because in renouncing personal enlightenment the adept can achieve a selflessness that is required for becoming enlightened.

An Emphasis on Practice over Belief

Attachment to self is a psychological attachment. Appropriately, overcoming attachment involves disciplined practice. Correct practice, more than correct belief, is emphasized in Buddhism for this is the primary means for realizing freedom from suffering. This emphasis on practice is why Mahayana and non-Mahayana monks were able to live peaceably in the same monasteries in the initial centuries of Mahayana's development. It is a reason why there have not been violent sectarian schisms in Buddhism as in other religions. Buddhism is, as Williams states, "an orthopraxy rather than an orthodoxy."[1] This chapter will close with two examples of this emphasis on correct practice over correct belief from the Buddha's life. Both are drawn from Harvey: "When Brahmins asked him [the Buddha] about how to attain union with the god Brahma after death, he did not say that this was impossible, but that it could be attained by meditative development of deep loving-kindness and compassion, rather than by bloody Vedic sacrifices."[2] The Buddha here shows a greater concern with moving people towards correct practice

---

1 Williams (2000), p. 99.
2 Harvey (1990), p. 29.

than correct belief. This emphasis on practice conveys that it matters less what belief someone holds, perhaps to the extent of it not mattering whether the belief is even true, as long as the practice is compassionate and selfless. Another example:

> A general Siha, who was a great supporter of Jain monks, once decided to become a lay disciple, but the Buddha advised him that such a prominent person as himself should carefully consider before changing his religious allegiances. Already impressed by the Buddha's teaching, Siha was even more impressed by the fact that he did not jump at the chance of gaining an influential disciple. On affirming that he still wished to be a disciple, the Buddha advised him that he should not deprive Jain monks by withdrawing his generous support, but continue this while also supporting Buddhist monks, as he now wished to do.[1]

General Siha was supporting good work with the Jain monks, and there would be a loss of this if he became a Buddhist disciple and patron. Again, the Buddha is less concerned with promoting true belief than good practice and its consequences.

We might think that the primary goal of a teaching is the transmission of truth (in the form of true beliefs), but the primary goal of Buddhist teachings is determined by the goal of the Buddhist path itself: delivery from suffering. Delivery from suffering and the transmission of truth are not exclusive objectives, to be sure, but they are not necessarily convergent either. The emphasis on correct practice over correct belief raises the question of whether or not a skillful presentation of teachings can countenance false or deceptive teachings as long as they help lead followers to freedom from suffering. The next chapter, which is the closing chapter of the book, will take up this question of the relation between truth and teachings – a question first raised in the Preface – in the context of a close discussion of the Parable of the Burning House from the *Lotus* sutra.

---

1 Harvey (1990), p. 30. See *Vinaya Pitaka* I 236, Vol. 4, p. 322.

XV

The Parable of the Burning House – A Closing Discussion

A SPECIFIC QUESTION, RAISED AT the end of the previous chapter, is whether the Buddha's employment of Skillful Means admits deceptive teachings if they are an expedient for attaining enlightenment. This is a question concerning the relation between practice and belief in Buddhism, and whether the emphasis on correct practice in Buddhism can outweigh the importance of correct beliefs. The following discussion addresses this question in the context of Mahayana Buddhism, and specifically by way of an examination of the Parable of the Burning House from the *Lotus* sutra. This discussion, which concludes the book, is a return to a discussion first broached in the Preface: the relation between truth and teachings in Buddhism.

The Parable of the Burning House, from the *Lotus* sutra, describes an application of Skillful Means. The parable begins with children inside a burning house. Their father calls for them to come out but they will not. The children are occupied playing games, and are unconcerned by the calls for them to come out and are oblivious to the danger of encroaching flames. They do not listen to their father. He thinks to himself: "The house is already in flames from this huge fire. If I and my sons do not get out at once, we are certain to be burned. I must now invent some expedient means that will make it possible for the children to escape harm."[1] The father, in an attempt to save his children from burning to their early deaths, tells them that there are gifts waiting for them outside the house. These are goat-carts, deer-carts, and ox-carts. The father declares: "They [goat-carts, deer-carts, ox-carts] are outside the gate now where you can play with them. So you must come out of this burning house now."[2] The children, in eagerness, rush out of the burning house to get their promised presents. As noted in the passage just quoted, the claim about the awaiting carts was an invention; it was an "expedient means." The promised animal carts were not waiting for the children. The father, by promising these gifts, is said to have used "skillful means" to bring his children to safety. When the children asked for their carts the father, who was a very rich man, reflected on how to respond: "There is no end to my possessions. It would not be right if I were to give my sons small carriages of inferior make."[3] So he gave his children something grander than the carts they were expecting: they were given a carriage, bedecked with jewels and fineries, and pulled by white oxen. The children do not get the carts they were promised, but they pay no mind to this when they are given a much grander carriage.

In the parable, the father stands for the Buddha.[4] The children are the unenlightened. The burning house is the condition of suffering. The goat, deer, and ox carts are vehicles that are supposed to lead to enlightenment (and it is worth noting that it is the promise of these vehicles, and not the vehicles themselves, which leads the children from the burning house, the condition of suffering – this will be elaborated later). The vehicles are Buddhist teachings, and the difference in carts is analogous

---

1 *The Lotus* sutra, p. 57.
2 *The Lotus* sutra, p. 57.
3 *The Lotus* sutra, p. 58.
4 The Buddha tells his disciple Sariputra: "I say this to you Sariputra, I am like this rich man." *The Lotus* sutra, p. 69.

to differences between teachings, suited to differences in spiritual needs and development among followers. These teachings provide guidance in overcoming suffering and the teaching given to the children at the end – represented by the bejewelled carriage pulled by white oxen – represents the Buddha's higher teaching. This is the way of the Bodhisattva, which in the view of the *Lotus* sutra, is the true way to Buddhahood.

The Parable of the Burning House, as with the Raft Simile discussed in the previous chapter, conveys that the Buddha's teachings are means that deliver freedom from suffering. At the end of the previous chapter, the question was raised as to whether skillfully employed means can include deceptive teachings if they help deliver freedom from suffering. This does seem to be the case in the Parable of the Burning House. That is, it does seem that the father lied to his children to get them out of the house. The father may have told a necessary lie, or a benevolent lie, but a lie nonetheless. It appears that deceptive teachings that lead to benevolent ends can be justified, and that using teachings in this way is actually "skillful."

However, this is not the way this Parable is interpreted in the *Lotus* sutra itself. It is asserted that the father did not lie to his children (and, by analogy, the Buddha does not deceive in his teachings). The Buddha asks Sariputra whether the father tells a falsehood to his children. Sariputra's unequivocal response is that he did not:

No, World-Honored One. This rich man simply made it possible for his sons to escape the peril of fire and preserve their lives. He did not commit a falsehood. Why do I say this? Because if they were able to preserve their lives, then they had already obtained a plaything of sorts. And how much more so when, through an expedient means, they are rescued from that burning house! World Honored One, even if the rich man had not given them the tiniest carriage, he would still not be guilty of falsehood. Why? Because this rich man had earlier made up his mind that he would employ an expedient means to cause his sons to escape. Using a device of this kind was no act of falsehood. How much less so, then, when the rich man knew that his wealth was limitless and he intended to enrich and benefit his sons by giving each of them a large carriage.[1]

The Buddha agrees with Sariputra's analysis: "Very good, very good. It is just as you have said." Sariputra's response, though, is puzzling. Sariputra states that the father – the "rich man" in the passage above – did not lie because the children got something in return, namely their lives, and because he knew, ahead of time, that his promise was an expedient means to get his children out of the house. Furthermore, according to Sariputra, it was even more so not a falsehood (if such a thing is sensible) because the children were rewarded with something better than the carts they were expecting. It is not denied that the father invented an expedient means but it is denied that this is a lie. This invention is not a lie because the children were given better carriages than those promised, and because the father intended for the promise of the awaiting carts to be an expedient means for getting the children out of the house. Nevertheless, the promise made by the father was not for something better, or for their lives. It was for goat, deer and ox carts, and these were promised to be waiting outside the house. Knowing that these claims were benevolent expedients does not mean they weren't deceptive. Despite Sariputra's defences, and the Buddha's agreement, the father does appear to be guilty of falsehood.

If the father deceives then, by analogy, the Buddha and the Dharma, at least in places, deceive. The deception may be benevolent and skillfully employed, but deception is still deception. Or so it seems. The Buddha and Sariputra, as presented in the passage from the *Lotus* sutra above, deny there is falsehood despite contrary appearances. It is worth considering further why it is maintained that there is no deception in this employment of Skillful Means. Considering this question is not just to focus on interpreting the parable. It is taken as an opportunity for reflecting more widely on the role of Buddhist teachings, and specifically on the role of teachings in leading to right practice and how this

---

1 *The Lotus* sutra, p. 58.

bears on the role of communicating truths. All teachings are rafts, says the Buddha, and as such are means towards ends. Thinking through this question, and how it can be answered, will shed further light on the Buddha's skillful use of teachings and the compassionate ends he aims to attain.

In the parable, the flames are the condition of suffering. They are Samsara. The flames represent craving and attachment to self, suffering in the Buddhist conception. The flames do not represent the suffering of pain, sorrow, sickness, death or unsatisfied desires generally (i.e., the sufferings of the first two groupings of the First Noble Truth). The presence of these would trouble and motivate the children. They would run out of the house to be free of pain and death. Instead, the flames are ignored. The parable conveys that there is a kind of suffering that is very dangerous but that may, for all its danger and peril, go unrecognized. The children are busy playing their games, undisturbed by the flames and unbothered to leave. The Buddha describes this: "They had no alarm, no fright, and in the end no mind to leave the house. Moreover, they did not understand what the fire was, what the house was, what danger was. They merely raced about this way and that in play ..."[1] By analogy, humans live in a condition of pervasive self-attachment and craving and do not even register that this is suffering. The parable conveys to the reader or listener that there is more to suffering than the unenlightened may ordinarily feel and think.

The father delivers his children from the burning house with the promise of gifts. Specifically goat carts, deer carts and ox carts. To say that the promise of carts leads the children out of the house is to say that the promise made in the teachings leads the children out. What, though, is this promise that delivers freedom from suffering? The Parable conveys that it is not the promise of freedom from suffering in the Buddhist sense of the word, since the children are oblivious to the flames. That is, it is not the promise of delivery from flames that leads the children out, and accordingly it is not the promise of delivery from attachment to self

---

1 *The Lotus* sutra, p. 57.

that leads an initiate along the Noble Eightfold Path. It is the promise of freedom from suffering in another sense – a personal self-attached sense – that is the motivator.

The promised animal carts that motivate the children to rush out of the flaming house are individual vessels and represent personal enlightenment. They are described as "inferior" compared to the bejewelled carriage pulled by white oxen that the father ultimately gives. This carriage is described as a "Great Vehicle," which is the meaning of 'Mahayana'. The "inferior" carts are lesser vehicles that carry only the individual. They are by definition 'Hinayana'. The children, who suffer from attachment to self, rush out of the house for these "inferior" carts. By analogy, it is the promise of personal enlightenment that motivates the self-attached novice to follow the Noble Eightfold Path. This path helps lead the follower out of the suffering of self-attachment just as it leads the children out of the house. When the children get out of the house they do not find the carts they were promised. Instead, they are given a bejewelled carriage pulled by white oxen which they prefer. The implication is that when the adept has sufficiently overcome attachment to self so as to not need personal enlightenment as a motivation – when he is out of these flames – then his preference for personal enlightenment can be replaced. He is ready to renounce personal enlightenment in favour of pursuing freedom from suffering for all. In other words, he is ready for the way of the Bodhisattva, the "Great Vehicle" of Mahayana that is symbolized by the white-oxen led carriage.

Now let us return to our question: does the father, and by analogy the Buddha, deceive? Again, on the surface the answer is clearly 'yes'. The "inferior" animal carts are not waiting as promised. Likewise, the claim that one can achieve enlightenment by pursuing it for oneself – i.e., Arhatship – is false (according to the Mahayana view presented in the *Lotus* sutra). It is not that the Noble Eightfold Path, which is supposed to lead to individual enlightenment, is a wrong path. Rather, a change in motivation is needed in following it. Specifically, a selfless motivation, supplied by the renunciation of the Bodhisattva, is needed for the path to work. With this in mind, and looking past the surface, the question of deceit can be answered with a 'no'. A reason for thinking the Buddha does not lie is because the promise of personal enlightenment is never betrayed. It is still delivered; only the vehicle of delivery changes. In the parable, the promise of personal freedom from suffering is represented by the "inferior" animal carts (they are Hinayana: individual vehicles of delivery). These vehicles, and the self-interested motivation they represent, will not lead all the way to enlightenment because they retain attachment to self. A change in motivation is needed to complete the journey, and this is represented by a change in vehicle: the white-oxen led carriage represents the selfless path to enlightenment. It is the "Great Vehicle" that delivers the promised freedom from suffering. The Buddha promises personal delivery from suffering, but the motivation that successfully leads one to this cannot be *for* personal delivery from suffering. At some point on the path the motivation needs to change to a selfless motivation for the original promise to be fulfilled.

To be clear, the idea here is that the change in vehicles – from the lesser, "inferior" carts to the "Great" white-oxen led carriage – does not constitute a lie because it is exactly what is needed to ensure the Buddha does not lie. That is, the key promise is delivery from suffering and for this the vehicle of delivery needs to change from a personal motivation to a selfless motivation. Personal enlightenment is never taken away from the follower; it is just that it needs to be renounced to be obtained. This way of answering the question of deceit involves thinking about just what is the original promise of the Buddha: is it that personal delivery from suffering can be attained, or is it more specifically that personal delivery from suffering can be obtained by following a self-interested motive? The Buddha asserts the former but not the latter. So there is no deception in calling for a personal interest in freedom from suffering to be renounced in favour of a selfless interest in freeing everyone from suffering. Again, this means the father does not lie in switching vehicles (although notice that we must look to the Buddha and the nature of his promise to see why the father does not lie to his children). The *Lotus* sutra conveys that the Arhat must sincerely renounce a personal interest in enlightenment in order to secure it. Since personal enlightenment remains realizable, the Buddha does not lie on this count.

Then what about on another count? Renunciation may be necessary on the path to enlightenment, but this is not made clear at the outset. This lack of disclosure does seem deceptive and misleading. The would-be Arhat who commits to following the Noble Eightfold path does not expect that, at some point, he will have to renounce his personal pursuit. He does not expect, at the beginning of his journey, that he will have to take on the much more onerous challenge of trying to help everyone overcome suffering. Analogously, the father could have communicated, up front, to the children that they would be presented a grand carriage for all to ride instead of small, individual carts. But he does not. It seems the would-be Arhat has a legitimate claim to being misled. Consider this analogy. Suppose a climber is told that the top of the mountain is only a little further on. Then after he climbs for a couple hours, he is told that it is much further on. This is deceptive. It is perhaps benevolent, done to boost the climber's drive, but it is still deceptive. Is the promise made to the would-be Arhat, who upon getting well-along on the path is told that he must now partake of the more challenging Bodhisattva path to reach the objective of enlightenment, not like this? Arhatship is presented as motivation but then, when the adept thinks he is getting close, he is told he has much further to go. He may happily accept this challenge, having reached a point on the path where he has overcome much of his self-attachment; similar to how the children are happy to receive the "Great Vehicle" once they get out of the burning house. But still, there is cause to say the would-be Arhat is misled at the beginning of the journey.

On the surface there is clearly deception. The goal line has been moved. But again, considered further, it can be reasoned that there is no deception. The point was already made that to fulfill on the promise of personal enlightenment, the self-interested desire for personal enlighten-ment, while useful for a novitiate, needs at some point to be renounced. This is represented by the father changing carts in the parable. A differ-ent point will be made here and this has to do with the kind of teaching a novice, as opposed to an adept, is open to understanding. In the *Lotus* sutra, the Buddha explains why the father does not deceive with this point in mind:

> Sariputra, that rich man first used three types of carriages to entice his sons, but later he gave them just the large carriage adorned with jewels, the safest, most comfortable kind of all. Despite this, that rich man was not guilty of falsehood. The Thus Come One does the same, and he is without falsehood … First he preaches the three vehicles to attract and guide living beings, but later he employs just the Great Vehicle [the Bodhisattva way] to save them. Why? … The Thus Come One possesses measureless wisdom, power, freedom from fear, the storehouse of the Law. He is capable of giving to all living beings the Law of the Great Vehicle. But not all of them are capable of receiving it.[1]

The Buddha conveys that at first the children — the unenlightened — are not ready for the "large carriage" or "Great Vehicle." The children, who are attached to self, will not make their way out of the house without thinking self-interestedly. This is how they see things. They are children, and so are we, the Buddha conveys, for thinking this way. The "large carriage" will deliver individual freedom from suffering, but not to those who are self-attached for they are not ready. When the children leave the house — that is, when they are out of the confounding flames in which they did not even see their cravings and self-attachment as suffered — final delivery from suffering and attachment becomes available to them. The Bodhisattva Way is not presented to the beginner and a reason this is not deceptive or misleading has to do with what the beginner is ready to understand. The idea is that being able to handle the full truth — which involves the renunciation of personal enlightenment in favour of the "Great Vehicle" — requires readying oneself. In the passage just quoted, the Buddha says of the Dharma of the "Great Vehicle," that "… not all of them are capable of receiving it." The Buddha conveys that

---

1 *The Lotus* sutra, p. 62.

he does not deceive because he gives as much truth as the follower can deal with at his or her stage on the path.

Attachment to self is a pervasive condition that manifests not only affectively but also cognitively, which is to say it is part of how we understand and make sense of things. Freedom from attachment to self is not only a difficult goal to motivate; it is a difficult goal to comprehend. Something is worth pursuing, we tend to think, if it benefits one's future self or other people's future selves. This is how we assess goals. We presume permanence or sameness of self over time. In this frame of mind, to work tirelessly towards an objective only to wholeheartedly renounce it would be difficult, not only to accept, but to understand. To be told that this is the way to a personal release from suffering would make sense, but then this would interfere with the renunciation being sincere and wholehearted; it would become an instrumental renunciation done for the reason of a personal release from suffering. The teaching of renunciation is thus for those who are further along on the path and sufficiently divested of self-attachment. This is needed to appreciate it. If a follower is unable to fully appreciate a part of the Dharma, then arguably it is not deceptive to not be given this Dharma. It would only be unskillful or impractical. In this Mahayana view, the journey to enlightenment is presented as having stages, and thus so is the Dharma. The Dharma, according to the Buddha, is a series of rafts. To be given the final raft, or all rafts together, is as impractical as carrying a raft on one's back after it has served its use. In the passage above, the Buddha, in his wisdom, conveys that partitioning the Dharma is not only the practical or skillful way of proceeding, it is necessary. It is the only way the Dharma can be taken in and comprehended by the unenlightened. The parable tells us that the unenlightened are like children who must learn and grow in stages. Since this is their nature, it should not be false to educate them according to it.

Furthermore, notice again that the great oxen-led carriage is presented as a much better gift than the smaller animal carts. One meaning to this contrast between carts has been noted: the smaller carts – representing Arhatship – will not lead all the way to enlightenment (or will lead only to a lesser enlightenment, depending upon the Mahayana interpretation of the Arhat). These lesser carts thus have a lesser value. There is also another meaning to the contrast, and perhaps more important: the oxen-led carriage is not simply a better carriage because it can lead to a better destination; in the Parable, it is represented as a better carriage in itself. Care is taken to describe how it is lavishly bejewelled, with ornamentation and finery lacking in the smaller carriages. The analogy thus conveys that the Bodhisattva path is a better way to live, and not just better because of the superior enlightenment to which it is alleged to lead. This is to say that the more toilsome path of having to be concerned with the suffering of all, rather than just the suffering of oneself, is to be viewed positively, as good in itself, rather than as just a means to a better end. Indeed, it is supposed to be seen as a great boon. The sacrifice required on this path is a challenge to be sure, but this sacrifice is not to be avoided or complained about as if one were under compunction to do a chore; on the contrary, it is to be welcomed. Sariputra, in defending the father, says the children were given a much better carriage than they expected. Likewise, the adept who is well along in Buddhist practice before being told that ending the suffering of others must come before ending his own, should not begrudge this. The Parable is telling us that he should happily prefer this, just as the children happily prefer the greater carriage to the lesser carriages (along with all the demands that this symbolizes). The Parable is telling us that the demands of self-sacrifice and compassionate service are to be viewed positively and with gratitude, as if a gift of jewels were being given to oneself. Our usual mindset tends to be quite opposite: when told to sacrifice our self-interests we demur and ask to what benefit it will lead. We do not see it as good in itself, analogous to a fine carriage. When the Buddha compares the unenlightened to children, he is conveying that they do not see service to others in this way.

Consider that we can appreciate why the would-be Bodhisattva chooses to renounce personal enlightenment if this is thought to be the very way to secure enlightenment. However, if the would-be Bodhisattva does not expect to gain enlightenment through renouncing it; if the renunciation is sincere and not a means to an end, then we might wonder why he would renounce a goal for which he has worked so hard. The Parable of the Burning House tells us why: the renunciation of personal enlightenment, and the outright commitment to alleviating the suffering of others that this involves, is good in itself. Compassion may lead to a better enlightenment, but the Parable conveys that it is an end in itself and to be desired as such.

So far, a reasonable case can be made that the father's, and thus the Buddha's, skillful use of means is not a deceptive use. But let us try one more time. The father promises delivery from suffering. However, the suffering the children are delivered from is not what they originally considered to be suffered. This is represented by the children's obliviousness to the flames which conveys they are oblivious to the dangers of cravings and attachment to self. Because the father delivers the children from something they did not recognize as being suffered, his promise of delivery from suffering may seem deceptive. The analogue would be promising delivery from pain, aging, sickness, death and unsatisfied desires generally and then only delivering freedom from craving and attachment to self. While freedom from self-attachment may make the pain, aging, etc., less displeasing, it is still not to give freedom from pain, aging, etc.

So let us consider whether this is a source of deception: the kind of suffering from which freedom is promised. Three different groupings of suffering are presented in the First Noble Truth, but only suffering in the third sense is to be eliminated. One might say that the promise that suffering can be eliminated (asserted in the Third Noble Truth) should be read to include all three groupings and thus the Buddha deceives when he does not deliver all this. However, while the First Noble Truth does include examples such as pain, sickness, aging, and death, the suffering that is focussed upon in these and other experiences is explicitly summarized as involving attachment to the aggregates. This means that what is suffered, in the Buddhist sense, when one experiences pain and sickness is not the events themselves but the cravings that accompany these experiences; that is, the attachment to self in these experiences is suffered.

Pain, aging, sickness and death are all plainly part of being human and mortal. Buddhism does not try to eradicate them. This should also be clear from the Buddha's life story. When Gautama first leaves his father's palace, it is not just the sight of the first three signs — old age, sickness and death — that disturbs him. It is their inevitability that disturbs him. His chariot driver successively tells him that he too will succumb to old age, sickness and death and with each telling Gautama is further unnerved. He realizes his palace life cannot shelter him from old age, sickness and death no matter how much diversion it offers. This is why he is so troubled by the signs, and so compelled to leave his luxuriant life (for it offers no real remedy). He knows he will not cure old age, sickness and death upon venturing out but he hopes to find a way to be undisturbed by their inevitability. He turns to asceticism to deal with his desires, and not to escape old age, sickness and death. The Buddha's life story, which is an important part of the pedagogy of the Dharma, is by itself enough to convey that the Buddha does not promise freedom from sickness, old age, or death. For some, Buddhism may seem to promise these — in a heavenly abode perhaps — but the life of the Buddha, including post-enlightenment, does not show this (for he did get sick, age, feel sorrow and pain, and die). Buddhism should not be thought to promise what was not attained by the Buddha himself. In short, the Buddha does not deceive his followers about the kind of suffering he promises freedom from; or at least, if they are deceived about this, they bear responsibility for deceiving themselves. This means that in the parable, in luring his children out of the burning house by promising individual animal carts, the father does not, by analogy, promise freedom from sickness, aging, and death. His promise is for personal enlightenment, and as described above, this promise remains in place through the change in vehicles.

Are these considerations enough to show that the father in the parable, and analogously the Buddha, do not deceive in using skillful means? The reader is left to decide for him- or herself. What is more important, for the purpose of this book, is to appreciate how the Dharma is used to lead the Buddhist aspirant along a path towards ever greater selflessness. This is its aim. And this is wherein the end of suffering is to be found.

This has been the primary theme developed in this book. We see this with each of the teachings discussed, including the lessons imparted in the legend and life story of the Buddha. All Buddhist doctrines and principles are rafts to be used to lead to the end of self-attachment and thus to the end of suffering. The Buddha finds a spiritually fulfilled life – an enlightened and awakened life – in a selfless life. It is towards this hopeful end that the Buddha's Dharma serves as means. And so it is entirely appropriate for the Buddha to try for this to be an expedient and skillful means. Indeed, this is just what should be expected of a Compassionate One.

Glossary of Select Sanskrit, Pali and Philosophical Terms

WHILE SANSKRIT TRANSLITERATIONS OF terms are generally used in this book, Pali transliterations are given in addition to, and occasionally instead of, Sanskrit where this is commonplace or in line with the source used. Diacritical marks and accents on transliterated words have not been included in order to help the reader who is not familiar with Buddhist or Indian terms, or with the use of these marks and accents and the spellings they can affect.

Abhidharma: Literally the higher teachings of the Buddha. A collection of texts and literature that provide systematic treatments of the Buddha's teachings. *Abhdiharma Pitaka* refers to the *Abhidharma* that make up one of the "three baskets" of the *Tripitaka*.

Aggregates: The psychophysical constituents of the self. They include bodily processes, sensations, perceptions, volitional and intentional activity, and consciousness.

Anatman/Anatta: Sanskrit/Pali for No Self.

Anitya/Anicca: Sanskrit/Pali for Impermanence.

Annihilationism: There is a self, permanent and independent of the ever-changing aggregates, that comes to an end at death.

Arhat/Arahant: Sanskrit/Pali for one who, by following the teachings of the Buddha, has achieved enlightenment as an individual goal.

Atman: The True Self of the Upanishads. Atman is not a personal self. Atman is identified with Brahman.

Bhikkhus: Buddhist monks.

Bodhisattva/Bodhisatta: Sanskrit/Pali for an enlightened being. The Bodhisattva pursues the end of suffering for all rather than just for him- or herself.

Brahman: The Ultimate Reality of the Upanishads. Brahman is monistic (i.e., essentially one, without fundamental distinctions). Brahman is identified with Atman, the True Self.

Buddha: One who is enlightened or awakened. That is, one who has obtained freedom from suffering.

Causal Determinism: Every event is fully determined by its cause.

Cravings: Desires that seek to satisfy an ego-self. More specifically, second or higher-order desires that seek to satisfy a first or lower-order desire in order to satisfy a self.

Dharma/Dhamma: Sanskrit/Pali for the teachings and truths of the Buddha. Dharma in the Indian tradition also has other related connotations such as duty, order, righteousness, or Natural Law.

Dharmas/Dhammas: Sanskrit/Pali for the impartite constituents of the world as experienced.

Duhkha/Dukkha: Sanskrit/Pali for Suffering. Other connotations include sorrowfulness and unsatisfactoriness.

Empiricism: School of philosophical thinking according to which judgements pertaining to what is true or real must be justifiable by experience.

Emptiness (*Sunyata*): Refers to the absence of independent or ultimate reality or own-being (*svabhava*, see below). Alternatively, refers to the conventional dependence of all things, concepts and truths.

Enlightenment: See Nirvana/Nibbana.

Eternalism: There is a self, permanent and independent of the ever-changing aggregates, that continues on after death.

Guru: Teacher.

Hinayana: The "lesser vehicle." A term used by Mahayana Buddhism to refer to schools that promote the ideal of personal enlightenment or the Arhat.

Karma: In Buddhism, karma refers to intentional actions and the theory of karma stresses the law-like causal connections between intentional actions and their effects.

Mahayana: The "greater vehicle or vessel." Refers to the ideal that enlightenment is to be pursued for all rather than just for oneself; this ideal is the way of the Bodhisattva.

Moksa: Liberation from suffering and the cycle of samsara.

Monism: The idea that everything is essentially one, without fundamental distinctions. In the Upanishads, this oneness or unity is called 'Brahman'.

Nikaya: A collection within the *Sutra/Sutta Pitaka*.

Nirvana/Nibbana: Sanskrit/Pali for the extinguishing of suffering. Treated as synonymous with Enlightenment or Awakening.

Non-Dualism: The experience or condition of being without subject-object dualism (see below).

Numerical Identity: Being one and the same thing as. The notion of personal identity over time involves numerical identity.

Parinirvana: Final Nirvana occurring at the end of a life and signifying the end of the cycle of rebirth. May also be interpreted as superior in quality to Nirvana.

Prajnaparamita: The Perfection of Wisdom. A perfect wisdom is "from beyond"; it reflects the enlightened viewpoint. Refers to the *Perfection of Wisdom* sutras such as the *Heart* sutra and *Diamond* sutra.

Qualitative Identity: Being the same in qualities or properties.

Rishi: Sage or seer.

Rita: The cosmic or universal order which serves to make the universe intelligible.

Samsara: The condition of suffering and the cycle of rebirth.

Skanhdhas/Khandhas: Sanskrit/Pali for the Aggregates.

Sramana/Samana: Sanskrit/ Pali for an ascetic.

Subject-Object Dualism: This is a dualism between our selves or our subjective awareness on the one hand, and the objects of our awareness on the other hand (these objects of awareness can be in the external world or states of our minds).

Sutra/Sutta: Sanskrit/Pali for a discourse of the Buddha. *Sutra/Sutta Pitaka* refers to the collection or "basket" of *sutras/suttas* that make up one of the "three baskets" of texts in the *Tripitaka*.

Svabhava: Own-being. Or self-being, essence, or ultimate existent. Dharmas are said to have *svabhava* in the *Abhidharma* literature.

Theravada: The "doctrine of the elders." A non-Mahayana Buddhist school.

Tripitaka/Tipitaka: Sanskrit/Pali for the "three baskets" of texts in the Pali canon. These are the *Sutra/Sutta Pitaka*, *Vinaya Pitaka*, and the *Abhidharma Pitaka*.

Trishna: Cravings.

Universal Causation: Every event has a cause.

Upanishads: A collection of discourses that literally translates as "Sitting down near" as in sitting at the feet of a teacher for instruction. Also known as Vedanta, or "end of the Vedas," both because they are concluding portions of the Vedas and represent the philosophical height of the Vedas.

Upaya Kaushalya: Skillful Means, or Skill in Means.

Vedas: Oldest and most sacred scriptures of Hinduism.

Vinaya: Texts that deal with monastic rules. *Vinaya Pitaka* refers to the *Vinaya* that make up one of the "three baskets" of the *Tripitaka*.

Wants: Desires that are not cravings (i.e., that do not seek to satisfy an ego-self).

Yoga: Bodily, mental and spiritual techniques of discipline.

Yogi: A master in yoga techniques.

Bibliography

Primary Sources

Anguttara Nikaya. F.L. Woodward (trans.). The Book of the Gradual Sayings or More Numbered Suttas. 5 vols. London: Pali Text Society, 1995–96.

Buddhism in Translations. Henry Clarke Warren (ed. and trans.). Delhi: Motilal Banarsidass, 1987.

Buddhist Scriptures. Edward Conze (trans.). Harmondsworth, UK: Penguin Books, 1959.

Buddhist Texts through the Ages. Edward Conze, I.B. Horner, David Snellgrove, and Arthur Waley (eds. and trans.). New York: Harper Torchbooks, 1954.

Dhammapada. Juan Mascaro (trans.). The Path of Perfection. London: Penguin Books, 1973.

Digha Nikaya. Maurice Walshe (trans.). The Long Discourses of the Buddha. Boston: Wisdom Publications, 1987.

Early Buddhist Discourses. John. J. Holder (ed. and trans.). Indianapolis: Hackett, 2006.

Jataka. E.B. Cowell (trans.). *Stories of the Buddha's Former Births.* 6 vols. London: Pali Text Society, 1995.

The Lotus Sutra. B. Watson (trans.). New York: Columbia UP, 1993.

Majjhima Nikaya. Bhikku Nanamoli and Bhikkhu Bodhi (trans.). *The Middle Length Discourses of the Buddha: A New Translation of the Majjhima Nikaya.* Boston, MA: Wisdom Publications, 2005.

Milinda Panha. T.W. Rhys Davids (trans.). *The Questions of King Milinda.* 2 vols. Delhi: Motilal Banarsidass P, 1965.

Mulamadhyamakakarika of Nagarjuna. Jay Garfield (trans. and commentary). Oxford: Oxford UP, 1995.

The Principal Upanishads. S. Radhakrishnan (trans.). New York: Harper & Brothers, 1953.

Samyutta Nikaya. Bhikkhu Bodhi (trans.). *The Connected Discourses of the Buddha.* Boston: Wisdom Publications, 2000.

The Short Prajnaparamita Texts. E. Conze (trans.). First Edition. London: Luzac & Co., 1973.

Udana. F.L. Woodward (trans.). *Verses of Uplift* in *The Minor Anthologies of the Pali Canon.* Part II. Oxford: Pali Text Society, 1996.

Vinaya Pitaka. I.B. Horner (trans.). *The Book of Discipline.* 6 vols. London: Pali Text Society, 1938-66.

Visuddhimagga of Buddhaghosa. Bhikkhu Nanamoli (trans.). *The Path of Purification.* Onalaska, WA: BPS Pariyiyatti Editions, 1999.

Secondary Sources

Bahm, Archie J. *Philosophy of the Buddha.* Fremont, CA: Jain, 1959.

Blackburn, Simon. *Think.* Oxford: Oxford UP, 1999.

Chisholm, Roderick. "On the Observability of the Self" in *Philosophy and Phenomenological Research,* Vol. 30, No. 1, Sept. 1969, pp. 7-21.

Collins, Steven. *Selfless Persons: Imagery and thought in Theravada Buddhism.* Cambridge: Cambridge UP, 1982.

Conze, Edward. *Buddhist Thought in India.* Ann Arbor: Michigan UP, 1967.

Davidson, Donald. *Essays on Actions and Events*. Second Edition. Oxford: Clarendon P, 2001.

Descartes, René. *Meditations on First Philosophy*. Third Edition. Donald A. Cress (trans.). Indianapolis: Hackett, 1993.

Ganeri, Jonardon. *Concealed Art of the Soul: Theories of Self and Practices of Truth in Indian Ethics and Epistemology*. Oxford: Oxford UP, 2007.

Garfield, Jay. "Dependent Arising and the Emptiness of Emptiness: Why did Nagarjuna Start with Causation?" in *Philosophy East and West*, 44 (2), 1994, pp. 219-50.

_____. "Emptiness and Positionlessness: Do the Madhyamaka Relinquish All Views?" from *Empty Words: Buddhist Philosophy and Cross-Cultural Interpretation*. Oxford: Oxford UP, 2002, pp. 46-68.

Gethin, Rupert. *The Foundations of Buddhism*. Oxford: Oxford UP, 1998.

Gombrich, Richard F. *How Buddhism Began: The Conditioned Genesis of the Early Teachings*. New Delhi: Munshiram Manoharlal, 1997.

Gowans, Christopher W. *Philosophy of the Buddha*. London: Routledge, 2003.

Harvey, Peter. *An Introduction to Buddhism: Teachings, History and Practices*. First Edition. Cambridge: Cambridge UP, 1990.

Hume, David. *Treatise of Human Nature*. Oxford: Oxford UP, 2000.

Kalupahana, David. *A History of Buddhist Philosophy: Continuities and Discontinuities*. Honalulu: U of Hawaii P, 1992.

Kim, Jaegwon. *Philosophy of Mind*. Third Edition. Boulder, CO: Westview P, 2011.

Koller, John M. *Asian Philosophies*. Fifth Edition. Upper Saddle River, NJ: Pearson Prentice Hall, 2007.

Mathur, D.C. "The Historical Buddha (Gotama), Hume, and James on the Self: Comparisons and Evaluations" in *Philosophy East and West*, 28 (3), 1978, pp. 253-69.

McIntyre, Jane. "Hume and the Problem of Personal Identity" in D.F. Norton and J. Taylor (eds.). *The Cambridge Companion to Hume*, Second Edition (pp. 177-208). New York: Cambridge UP, 2009.

Mishra, Pankaj. *An End to Suffering: The Buddha in the World*. New York: Picador, 2004.

Nanamoli Bhikkhu. *The Life of the Buddha: According to the Pali Canon*. Third Edition. Kandy: Buddhist Publication Society, 1992.

Parfit, Derek. "The Unimportance of Identity" in H. Harris (ed.). *Identity: Essays Based on Herbert Spencer Lectures Given in the University of Oxford* (pp. 292-317). Oxford: Oxford UP, 1995.

Penelhum, Terence. "Hume on Personal Identity" in *The Philosophical Review*, 64 (4), 1955, pp. 571-89.

Plato. *Phaedo* from *Five Dialogues*. Second Edition. G.M.A Grube (trans.). Indianapolis: Hackett, 2002.

Radhakrishnan, S. *Our Heritage*. Delhi: Orient Paperbacks, 1984.

_____ and C.A. Moore (eds.). *A Sourcebook in Indian Philosophy*. Princeton, NJ: Princeton UP, 1957.

Robinson, Wade L. "Hume's Ontological Commitments" in *The Philosophical Quarterly*, Vol. 26, No. 102, Hume Bicentenary Issue, Jan. 1976, pp. 39-47.

Siderits, Mark. *Buddhism as Philosophy: An Introduction*. Indianapolis: Hackett, 2007.

Singer, Peter. *Practical Ethics*. Second Edition. Cambridge: Cambridge UP, 1993.

Strong, John S. *The Experience of Buddhism*. Second Edition. Toronto: Wadsworth, 2002.

Thomas, Edward J. *The Life of Buddha as Legend and History*. Third Edition. London: Routledge & Kegan Paul, 1949.

Westerhoff, Jan. *Nagarjuna's Madhyamaka: A Philosophical Introduction*. Oxford: Oxford UP, 2009.

Williams, Paul. *Mahayana Buddhism: The Doctrinal Foundations*. London: Routledge, 1989.

_____, with Anthony Tribe. *Buddhist Thought: A Complete Introduction to the Indian Tradition*. London: Routledge, 2000.

Index

from the publisher

A name never says it all, but the word "broadview" expresses a good deal of the philosophy behind our company. We are open to a broad range of academic approaches and political viewpoints. We pay attention to the broad impact book publishing and book printing has in the wider world; we began using recycled stock more than a decade ago, and for some years now we have used 100% recycled paper for most titles. As a Canadian-based company we naturally publish a number of titles with a Canadian emphasis, but our publishing program overall is internationally oriented and broad-ranging. Our individual titles often appeal to a broad readership too; many are of interest as much to general readers as to academics and students.

Founded in 1985, Broadview remains a fully independent company owned by its shareholders—not an imprint or subsidiary of a larger multinational.

If you would like to find out more about Broadview and about the books we publish, please visit us at **www.broadviewpress.com**. And if you'd like to place an order through the site, we'd like to show our appreciation by extending a special discount to you: by entering the code below you will receive a 20% discount on purchases made through the Broadview website.

Discount code: **broadview20%**

Thank you for choosing Broadview.

Please note: this offer applies only to sales of bound books within the United States or Canada.